Affirmative Aesthetics and Wilful Women

Maud Ceuterick

Affirmative Aesthetics and Wilful Women

Gender, Space and Mobility in Contemporary Cinema

Maud Ceuterick
University of Bergen
Bergen, Norway

ISBN 978-3-030-37038-1   ISBN 978-3-030-37039-8   (eBook)
https://doi.org/10.1007/978-3-030-37039-8

© The Editor(s) (if applicable) and The Author(s) 2020 This book is an open access publication.

Open Access   This book is licensed under the terms of the Creative Commons Attribution 4.0 International License (http://creativecommons.org/licenses/by/4.0/), which permits use, sharing, adaptation, distribution and reproduction in any medium or format, as long as you give appropriate credit to the original author(s) and the source, provide a link to the Creative Commons licence and indicate if changes were made.
The images or other third party material in this book are included in the book's Creative Commons licence, unless indicated otherwise in a credit line to the material. If material is not included in the book's Creative Commons licence and your intended use is not permitted by statutory regulation or exceeds the permitted use, you will need to obtain permission directly from the copyright holder.
The use of general descriptive names, registered names, trademarks, service marks, etc. in this publication does not imply, even in the absence of a specific statement, that such names are exempt from the relevant protective laws and regulations and therefore free for general use.
The publisher, the authors and the editors are safe to assume that the advice and information in this book are believed to be true and accurate at the date of publication. Neither the publisher nor the authors or the editors give a warranty, expressed or implied, with respect to the material contained herein or for any errors or omissions that may have been made.
The publisher remains neutral with regard to jurisdictional claims in published maps and institutional affiliations.

Cover illustration: Sibel Kekilli in *Gegen Die Wand* (2004)

This Palgrave Macmillan imprint is published by the registered company Springer Nature Switzerland AG.
The registered company address is: Gewerbestrasse 11, 6330 Cham, Switzerland

Preface

This book was formed through travel and habitation of cities in Belgium, Spain, Ireland, New Zealand, and Norway. As I was trying to find my way across the globe through the academic maze, I observed the differences in treatment I received as a woman compared to my male counterparts, whether in the streets, at the wheel of a car, in private houses, or in 'public' places such as restaurants, cafés, or workplaces. If the sexist comments and attitudes in Brussels were in appearance much more frequent and violent than in Spain, New Zealand, or Norway, sexism and misogyny in these countries remain pervasively ubiquitous and institutionalised, albeit in surreptitious ways. The categorisation of subject identities according to gender, ethnicity, sexuality, and social class determines spatial perceptions and experiences and affects mobility. As a film and media scholar, I feel that art has a responsibility to make visible how space and mobility are gendered and racialised, as well as to stimulate imagination and create the new. This book argues that films and media have the power to critique the status quo and generate future possibilities by formally creating fluid spaces and wilful bodies. I have come to categorise these wilful and fluid forms as instances of 'affirmative aesthetics'. Before going into more detail on the origin and implications of affirmative aesthetics, however, I want to recount an anecdote that touches on the major themes of this book and reaffirms its cross-disciplinary and cross-cultural aspects.

Lowering her voice to a whisper, a friend at a party asked me: 'are you a *feminist*?' I laughed and asked her why she seemed so ashamed to utter the 'f-word' as if it was a swear word. She proceeded to tell me her story about how traditional views of gender roles and power structures shaped her life. My friend J. was raised in a small Chinese town where she was exposed to strong cultural traditions which posited girls' mobility (their necessity for and capacity of) as inferior to that of boys. Under her mother's guidance, she took up competitive running. Her fellow male students were perplexed about her competitive nature; they believed that competitiveness was a male trait and that she did not need to be competitive because she would ultimately be expected to find a husband who would provide for her. Later, when she talked about her Swedish boyfriend, people 'back home' would blame her for having a foreign partner and not keeping the Chinese genes 'pure' or within the nation. As an answer to these accusations, she would joke that foreigners are fearful of China taking over the world and that by marrying a foreigner she was playing her patriotic part in the conquest of the world. However, this explanation was not acceptable to her fellow citizens, since for them 'Chinese ethnicity' was transmitted through the father, and thus, because she was a woman, her children 'would not be Chinese'.

Because she perceived the injustice of not being accommodated by space, of having to 'insist on what is simply given to others' (Ahmed 2014, 149), J. experienced the wilfulness to put her body in the way of the patriarchal and sexist division of space and social rights. Instances like the ones mentioned appear to have structured her young life and raised her awareness of an unequal gendered existence. My friend's story resonates with me as similar to the story of the young character in Haifaa Al Mansour's film *Wadjda* (2012) who, because of her gender, is prohibited from riding a bicycle as the boys of her age do (see Chap. 4 on *Wadjda*). Feminist scholar Sara Ahmed writes that wilfulness is '*a matter of how we are affected*', namely by social and spatial constraints; Wadjda's and my friend J.'s wilful bodies would '[get] in the way, when spaces [were] not made "accessible" to [their] bodies' (2014, 76; 147, emphasis in original). Experiencing wilfulness is about endorsing 'the capacity to say or enact a "no" to what has been given as an instruction', to 'what has been willed by others' (14; 65). It is also to walk *freely* through the city so as to inhabit it *fully*, despite not being naturally accommodated, just as Hannah Arendt notes when writing that 'one inhabits a city by strolling through it without aim or purpose' (cited in Solnit 2001, 211). Inhabiting space through walking without aim or purpose may manifest as a wilful gesture, not a conscious one, but one that is experienced.

As this book explores, wilfulness is not a matter of individual will but rather of collective affects. I questioned J. further about her surroundings and her education, whether her Chinese friends 'at home' were *feminists* too, and how she interpreted the way she had become so wilful in comparison to earlier generations of women. J. perceived her family as different from most traditional Chinese families because her father would generally perform the domestic tasks, although her paternal grandmother would blame J.'s mother for not doing them herself. Now and again, her mother would tell J. stories of her experiences in the army where, she insisted, there was nothing physical that she could not do that the men could. Her mother enlisted to escape the domestic space, where she had the responsibility of maintaining the household and raising her numerous siblings (despite having an older brother). Going back one more generation, J. recognised that although her grandmother was very respectful of traditional gender roles, she valued her own intellectual capacities highly, went to school for longer than what was common for women at the time, and became an accountant in the army (the biggest employer in China in the 1940s), which ensured her a role in the public sphere.

J. repeatedly emphasised how the increase of media and larger diffusion of information were important catalysts to her wilfulness. Many women of earlier generations were illiterate and so, even if feminist groups existed before, it was not as easy to transmit their thoughts and behaviour widely. Above all, J. underlined the important role films had played in her feminist formation; the visual component of films triggered her imagination more thoroughly than the books she accessed at the local library. Her story confirmed the hypotheses I had in mind while studying *Wadjda*, namely that Wadjda's wilfulness arose out of creative works, 'works of imagination' (Appadurai 2002), that encouraged her to think outside of the constraining limits imposed upon her by a particular cultural form of patriarchy that forbids (or socially disapproves of) women riding bikes or driving. Arjun Appadurai underlines the relational and dynamic dimension of culture, which only exists in its 'difference from something else', namely, its difference from other cultural expressions. According to Appadurai, culture is also 'a terrain of possibilities, constructed through the work of imagination, ... [which infuses] life with meaning, with value, with belief' (2002, 45). J.'s different conception of gender and space from traditional Chinese culture arose from films, books, and media, as well as from social and affective relations. Albeit to a different extent, the resistances of J., her mother, and her grandmother against established gender roles counteract what Doreen Massey calls the 'power-geometries' of space, whereby women and other discriminated groups have less control over mobility, movement, and networks of communication than men (Massey 1994, 149–150). Wilful women like Wadjda and J. continually negotiate spatial and social structures invested with power, cultural meanings, and practices.

The story of J.'s family also reminded me of my own Flemish-speaking grandmother, who feels a profound regret that she did not have the opportunity to continue her formal education beyond primary school. Like my friend's mother, she was the eldest girl of a large family. She was forced to leave school to work in the fields and help her mother with domestic tasks. She learned French from comic books, established a farm with my grandfather, a Walloon farmer, and gave birth to my mother. As was common in farming families, my grandmother and grandfather expected my mother to work on the farm after she completed her compulsory high school education at the age of 18 and to find a husband who would increase the farm's value through his own family's land. My mother, however, had different ideas for her future and wanted to pursue higher education, which she did, in spite of my grandparents' wishes. When my mother questions the origins of my own wilfulness, I say that she was the one who showed me how to go against the flow of gender expectations. However, this simple explanation does not amount for all the other influences that contribute to wilfulness.

Wilfulness does not emerge from one's will or individual situation, but rather from the negative affects sexism, racism, and classism have on a determinate group's mobility, social role, and spatial habitation. Wilfulness manifests as a praxis or activity to will 'what has disappeared from view', or in other words, 'a modification of what seems reachable' (Ahmed 2014, 16; 140). We inhabit space from an affective position, one that has been, and is being, nourished by our contacts with others, by the wilful actions and thoughts of generations before us, and, most importantly for the purposes of this book, by the films we watch and the media we consume. The women in this book wilfully wander in spaces that have been legitimated as masculine arenas and from which they have typically been excluded. Films have the power to denounce, challenge, and counteract unbalanced relations of power, through both their diegesis and their aesthetic choices. The wilfulness to go against the flow that I, J., our mothers, and grandmothers experienced certainly emerged from environments that failed to accommodate us for who we were and are, and for how we strolled across prohibited grounds. If these negative affects pervade generations and cultures, wilfulness and affirmative forms similarly pass from one generation to the next, reach from one culture to another, and change representation into desire.

This book aims to follow my grandfather's motto that optimism is good for our health and well-being (*L'optimisme, c'est bon pour la santé*) and is dedicated to the women of my family, who (including myself) struggle to live by that principle: my grandmother Mariette, my mother Martine, and my sister Aline. All in their own ways, they have taken wilful paths and contributed to who I am and to the thoughts that went into this book.

Bergen, Norway   Maud Ceuterick

Acknowledgements

This book could not have been completed without the University of Otago Doctoral Scholarship that funded my doctoral research, from which this project emerged. I received an individual research fellowship from the European Marie Skłodowska-Curie Actions, which allowed me to devote my time to research and write this book. I also received generous funding from the University of Bergen's Open Access Publication Fund, which made it possible to publish this book under a Creative Commons licence. An early version of Chap. 3 has been published in Baschiera, Stefano, and Miriam De Rosa (eds.), *Film and Domestic Space: Architectures, Representations, Dispositif*, Edinburgh: Edinburgh University Press, 2020. Many thanks go to the editorial team at Palgrave, Lina Aboujieb, and Emily Wood, and to my peer reviewers for believing in this project and for their extraordinary efficiency. Thanks to William Gillis for his careful re-reading of this book. Thanks are also due to Anja Padge at Wüste Film, Jennifer Bredtmeyer, and Sibel Kekilli for the cover image.

The ideas in this book result from my interactions with wonderful friends and colleagues at the University of Otago, New Zealand. My deepest and unreserved thanks go to my supervisor and mentor Cathy Fowler, for her inestimable generosity, kindness, continuous support, and insight. I am grateful to my peers and mentors in the Department of Media, Film, and Communication, whose inspiring and stimulating conversations have nourished my research, especially my co-supervisor Cecilia Novero, Vijay Devadas, Brett Nichols, Anne Begg, Sally Milner, Alex Thong, Rosemary Overell, Peter Stapleton, and Massimiliana Urbano.

For their support, editing advice, and general insight, I wish to thank Sam Spector, Nick Reeder, and Chris Ingraham. Thank you to my colleagues in the Digital Culture Research Group and Media Aesthetics Research Group at the University of Bergen, in particular Jill Walker Rettberg, Asbjørn Grønstad, Øyvind Vågnes, and Anders Lysne.

I am also indebted to a great number of friends who have made and continue to make my life a plentiful and colourful one, whether in Dunedin, Belgium, or Bergen, and in particular to Manon de Decker who has been there for me since our first years at university.

Most of all, my tender thanks go to my family for their unwavering support: Aline, Robin, and Michel Ceuterick: and Martine, Mariette, and Georges Eliard. Thank you to André Ceuterick for transmitting his passion for socially engaged cinema.

Finally, I thank Gon Nido, for his wit, love, and delicious breakfasts that enliven my life on a daily basis.

Contents

1 Introduction: Gender, Space, and Affects in Film   1
   An Inter-disciplinary Approach to Mobility, Space, and Gender
   on Screen   5
      Space-Time and Power-Geometries   5
      Forms, Bodies, and Affects on Screen   8
      Affective Cinematic Spaces   13
   Filmic Affects as Affirmative Aesthetics   17
      Wilfulness and Affirmative Politics   19
      Book Structure   23
   References   30

2 Women's Road Movies and Affirmative Wandering: *Messidor*   37
   References   54

3 Cars: A Micro-analysis of Space and Bodies in *Vendredi soir*   57
   Windows, Wandering Camera, and Magical Realism   62
   A Space of Intimacy: Recollection Objects and Haptic Cinematic
   Space   67
   The Car, a Vehicle of (Im)Mobility   70
   Affirmative Wandering   74
   Gendered Contacts, Affective Contacts   78
   Desiring Bodies   82
   Rewriting Spatial Habitation: A Place Called Home?   87
   References   95

4 Houses and Wilful Women: *Wadjda* — 99
Wadjda *in Context* — 101
In the Streets of Riyadh — 104
A Passport to Be Mobile — 107
Bending Lines — 109
Wilful to Appear Docile — 112
A Space of One's Own — 116
Housing Wilfulness — 119
References — 121

5 Streets: Freedom, Diaspora, and the Erotic in *Head-On* — 125
A Rewriting of Space-Time — 128
Freedom and the Erotic as Power — 130
Dance and Diaspora — 137
Punk and Abjection as Affirmative Forms — 144
Windows, Hotels, and a Space for Pausing — 151
Domestic Space and Gender Roles — 158
References — 160

6 Conclusion: Forms of Affirmative Aesthetics — 163
References — 174

Index — 177

List of Figures

Fig. 2.1	*Messidor*: First misogynist driver	43
Fig. 2.2	*Messidor*: Jeanne answers back	44
Fig. 2.3	*Messidor*: Long shot of Jeanne and Marie walking up the mountain	48
Fig. 2.4	*Messidor*: Jeanne and Marie seamlessly inhabit their spatial environment	48
Fig. 2.5	*Messidor*: The road forms a social border difficult to cross for Jeanne and Marie	49
Fig. 2.6	*Messidor*: 'We're moving through empty space'	50
Fig. 2.7	*Messidor*: A weapon is a penis and vice versa	52
Fig. 3.1	*Vendredi soir*: Laure looking out from the window of her apartment	64
Fig. 3.2	*Vendredi soir*: Laure looking towards or imagining lit windows that pierce the darkness of the night	66
Fig. 3.3	*Vendredi soir*: Frightening man mockingly waves to Laure	72
Fig. 3.4	*Vendredi soir*: Close-ups and frames within the frame contain Laure in her car, which drives forward without Laure watching	74
Fig. 3.5	*Vendredi soir*: Claire Denis' ballet of cars	76
Fig. 3.6	*Vendredi soir*: Laure watches Jean passing his hand inside the collar of his shirt	81
Fig. 3.7	*Vendredi soir*: Focus on a younger woman's gaze and hands in a café	84
Fig. 3.8	*Vendredi soir*: Laure's and Jean's faces become almost indistinguishable as they kiss	85
Fig. 3.9	*Vendredi soir*: Body parts in extreme close-up in the motel room	86
Fig. 3.10	*Vendredi soir*: Laure runs through the street towards the camera	90

Fig. 4.1	Closing a street sequence in *Wadjda*: Shots of Abdullah and Wadjda	106
Fig. 4.2	The veil takes a wilful form in *Wadjda*	109
Fig. 4.3	Wadjda's class is straightened out in her absence	111
Fig. 4.4	*Wadjda*: Micro-instances of wilfulness	111
Fig. 4.5	*Wadjda*: Wadjda's mother eats after the men have left	113
Fig. 4.6	*Wadjda*: A formalist confrontation	115
Fig. 4.7	*Wadjda*: Crossing boundaries	118
Fig. 5.1	*Head-On*: Chanting tableaux opening and closing the film	129
Fig. 5.2	*Head-On*: Sibel looking directly into the camera and at Cahit	132
Fig. 5.3	*Head-On*: Sibel being submissive in front of her father and brother	134
Fig. 5.4	*Head-On*: Fluid dynamics of power in the cinematic space	135
Fig. 5.5	*Head-On*: Sibel walking in the street	137
Fig. 5.6	*Head-On:* Sibel performing masquerade while dancing in a nightclub	139
Fig. 5.7	*Head-On:* Sibel drinks and dances until she falls to the ground, unconscious	142
Fig. 5.8	*Head-On*: Parallel editing of Sibel enjoying the city and being confined in gender expectations	147
Fig. 5.9	*Head-On:* Sibel bleeding after cutting her veins open	148
Fig. 5.10	*Head-On:* Sibel in a gesture of abjection	150
Fig. 5.11	*Head-On:* Sibel enjoying the sun on her face as she confidently looks over the city	153
Fig. 5.12	*Head-On:* Sibel and Cahit making love and disturbing the spatial symmetry	156
Fig. 5.13	*Head-On:* Sibel and Cahit looking at the city from above	157
Fig. 5.14	*Head-On:* Sibel's limitation to freedom expressed through her habitation of cinematic spaces	159
Fig. 6.1	*Roma*: The family surrounding Cleo as a member of the family	166
Fig. 6.2	*Roma*: Ending image after Cleo has left the frame	166

CHAPTER 1

Introduction: Gender, Space, and Affects in Film

When we look for films that 'imagine' mobile female characters and examine the scholarship related to these films, we encounter binaries in both, binaries that confine women through gendered considerations of mobility. Filmic narratives of travel, such as the road movie, tend to situate their characters within dichotomous systems that oppose, for instance, 'masculine' / 'feminine', mobility / stasis, road / house, traveller / strayed wanderer,[1] desiring / aimless, and autonomy / dependency. Meanwhile, scholars writing about gender and space on screen also seem to overtly focus upon how female characters seem trapped in both passive roles and within domestic space. Having noted the prevalence of binaries, we need to ask how the patriarchal status quo *affects* women's (as in those who identify or are identified as 'women') freedom of movement and habitation of space.

In this book I am looking for both 'new images' that will transmit women's wilful habitation of space along with a new vocabulary through which to theorise gender and space in film affectively. The logical starting point, with the road movie, is in fact problematic for female protagonists for reasons I discuss in Chap. 2; therefore, what we need to examine is not the 'mobility' of these women but their bodily habitation of their spatial environments. Similarly, in order to find wilful models of women who are able to move and act with as much 'freedom' as men do, we have to start looking at 'mobility' through a different lens.[2] For what stands out from the real-life stories in my preface is the 'problem' that bodies indentified as female seem to pose to patriarchal societies.

The way mobility is perceived and analysed in the cinema needs to change. Departing from the romantic and gendered aspects of travel, the *freedom* found on the road, or the seemingly *transformative potential of mobility* can instead be found in the habitation of space itself, of spaces currently dominated or controlled by men, such as the ones I consider in this book: the street, the house, and the car. Rather than forming a distinct category of works or a filmic genre, the films examined here are examples of films that show women's spatial habitation as 'affirmative', a term to which I will return; hence, the women characters in the films studied break away from the spatial and gendered binaries that maintain them on the 'right path' under patriarchy. From this starting point the book follows two ideas: first, we take a journey into filmic (affective) representations of women's spatialities; second, we look for an appropriate language to extract affirmative movement from these representations, evacuating the negativity that has continually re-placed women within binary models of gender and mobility. Wilfulness, habitation, affirmative, and affective are some of the key terms through which a model for gender and space in cinema will be plotted in order to recognise the fluidity, affectivity, and plurality of spaces and subjectivities. To begin, it is necessary to rehearse some of the critical terrain upon which this book builds. This introductory chapter is divided into two parts. The first part provides a methodological journey through which I explore the ideas of space as a kind of space-time that is in continual transformation, examine how cinema produces transformative affects and discourses, and consider how spaces on screen are created through filmic forms and bodies. In the second part, I return to the terms that I introduce here and adopt Rosi Braidotti's affirmative politics and Sara Ahmed's wilfulness as ways to analyse women's wanderings from prescribed paths and habitation of different spaces as affirmations of *fluid* identities. I refer to fluid as unbounded; the representation of characters' subjectivities is essentially liminal, on thresholds, and in continual transformation, rather than bound to fixed categories of gender, race, space, or sexuality.

If we retrace scholarship on gender and space, we typically find ourselves back at the turn of the twentieth century, out in the streets, in an emerging public sphere. Due to their continual sexualisation, women had to deploy several tactics to inhabit the public sphere. In her revision of her essay 'The invisible flâneuse' (1985), Janet Wolff highlights how only men had 'the privilege of passing unnoticed in the city' while women's 'presence on the streets would certainly be noticed' (2006, 19). Women's difficult habitation of space is opposed to the privileged abilities of men to cross spatial boundaries unrestricted. While male *flâneurs* such as Baudelaire were roaming the streets for pleasure or in search of artistic inspiration, female *flâneuses,* such as Virginia Woolf, needed a clear aim that justified their movement in so-called 'public' spaces (1942). As has been well recorded, middle-class female *flânerie* became possible with the apparition of the department store, as it allowed women to go into the streets unchaperoned, and consume goods in a semi-private, protected area.[3] As Rebecca Solnit puts it in her book *Wanderlust,* 'women legitimised their presence [in urban life] by shopping—proving they were not for purchase by purchasing... as either commodities or consumers' (2001, 237).

For many of these early writers, the streets were seen to have a negative impact upon women's lives. Ironically, in order to escape the commodifying male gaze, women had to *haunt* the urban space like unwelcome ghosts,[4] for they embodied all the sexual 'uncanny' that the city space represented (Wolff 2006, 27). In particular, Wolff notes that:

> the lives of women in the modern city—in private as well as in public (for the sociology of modernity has paid little attention to the domestic sphere) are thus, as [Avery] Gordon puts it, 'barely visible, or seemingly not there'. As a result, they haunt the discourse and the city itself—uncanny because not admitted to language and thought. (2006, 27)

Despite the tendency to dwell upon the problems city spaces pose to women, less pessimistic readings do exist. Elizabeth Wilson describes how women's resistance to ideological and spatial boundaries '*flourished* in the interstices of the city' (1991, 8, emphasis mine). Whereas Wilson writes that cities of the early twentieth century were simultaneously feared and desired for all the sexually and morally forbidden activities that became possible, and that women were (and arguably continue to be) seen as problems that needed to be controlled. Yet Wilson also celebrates the potential of cities to offer women, in particular, 'greater freedom and diversity than life in small communities' (5–6; 156). Although in the city '[women] were and continued to be defined in terms of their sexuality in a way that most men were not', urban life undermined patriarchal authority, as it gave birth to employment and subsequent relative economic independence, as well as entertainment, with all the ideas of immorality and illegitimacy that it conveyed (2001, 137; 73).[5] In her work, Wilson identifies acts of resistance that bring about transformative practices and affirmative narratives of space.

A reading of gender and space that begins with the *flâneur* leads us down the cul-de-sac of binaries to which I referred earlier. Such discourses emphasise women as being negatively affected and unable to transform their negative affection into productive forces, as Rosi Braidotti would advocate. Braidotti's work on 'affirmative politics' echoes my frustration with critical theory that is anchored in negation, in 'quests for meaning' (Braidotti 2011a, 292); instead, Braidotti advocates '[starting] from *micro-instances* of embodied and embedded self and the complex web of social relations that compose the self... [building] upon *micropolitical* instances of activism, avoiding overarching generalisations' (2011b, 268–69, emphasis mine). In an article titled 'The new activism: A plea for affirmative ethics', Braidotti advocates '[actively working] towards the creation of alternatives ... [thereby] abandoning dualistic oppositional thinking ... [and creating] an ethology of forces ... not tied to the present by negation' (2011b, 267). Through 'untapped' resources such as 'desires and imagination', Braidotti champions thinking differently about ourselves and others, in a non-dichotomous way, as 'a question of and/and, not of either/or' (268). Her call for 'affirmative ethics' aims to establish 'transformative politics' and 'sustainable futures' by rewriting a new 'cartography' (270).[6] Similarly, transformations of women's spatial *imaginaries* beyond patriarchal boundaries rely upon a combination of wilful and imaginative spatial habitation on screen and affirmative ways of considering them. Affirmative aesthetics on screen and in the scholarship amounts to 'enduring' patriarchal systems rather than being 'dispossessed' by them (in Braidotti's words). In her book *Nomadic theory*, Braidotti writes that affirmative ethics produce:

> a number of significant shifts: from negative to affirmative affects, from entropic to generative desire, from incomprehensible to virtual events to be actualised, from constitutive outsides to a geometry of affects that require mutual actualisation and synchronisation, from a melancholy and split to an open-ended weblike subject, from the epistemological to the ontological turn in philosophy. (2011a, 290)

For Braidotti, affirmative ethics functions as a way to relate to life through its 'potentia', its 'generative force of becoming', instead of through what she calls 'negative passions' such as entropy or melancholy, in other words, yielding to negative affects 'as a result of a blow, a shock, an act of violence, betrayal, trauma, or just intense boredom' (2011a, 288).

My approach to gender and space makes visible what I call *affirmative aesthetics,* as a cinematic way out of the restrictive dualistic oppositions that *freeze the present* into negative politics. The films chosen, *Messidor* (Alain Tanner 1995 [1979]), *Vendredi soir* (Claire Denis 2002), *Wadjda* (Haifaa Al-Mansour 2012), and *Head-On* (Fatih Akin 2004) enable the study of women's *micro-relations* to space through an 'affirmative' lens, examining their bodily and affective spatial relations rather than focusing upon the (lack of) 'success' of their travel. However, as the recourse to Braidotti might suggest, such an approach demands that the tools of film studies are combined with those of other disciplines—namely cultural geography and feminist critical theory—so as to reconceive of space as space-time and to understand the affective dimensions of spatial relations.

AN INTER-DISCIPLINARY APPROACH TO MOBILITY, SPACE, AND GENDER ON SCREEN

In the search for an affirmative vocabulary through an examination of the body's relation to space as lived experience, we need to consider space as fluid, practised, and affective rather than conceived and fixed. Feminist geographer Doreen Massey's concepts of space-time and power-geometries offer useful starting points.

Space-Time and Power-Geometries

Narratives and affective images 'involving' relations to space, such as the street, the house, and the car in particular, affect how people experience and inhabit these spaces. Spaces exist in time and in representation: they are *lived* through historical and affective imaginaries. For Henri Lefebvre, spaces are threefold: an interweaving of this 'lived space' (*espace vécu*) just mentioned, the space 'conceived' (*l'espace conçu*) by planners and urbanists, and the space 'perceived' (*l'espace perçu*) through daily practices (Lefebvre 1974, 49–52). Although space is conditioned by how places were initially conceived and by current practices (with all the restrictions of mobility related to gender, class, and 'race'), films produce spatial imaginaries—or in Lefebvre's words, lived spaces, 'spaces of representation'—within which processes of change may occur. We are not interested here in the 'conceived space', which implies planning and regulations, but in the lived space, made of social relations that continually change through time, as defined by Doreen Massey. The three spaces that Lefebvre distinguishes are contingent, so that one could consider that filmic representations of space and bodies have an impact on lived, perceived and, ultimately, conceived places.

In this book, I refer to space as 'practiced places', socially constructed and in constant transformation (de Certeau 1984, 117). For Michel de Certeau, narratives constantly transform places into spaces and, vice versa, the social idea of a space into a specific place (118). De Certeau explains that these narratives emerge as strategies, deeds of a 'subject of will and power (a proprietor, an enterprise, a city, a scientific institution)', or as tactics, the weak's (the 'other') resistance to hegemonic structures (xix). It seems here that strategies *conceive* space and participate in the *perception* of space, while tactics progressively determine *lived* spaces. According to de Certeau, the binary separation of space that depends on actions of the strong and the weak impacts how space and time are perceived, ranked, and appropriated: strategies are spatialised and tactics depend on time.

In the essay collection *Entanglements of Power: Geographies of Domination/Resistance* (2000), Tim Cresswell and Doreen Massey critique de Certeau's binary divisions between strategies and tactics, and domination and resistance. As opposed to subjects 'with will and power' managing space and its inhabitants, de Certeau describes very pessimistically the position of the 'weak', or the 'other', who lacks a proper place and can only resist strategies of power through micro-tactics (1984, 36–37). Massey argues that a more 'egalitarian map of power' requires thinking about power in terms of both possibilities and responsibilities by practising 'active spaces of action, [which are] continually being made' (2000, 284). While power configurations are not as totalising and all-coherent as de Certeau argues, Massey warns: 'a recognition that power is everywhere – and that we must pay attention to the micro-politics of power (which we must) – should not lead to a position where the real structural inequalities of power are lost, dissipated in a plethora of multiplicities' (280).

According to Massey, space should be considered as space-time affected by 'power-geometries': a practised, inhabited, and 'ever-shifting social geometry of power and signification' (1994, 3). Massey contends that space is not neutral, 'fixed and unproblematic in its identity' (5), but is instead an evolving source of meaning and social relations produced and reproduced within power configurations. While these power-geometries may seem immutably established within social relations, fixed in time, it is essential to retain Massey's idea that space always remains in a continual process of becoming. In her essay 'A global sense of place', Massey argues that not only 'capital' but also race and gender characterise our sense of space, time, and mobility (1994, 147). She describes our 'sense of place' as a place of rootedness as well as a progressive sense of place that accounts for our current 'global-local times', and the networks of power and control over mobility present within places and communities (150–52). Although people's sense of place often relates to their need for attachment, Massey contends that space should be detached from reactionary nationalisms, obsessions with 'heritage', or the idea that it conveys unproblematic stable identities (151). Instead, what matters is a 'geography of social relations': thinking of places as 'articulated moments in networks of social relations and understandings' not restricted by boundaries but positively linked to a consciousness of the wider world (Massey 1994, 154–55). Massey defines the concept of place as follows:

> what gives a place its specificity is not some long internalized history but the fact that it is constructed out of a particular constellation of social relations, meeting and weaving together at a particular locus. ... [Place] is absolutely not static. If places can be conceptualised in terms of the social interactions which they tie together, then it is also the case that these interactions themselves are not motionless things, frozen in time. They are processes. ... places are processes, too.... clearly places do not have single, unique 'identities'; they are full of internal conflicts. (1994, 154–55)

Cultural geographers have provided the tools to reconsider places that were previously seen as unproblematic (such as streets, houses, and cars) in a framework that considers the dynamic socialities of gender, class, 'race', and culture (Massey 1994, 2000; Rose 1993; McDowell 1999; Spain 1992; Thrift 2008; Uteng, and Cresswell 2008).[7] In her reformulation of space as social and contextual, Massey powerfully advocates the need to consider space as 'space-time', since the spatial is interrelated with the social, on a local and a global scale, and 'is integral to the production of history, and thus to the possibility of the politics' (1994, 269). Later I will argue that we should perceive of gender as a social construct and a foundation for unequal power-geometries rather than as a valid category of identity; similarly, we must reject the binaries that separate public from private, home from travel, and space from time.[8] Instead, space must be considered as in continual transformation, a transformation that, I argue, may occur through films, among many other sociocultural instances. In the next section, I explore the affectivity of spatial habitation, which films build upon, thereby making and remaking space.

Forms, Bodies, and Affects on Screen

If we are to see space as in continual transformation and constructed through fluid social relations, as Massey and Lefebvre argue, then we also need to understand that space is constructed through the affects (human and non-human) bodies have on one another. The recent (re)turn to affect theory in screen studies seems appropriate to account for the embodied aspect of power dynamics beyond binary patriarchal narratives, especially seen through the lenses of feminist scholars of affect (see Ahmed 2004, 2010; Berlant 2011; Brennan 2004; Butler 1997; Hemmings 2005; Sedgwick 2003; Stewart 2007).[9]

For Brian Massumi, affect encompasses three interrelated dimensions: a personal but collective bodily experience, a present potential to experience life, and an affective reflection. Massumi follows Baruch Spinoza's definition of affect: 'emotions *(affectus)*... [are] the affections of the body by which the body's power of activity is increased or diminished, assisted or checked, together with the ideas of these affections' (1982 [1677], 104). There is, in Spinoza, the double notion of being affected (having a decrease or increase of power of activity) and the accumulation of these affects. Cinema creates affects insofar as it is a mediated form, or in Lauren Berlant's words in *Cruel Optimism*, a 'recording form [that] not only archive[s] what is being lost but track[s] what happens in the time that we inhabit' (2011, 7).

Films aesthetically produce affects as they give shape to space and bodies. Following Massumi and Teresa Brennan, Lauren Berlant writes that 'bodies are continually busy judging their environments and responding to the atmospheres in which they find themselves' (2011, 15). If we consider the film as a body similar to the ones of the characters (see Barker 2009), the film *embodies* affects that give shape to space, characters, and situations. As the camera changes angle or lets in more or less light, for instance, it *gives form* to specific affects (see Brinkema 2014). In fact, when Spinoza refers to affecting and affective bodies, he is not only referring to the affect one human body can have on another, but also to affects produced by and to non-human bodies, objects, situations, and processes. Referring to Spinoza, Massumi explains that affect is 'the experience of a change, an affecting-being affected, redoubled by an experience of the experience' (2002, 4).[10] In other words, affect is the body's transiting 'power of activity' and the experience of that transition: a bodily experience that is at once personal and collective, affecting, and affected.

If affect is personal because people are individually affected in their own way, it is also collective because events or situations affect people collectively and have a similar bodily impact on a group of bodies, bodies that collectively affect each other (see Brennan 2004). Affects then form a 'visceral' memory that conditions our actions and reactions; this memory takes aesthetic forms on screen and may ultimately contribute to the building of collective cultural affects. Affects accumulate as 'perpetual bodily remainders', which 'expand our emotional register, or limber up our thinking', building potential 'ways of *connecting*', 'angles of participation in processes larger than ourselves' (Massumi 2002, 7; 5). In this sense, affect is *potential,* using a Deleuzian vocabulary, it is 'the *virtual co-presence* of potential' (5); in other words, accumulated ways of living that can become actualised. In Deleuze's interpretation of Spinoza, affect *(affectus)* is variation, 'the continuous variation of the will to exist (or the power of activity) of an individual, a variation that is determined by the 'ideas' that one has' (Deleuze 1978–1981, 9),[11] and is thus determined by previous affects. This brings us to another dimension of affect, as 'thinking, bodily', a 'thinking movement', 'the passing awareness of being at a threshold', which is not reflection (Massumi 2002, 8), but which, I argue, informs our consciousness and continually, subconsciously, transforms the ways in which we act, think, reflect, react, and feel, in the present. As Spinoza writes, 'whatsoever increases or diminishes, assists or checks, the power of activity of our body, the idea of the said thing increases or diminishes, assists or checks the power of thought of our mind', and transforms our imaginaries (Spinoza 1982 [1677], 111).[12]

Massumi explains that emotion and conscious thought are 'very partial [expressions] of affect', as 'the way we live… is always entirely *embodied, and*… is never entirely personal—it's never all contained in our emotions and conscious thoughts' (2002, 4; 5). In my embodied position as a spectator and as a researcher, the affects films produce—or embody—may modify such (affective) positions as suggested in the preface of this book; film may thus modify our 'margin of manoeuvrability, the "where we might be able to go and what we might be able to do" in every present situation' (in Massumi's words, 3). In the films I explore, affects *take form* through space and bodies, as aesthetic and narrative *passages* and connections. Similarly to Natalie Fullwood's work on gender and space in Italian cinema, this book explores 'how ideas of gender affect profilmic [that is, the spaces in the world chosen for settings] and filmic [that is, fictional, cinematic images] spaces, and the relation between the two' (2015, 5–6). *Affirmative Aesthetics and Wilful Women*, however, takes a reversed approach, as it considers how cinematic constructions of space and bodies give form to fluid genders, and everyday spaces (what Fullwood calls 'profilmic' spaces).

I disagree with Massumi's take on affect as asocial and outside discourse. Instead, I concur with Clare Hemming's idea that affect does not exist outside of social relations. Along with Lauren Berlant (1997), Audre Lorde (1984), Franz Fanon (1967 [1952]), and Sara Ahmed (2004), Hemmings emphasises that 'affective responses are bound by the early contexts in which [we] learn the codes and practices of gender and sexuality', among other social practices (2005, 560). Hemmings adds that certain subjects 'are so over-associated with affect that they themselves are the object of affective transfer', such as through sexualisation and racialisation (561). Hemmings refers to Jennifer Biddle's example of the woman prostitute, who has been inflected with being shameless, and to Franz Fanon's and Audre Lorde's accounts of black bodies as inspiring disgust in others and thus being affected with shame. As an example of affect, shame and disgust are linked to the social world through an 'ongoing, increasingly altering chain—body - affect - emotion - affect - body—doubling back upon the body and influencing the individual's capacity to act in the world' (Hemmings 2005, 564). Lorde's response to the ongoing spiral of shame may be interpreted as a wilful response, and as such, as an affirmative political act, whereby she 'reinvents her body as hers not theirs [such as through the erotic as Lorde argues elsewhere (1984)]... and connects to other bodies by shared judgments of the social' (Hemmings 2005, 564). As we will see throughout the book, and as Chap. 5 explores in more detail, the accumulation of negative affects (for instance as a woman, who is not accommodated by patriarchal structures) has an impact on one's habitation of space and gives form to space and bodies on screen. As Lorde's story exemplifies, these affects can also be appropriated and transformed (although not necessarily consciously), and thereby take affirmative forms.

In her book *The Cultural Politics of Emotion*, Sara Ahmed also interweaves affects with social relations and discourses. As she puts it, 'emotions shape the very surfaces of bodies, which take shape through the repetition of actions over time, as well as through orientation towards and away from others' (Ahmed 2004, 4). Affects orient our bodies into space, both through the presentness of the situation—the bodies we encounter—and how we are made to feel: our intentional emotions, which 'move us "toward" and "away" from such objects [we come into contact with]', in Ahmed's words (2006, 2).[13] In her book *Queer Phenomenology* (2006), Ahmed writes that bodies also take different shapes as they are being nominalised. Drawing on Butler's and Althusser's work on nominalisation, Ahmed explains that 'hearing oneself as the subject of [a gendered, sexualised or racialised] address' forces upon the subject a particular view of the world, orients bodies in a certain direction while hiding other directions from view (15). The body's power and will to persevere in a certain direction is in continual transformation, depending on how one affects and is affected by other human and non-human bodies. Certain spatial encounters and situations may create new connections and new ways of reaching out, and thereby turn the body in a different direction. As Ahmed eloquently describes in her later book *Willful Subjects* (2014), the subject may, for example, experience wilfulness out of not being accommodated.[14] Wilfulness may bring into sight lines and paths that have disappeared or have been concealed from view. Bringing these lines into view on screen, as I argue throughout this book, is affirmative, in so far as it *reaffirms* the fluidity of experience, and social and spatial relations.

In his second cinema book *L'image-temps,* Gilles Deleuze explains that film works as a mind, as a consciousness of the world and provokes a creative thinking *towards the world,* the unthought, the unseen (1985, 218). For Deleuze, through cinematic time ('durational' shots), film activates potentialities of the world which we fail to see in reality, producing a thinking towards the 'virtualities' within the real, in a similar manner as other philosophical 'tools' (see also Claire Colebrook 2000). Prior to this book, in *Différence et répétition,* Deleuze takes up the Bergsonian idea of 'duration' to explore continuous change, the process of becoming that things undergo through time (1976). Along the same lines, Elizabeth Grosz explains that 'each object is more than itself, contains within itself the material potential to be otherwise' (2005, 10).[15] Deleuze and Grosz argue that the real contains endless virtualities, the present being thus unfixed, ever-altering, and always in becoming; Deleuze adds, however, that the actualised form of these virtualities in the present space-time makes them appear (mistakenly) fixed and immutable (1976). Following Deleuze's thoughts, filmic representation may present both a version of reality that seems fixed and immutable and the virtualities of the same reality. While cinema has the potential to *fix* spatial habitation within racialised and gendered ideas, it may also affirmatively *suspend* these ideas of space and bodies and actualise alternative forms.

Following the notions of affect and cinema developed by Deleuze, Massumi, Berlant, Hemmings, and Ahmed, I would like to conclude that cinema acts as a 'way of thinking' towards the world and towards socio-spatial power relations. Although realist cinema is anchored in the actually existing, it may also reveal other perspectives: of a world in constant transformation. This book adopts Spinoza's and Deleuze's reading of affect as non-representative thought, as duration, as a passage: 'the continuous variation or the passage from one degree of reality to the next' (Deleuze 1978–1981, 10, translation mine).[16] In film theory, affect has often been considered as *being there* for the spectator, or as an exchange of potentialities between film and spectators (Sobchack 1992, 2004; Barker 2009). As Steven Shaviro writes, many film theorists have linked cinema and other media and art works to the production of affects, as *'machines for generating affect,* and for capitalizing upon, or extracting value from, this affect…. [films and music videos] lie at the very heart of social production, circulation, and distribution. They generate subjectivity' (Shaviro 2010, 2–3, emphasis in original). Rather than concentrating on the potential exchanges between film and viewers, this book focuses on the textures, light, objects, colours, sounds, and bodies that give shape to the film world, to space on screen. In his book *Non-Representational Theory: Space, Politics, Affect,* Nigel Thrift argues that it is by going beyond representation, beyond anchoring narratives and dialogues, that space, time, and gendered bodies become reconfigured (2008, 113–119). It is by focusing on affects as filmic forms that we can sense how this happens. In the genre of musicals, Richard Dyer finds great importance in recognising how 'non-representational signs' (colour, texture, movement, rhythm, melody, camerawork) 'embody feeling' and 'suggests an alternative to the narrative' (Dyer 2002 [1992], 21; 28). I contend that cinematic forms may create affirmative 'cracks' in the patriarchy that emerges from realist narratives; they may create what entertainment offers for Dyer: 'what utopia would *feel* like rather than how it would be organized' (20, emphasis mine). On a similar line, Eugenie Brinkema's model of close analysis ('reading for form') is appealing. In an authoritative and convincing manner, Brinkema writes in favour of 'treating affects as structures that work through formal means, as consisting in their formal dimensions (as line, light, color, rhythm, and so on) of passionate structures' (2014, 37). In her formalist film analyses, Brinkema reads affects as 'a matter of form, composition and structure [that] requires leaving behind narrative thematics', looking for the 'affective commitment' of a film (99). Her book *The Forms of the Affects* (2014) opens with detaching Marion's tear in Hitchcock's film *Psycho* from what it generally invokes: an emotional expression, a symptom of sadness. Brinkema reads the tear as form, as a structure: 'a texture', 'a distortion or culmination of pattern', or 'a method of reflecting light' (21). The tear becomes a form of affect, the form of a 'force more than transmission, a force that does not have to move from subject to object but may fold back, rebound, recursively amplify' (Brinkema 2014, 24). Reading affects as forms amounts to looking at virtual potentialities, at how transitions within space and bodies *take shape* on screen. Wilful affects should thus not be read as conscious mobilisation of the body against patriarchal dominance or oppressive representation, but rather as openness, transitions, and aesthetic actualisation of the virtual possibilities that exist within the real, and create the new against dichotomies of gender, space, and power.

Affective Cinematic Spaces

In this book, I regard characters and films as bodies of affects that constitute space. In his article 'On the role of affect and practice in the production of place', Cameron Duff underlines the recent turn whereby 'affects come to *actively constitute or produce place*' (2010, 884, emphasis in original). Referring to Nigel Thrift's *Non-Representational Theory*, Duff underlines how 'bodies are affected [both] *in place*... [and] *by place*', such that 'place always already conjures the lived, felt, and relational experience of a thinking, feeling body/subject' (885). If we refer to Maurice Merleau-Ponty's idea, there is no existence outside of our existence in space:

> Every sensation is spatial... sensory experience as the taking up of a form of existence ... It would be contradictory to say that touch is without spatiality, and it is *a priori* impossible to touch without touching in space since our experience is the experience of a world ... each sensation gives us a particular manner of being in space and, in a certain sense, of creating space. (Merleau-Ponty 2012 [1962], 230)

Whereas for Duff (referring to de Certeau) space is made through practice, for Merleau-Ponty it is our sensuous experiences of the world that lead us to 'create space'. Merleau-Ponty's understanding of the body as giving access to the social world through sense experiences enables us to consider how affects, that is, physical sensations towards another body that accumulate as ways of being in the world, are produced *in space* and in turn produce space.

Through the concept of power-geometry discussed earlier, Massey suggests that it is not only access to economical and transport resources that affects our experience of space but also social relations, which convert spaces themselves into sites of meaning and power (1994, 146–156). Although Massey situates the complexities of spatial experiences within social interactions determined by power rather than in affects, her text nonetheless suggests the affectivity of spatial existence: 'women's mobility, for instance, is restricted – in a thousand different ways, from *physical* violence to being ogled at or made to *feel* quite simply "out of place"—not by "capital", but by men' (1994, 148, emphasis mine). Both direct physical contact and mediated (such as filmic) experiences certainly affect us physically and therefore condition our reactions, behaviour, habitation of space, and indeed our whole social existence.

For instance, when I walk alone in the city (especially one unknown to me, and at night time), it is how I have been affected personally and collectively (as a woman) and how these affections have also been culturally mediated to me (through films for example) that orient the way I inhabit urban spaces: with fear, distrust, and a general feeling of being out of place. The many online and offline feminist movements against harassment in the post-2000s—such as Stop Street Harassment, the Slut Walks across the globe, the French Ni Pute Ni Soumise, Reclaim the Night, the Everyday Sexism Project, and the #metoo movement and its French equivalent #BalanceTonPorc—in fact reveal the collective, institutionalised, and ubiquitous dimensions of sexism and misogyny that negatively affect women's habitation of so-called 'public' spaces. Many women around the world have used their digital cameras to document sexual assaults and the many obstacles women have to overcome in the streets or before they go out of the house, such as in Brussels through "Femmes de la rue" (Peeters 2012), "10 Hours of Walking in NYC as a Woman" (Rob Bliss Creative 2014), and in Cairo, "Creepers on the Bridge" (Loon and Ghunim 2014). On the one hand, the digital sphere overflows with platforms that gather women's testimonies of being harassed, not feeling welcome, or not being *accommodated* in the urban space—thereby focusing on the negative affects of power-geometries. On the other hand, a plenitude of digital artists denounce what has come to be known as 'rape culture' in an array of creative and affirmative ways.

These range from comics to photography projects, creative essays, and social media posts, such as 'Projet Crocodiles' (Boutant and Mathieu 2013), 'Sexual Harassment in the Subway of Paris' on Eros-Sana.com (Sana 2015), 'Except, All of Us: Women and the Myth of Safety' (Foreman and Wong 2016), and a recent viral Twitter post that asks women, 'What would you do if all men had a 9pm curfew?' (Muscato 2018), which garnered thousands of answers from women who said they would take walk in parks without fear and with music on, leave their windows open at night, and enjoy doing activities alone. Instead of lamenting the limitations upon women, I argue that these creative instances affirmatively produce forces of potential change, open up a relational dialogue, and give us hope that things could be otherwise.

As Massey's work makes clear, the perception, practice, and production of space, and hence power-geometries, are contingent on a variety of social and cultural factors, and cinema certainly figures as a source of mediated experiences that affect in one way or another our view of the world. For film phenomenologists Vivian Sobchack and Jennifer Barker, films create a 'habitable *world* ... a space that is deep and textural, that can be materially inhabited' (Sobchack 2004, 151). Barker affirms that attention to texture, space, and rhythm allows us to determine 'the fleshy, muscular, and visceral engagement that occurs between films' and viewers' bodies' (2009, 4). For Barker, the transformative power of cinema lies in these affective exchanges between the film and the spectator. Rather than posit a direct (affective) transmission between film and viewers, I concur with film theorist and phenomenologist Kristin Lené Hole's idea that cinema makes us think about the world differently:

> [Cinema] fine-tunes our ethical sensibility with repercussions beyond the cinema doors. Cinema can alter our way of seeing and being in the world. Watching can be a kind of ethical training. Unfortunately, our codified ways of viewing tend to shut down an opportunity to encounter the unmasterable in the world and to see the other, for whom we are responsible, in all her singularity, surprise and wonder. (Hole 2016, 30)

Films force us to see differently and approach the world with wonder and desire. For Kristin Lené Hole in her book *Towards a Feminist Cinematic Ethics*, the emancipatory character of art lies in its interruption into the illusion of an objective knowledge. Cinema brings our senses to take different directions and constantly re-orientates ourselves, as it shows the world's ever-altering and dynamic existence (Hole 2016, 19).

My idea of affirmative aesthetics shares Hole's feminist ethics, as demonstrated in her exploration of Claire Denis' films, which she suggests are expressive of the idea that the world and the subject always exist in absolute alterity. As Hole writes, Denis' films 'both visually [register] "difference" or the classifications of gender and race that we use to understand the world, while also emptying them of their assumed or expected content' (2016, 9). Similarly, affirmative aesthetics refuse inadequate categories to make sense of the world and of spatial habitation, and thus interrupt totalising ideas of space and subject identity. As we will see, the affirmative films of this book both formulate a diegetic critique of how gender, sexual, and racial categories affect the characters' habitation of space and aesthetically dismantle or *suspend* the usefulness and inhabitability of these same categories.

An affirmative critique of films starts with the feminist consideration that cinema is an artistic practice that has the potential for emancipation, creation of the new, and raise possibilities that the status quo (reflected through realist narratives) obscures. Sometimes, by walking new paths and taking directions that are unexpected, wilful women characters transform the spaces they inhabit on screen, modifying—within the diegesis—the power-geometries of streets, houses, and cars, and they somehow *build* spaces that accommodate them. In other occasions, when characters may not appear to transform the structures of power that negatively affect their spatial habitation, the mise-en-scène, sound, montage, and rhythm of the film may *soak* the screen space with affirmative imaginaries that may be seen through the work of spectatorship. While philosopher Gaston Bachelard brings phenomenological attention to the possible exchanges between the poems' and readers' *bodies*, his topoanalysis emphasises the affective dimension of poetic images and their potential to produce the new. Bachelard explains that the affectivity of the poetic image arises in the unexpected character of a new image—in its creation of movements, 'spaces of language', and intimacies that carry the imagination along (1961, 8). If filmic images are always embedded within a collection of past images (the history of cinema), their particular aesthetic gives shape to different affects and constitutes its potential for expressing the new. In their book *The Forms of Films* (2004), Leo Bersani and Ulysse Dutoit emphasise that a major virtue of the visual arts is their capacity to make the invisible visible' (2004, 8). In order to see what visual arts make visible, however, Bersani and Dutoit suggest that it is necessary to read for forms and aesthetic choices rather than characters, which often take central stage. This may unveil 'what is *en-deça* ... an invisible non-event, which, however, we can, with some effort, see. That effort is the work of spectatorship' (Bersani and Dutoit 2004, 8). What matters, then, is looking for the invisible, that which is *en-deça,* that which comes to the side or 'before' the sanctioned individualities that cinema tends to make the most visible (and sometimes unforgettable, as the film star is the ultimate example of 'a sharply individualised presence') (8):

> We cannot become permanent works of art; the aesthetic subject is not a monumentalising of the self, but rather should be thought as a renewable retreat from the seriousness of stable identities and settled being. (9)

Looking for films' affirmative aesthetics is looking for the absolute alterity of bodies and spaces on screen, that which unsettles categories and our visual habits. A microanalysis of space and bodies on screen may thus reveal an affirmative potential that a strict analysis of characters, narrative, and dialogue may bury.

Filmic Affects as Affirmative Aesthetics

In both cinema and film theory, the dichotomous and hierarchical gendering of women's and men's bodies manifests as the first dimension that conditions mobility and spatial imaginaries. The fluid approach to space I explore above is designed to accommodate a different perspective on gender on screen. Given my focus upon women characters and their mobility, some kind of review of literature upon these topics might be expected. Yet feminist film theory is lacking an affirmative approach in this respect. In her essay 'Visual pleasure and narrative cinema', Laura Mulvey divides up cinematic spaces (1975): The woman's space is 'flat', she appears on screen, fetishised as an object of the male gaze (by the spectator and the character on screen), her 'beauty ... and the screen space coalesce; she is ... a product ... whose body [is] stylised and fragmented by close-ups... [at once] the content of the film and the recipient of the spectator's look' (1975, 14). By contrast, men are given a three-dimensional space, a seat as spectator, and the 'illusion of natural space', as 'the limits of the screen space' are blurred between the male spectator who through the male character can '[gain] control and possession of the woman within the diegesis'

(Mulvey 1975, 13). In spite of Mulvey's undeniable contribution to film theory, such an approach to representation through Lacan's psychoanalytic theories situates cinema as a mirror of a binary reality and the woman's body as a castrated version of the male's, which does not leave room for transformation. It ultimately reinforces men's spatial control and women's immobility within seemingly fixed and gendered socio-spatial binaries. This draws an opposition between subjects and objects of the gaze, the space on screen and the natural environment, and female characters and male spectators. This vision also focuses on the negative affects of deterministic heteronormative ecologies of cinematic desire.

While numerous film theorists have formulated the same concern, they often come short of answers. Both in cinema and in film theory, I have come across models that lament women's oppression and lack of freedom of movement (Bovenschen 1977; De Lauretis 1984; Irigaray 1977; Johnston 2000 [1973]; Mulvey 1975; Pidduck 1997, 1998), and very few that went beyond that lamentation. In order to take women away from their flat image and replace them in a material world that is perceived, sensed, and lived, many feminist film theorists have attempted to challenge the patriarchy of cinema by developing the idea of a possible 'feminine aesthetics' or a feminine 'language'. When Silvia Bovenschen discusses, a few years later, the idea of a 'feminine aesthetic', she simultaneously refers to a mode of *sensory perception* and a 'movement by women for women'; that is, an 'art with feminist intentions' (1977, 136). Bovenschen thus promotes a feminist *and* feminine aesthetic that would free women's imagination while resisting 'all the weeping and wailing' over the oppression of women (111). Echoing Bovenschen's call, Sue Thornham asks whether being the hero of a film's story empowers women and contributes to their unthinking themselves as victims. Like Teresa De Lauretis, Julianne Pidduck, and Natalie Fullwood, Sue Thornham dedicates her work to women and space on screen and warns us of the spaces that *contain* women. She warns us that post-feminist representations in particular, which Hilary Radner also explores, tend to replace women's quests, albeit heroic, within normative models of femininity (2012, 2–4).

In feminist theory and film theory, and in particular the writings of Bovenschen, Claire Johnston (1973), Luce Irigaray (1977), and Lucy Bolton (2011), there is an idea that women need to bond: collectively create narratives that place them into language from which they have been left out, so as to invent their own ('feminine') language. These considerations imply that women would have a particular way of being in the world compared to men; according to Irigaray, a way that is more centred on touch as opposed to vision (1977). This separates women and men in two opposed spaces. Instead, as I have discussed, I consider space and spatial habitation as affective, fluctuating with social relations and dynamics of power, which change with affects between bodies. Intervening in this lineage, affirmative politics 'aims at keeping life immanent, nonunitary' in Rosi Braidotti's words:

> This requires a double shift. Firstly, the affect itself moves from the frozen or reactive effect of pain to proactive affirmation of its generative potential. Secondly, this line of questioning also shifts from the quest for the origin or source to a process of elaboration of [ethical] questions that express and enhance a subject's capacity to achieve freedom through the understanding of its limits. (2011a, 294)

By 'mobilising resources that have been left untapped, including our desires and imagination', Braidotti emphasises how political and ethical agency become 'affirmative and geared to creating possible futures [instead of] ... oppositional and tied to the present by negation' (286). Similarly, rather than portraying gendered bodies as negatively affected by the patriarchal construction of space, I argue that films become affirmative when they imagine wilful bodies inhabiting fluid spaces and subject identities.

Wilfulness and Affirmative Politics

Referring to Foucault, Braidotti writes that 'the material that damages is also that which engenders positive resistance, counteraction, or transcendence' (2011a, 285). The idea that being negatively affected 'engenders positive resistance' strongly echoes Sara Ahmed's concept of wilfulness, which the preface of this book introduced. As Ahmed underlines, 'willing is *a matter of how we are affected*' (2014, 76). Because of the negative affects produced by gendered restrictions on their mobility, the protagonists of my chosen films act according to these principles (although wilfulness is an affective experience rather than a conscious decision). As well as the models of 'dangerous women' and/or 'lost' wandering women that road movies epitomise (as the following chapter will show), we can find wilful women who refuse to be 'straightened out', to be put back on the *right path* of happiness (as Sara Ahmed would put it). In a certain way, they find what Lauren Berlant calls 'adjustments' to not reaching the neoliberal fantasies of 'the good life', much like the characters in the films *La Promesse* (1996) and *Rosetta* (1999) by the Dardenne brothers (Berlant

2011, 2–3). Reading Ahmed reminds me of a series of filmic characters: wilful wandering women demanding spatial power, such as the iconic Thelma and Louise, Wanda in the film of the same name (Barbara Loden 2006 [1970]), Anna in *Les rendez-vous d'Anna* (Chantal Akerman 1978), Jeanne and Marie in *Messidor* (Tanner 1995 [1979]), Helene in *Germany, Pale Mother* (Helma Sanders-Brahms 2008 [1980]), Rosaleen in *The Company of Wolves* (Neil Jordan 2002 [1984]), Mona in *Sans toit ni loi* (Agnès Varda 1985), Radha in *Fire* (Deepa Mehta 1996), Have, Ahoo, and Hoora in *The Day I Became a Woman* (Marzieh Meshkini 2000), Cathy Whitaker in *Far from Heaven* (Todd Haynes 2002), the women of *The circle* (Jafar Panahi 2000) and *Offside* (Panahi 2006), Munis, Faezeh, Farrokhlagha in *Women Without Men* (Shirin Neshat 2009), and the three female protagonists of *678* (Mohamed Diab 2010), among many others. These wilful wanderers persist in inhabiting the street space, even as they recognise it as being a male arena that does not accommodate them.

While Braidotti calls for the endurance of the subject, who is '[pointing] to the struggle to sustain the pain without being annihilated by it' (2011b, 289), Sara Ahmed asserts that 'wilfulness involves persistence' (2014, 2). Ahmed underlines the difficulties in wilful persistence, as seen in many 'female road movies' and in a majority of the films mentioned above. It is often easier to obey than to disobey, such that 'a subject can be willing [to obey] in order to avoid being forced' (139). Just as 'persistence can be an act of disobedience', wilfulness tends to be perceived as a problem, of someone who wills too much or wills wrongly (Ahmed 2014, 2). As I will explore in my analysis of *Messidor* in the next chapter, it is by persistently inhabiting a space dominated by men to which they do not belong that Jeanne and Marie are identified as willing too much or willing wrongly, and are portrayed as 'dangerous women'. In road movies, it seems that it is the wandering of 'unaccompanied' female bodies that is identified as a danger for patriarchy and thus needs to be annihilated within the narrative. In order to extract the affirmative politics of films that portray women's wilfulness instead of their alienation, we must look for a new vocabulary, one that recognises wilfulness as affirmative spatial habitation and social existence.

In their theories both Braidotti and Ahmed underline the importance of generational lines and spatial movement. While Braidotti places emphasis on the activity of 'a group project that connects active, conscious, and desiring citizens… and [constructs] social horizons of hope' (2011a, 294–95),[17] Ahmed insists on the importance of creating new wilful paths for women to follow. The wilful subjects creating these paths may already be following others before them (2014, 153–54). Both Braidotti and Ahmed appear to situate affirmative politics and wilfulness, respectively, within space: both practices require the spatial movement of one group or individual and their 'democratic' access to the public sphere (see Sheller and Urry 2000).

Ahmed develops her concept of wilfulness across two books, *The Promise of Happiness* (2010) and *Willful Subjects* (2014), which both rely on her first book *The Cultural Politics of Emotion* (Ahmed 2004). Ahmed often describes wilful subjects as wanderers '[straying] from official paths, [creating] desire lines' that they hope others will follow (2014, 21). Following Ahmed's work in her book *Queer Phenomenology,* wilful subjects may be 'disorientated', attempting to orient themselves on a different path than the one prescribed for them; in this sense, wilful subjects *queer* expected lines. Looking at travelling women in the road movie, we find wandering women, not on a journey of self-transformation, like male protagonists, but in a sphere that is not theirs and in which they struggle to exist. They are not 'naturally' accommodated by the public sphere, as men are; instead, they struggle to move around and lack hope of finding an answer or destination through their movement, as men usually do.

The women protagonists of *Messidor*, *Head-On*, *Wadjda,* and *Vendredi soir*—the films I analyse in this book—inhabit space in a wilful way and from an affirmative position. The three protagonists also engage in processes of transformation of the power-geometries that subjugate them. They experience wilfulness to create different paths for themselves and other women to follow, while already following paths of women before them. Instead of the patriarchal binaries of realist films bounded by the present space-time, these films express the wilfulness of their female characters through affective forms, giving shape to an aesthetics of affirmation. From one generation to the next, and from one culture to another, the wilful paths of women on screen open up possibilities, transforming spatial imaginaries and ultimately perhaps spaces themselves.

Much like Braidotti's call for affirmative politics, Ahmed's concept of wilfulness implies that the negativity of one's affective position is transformed into a productive, affirmative force. For Ahmed, wilfulness emerges as a political act, in which wilful subjects are happy to cause trouble, happy to 'be the cause of unhappiness' (Ahmed 2010, 15). As they become identified as 'feminist killjoys', the protagonists of the films in this book (Jeanne and Marie, Laure, Wadjda, and Sibel) manifest, in Ahmed's words, as 'wilful women, unwilling to get along, unwilling to preserve an idea of happiness' (2014, 2). As wilful subjects, they refuse to follow the path they are asked to follow in a sexist and patriarchal society, they have the will to 'not to go with the flow', and they will 'what is not present' as they march 'with angry feet' and 'put their bodies in the way' of patriarchal imaginaries (Ahmed 2014, 11; 8; 163). As such, wilfulness involves spatial movements and 'full', lived, embodied habitation of one's space. It is through aesthetic choices (mise-en-scène, sound, cinematography) that the films give shape to space and to the protagonists' empowered habitation of these spaces.

Ahmed defines becoming wilful as being involved in an affective project, a project to overcome an obstacle that we encounter, to reach for what seems out of reach (37; 41). Like Braidotti's affirmative project, the wilful project is oriented towards 'objects of hope': founding alternative paths, opening up possibilities and imagination, and finding 'space to breathe'— be it as a person of colour in a racist world or as a woman in a misogynistic world (Ahmed 2010, 120). In both Braidotti's and Ahmed's work, and as for Spinoza, Massumi, and Deleuze, imagination appears as a source for transformation. Desire and imagination manifest as 'resources that have been left untapped' and have the potential to 'create possible worlds' (2011a, 286), or to reach for what seems out of reach, to reach for the virtual within the real.

Both Ahmed's wilfulness and Braidotti's affirmative politics advocate in a very similar fashion (albeit without acknowledging each other) the production of (positive) resistance to the injustices of the present through the transformation of negative affects into wilful or affirmative forces. While wilfulness tends to the actions (affective, unconscious) of characters, affirmative refers to the forms of the film: its aesthetic production of spaces and bodies that escape or suspend *fixed* ideas of gender and power-geometries. The films chosen bring women's 'mobility' under an 'affirmative' light, by portraying their wilful bodies' habitation of space-time in continual transformation. When Braidotti writes her 'Plea for affirmative ethics', she calls for affirmative critical thinking and activism which understands humanity as not rising from freedom, 'but rather that freedom is extracted out of the awareness of our multiple limitations … affirmation [being] about freedom from the burden of negativity, through the understanding of these limitations' (2011b, 269).

It is due to the limitations on their 'freedom' within the patriarchal status quo that the protagonists of *Messidor, Vendredi soir, Wadjda,* and *Head-On* experience wilfulness. It is also through each film's understanding of the patriarchal limitations on space and mobility for women that their cinematic spaces become 'spaces of wilfulness', spaces that the women protagonists fully inhabit. Similarly, albeit in different measures and forms, if one looks beyond representation, the filmic aesthetics of *Sans toit ni loi, Marseilles, Les rendez-vous d'Anna, 678, Ten,* and *The Day I Became a Woman,* among others, may appear to share similarities with the films analysed here, as they affirmatively transform the gendering of space through the 'wilful wandering' of their women subjects. I argue that the films' affirmative images of spatial habitation and 'mobility' perform a 'remapping of dwelling', as Giuliana Bruno suggests: re-writing streets, cars, and houses as ever-changing space-time, lived, experienced, and inhabited affectively.

Book Structure

My quest for affirmative aesthetics explores how cinematic representations of specific diegetic spaces contribute to the disentanglement of space from seemingly fixed and determined power-geometries on screen. I am looking for forms, light, textures, rhythms, and sound that give shape to affirmative affects: cinematic aesthetics that counteract the established relations between subject, gender, and space. The affirmative aesthetics of film include both wilful women characters, which inhabit space against normative flows, and aesthetic choices (rhythm, colours, mise-en-scène, cinematography, sound) that unveil spaces and bodies as fluid and unbounded. As the films' aesthetics produce specific affects, they also create narrative content and convey sociocultural meanings. More than 'positive representations of women doing positive things', I refer to affirmative aesthetics as feminist works that dismantle binaries and give form to fluid genders, spaces, and identities. A micro-analysis of cinematic spaces and characters' relations to space reveals the affirmative aesthetics of films such as *Messidor* and *Head-On* (in Chaps. 2 and 5), which may otherwise remain buried in negativity. Although in appearance these films may seem to focus overtly on how the power-geometries of streets and other 'public' spaces negatively affect women, they aesthetically give form to micro-instances of affirmation wilful women that inhabit space 'freely'—and spaces that offer new configurations. While not all feminist works can be deemed affirmative, the affirmative aesthetics of films is a spectrum rather than a binary division. This book also hopes to open the reflection towards an affirmative form of critique, one that critically *reads for* forms that establish subjects and space as fluid, relational, and in constant transformation. *Affirmative*

Aesthetics shows how this happens in spite of the negativity and apparent fixity that may characterise realist narratives.

Women's wilful habitation of space takes various forms that are worth exploring. The films of this book, from a diversity of cultural contexts, in fact engage with very different cultural forms of patriarchy. While the concepts of mobility, space, and gender adopt distinct shades, they each speak affectively to women's spatialities. In his work on imagination as a social practice, Appadurai celebrates the cross-cultural aspect of imagination 'for the creation of multiple horizons of possibility' (2002, 34). As the book looks for models of films that situate spatial habitation within fluid—unbounded—social and affective relations, it looks at a cross-cultural corpus of films so as to broaden the diversity and plurality of aesthetic 'acts of resistance' and of 'margins of manoeuvrability' (echoing Massumi's words, 2002, 3). The four films chosen are case studies of affirmative aesthetics: filmic transformation of gendered spatial imaginaries. The films give different aesthetic forms to spaces, identities, and the wilfulness of their women characters: *Messidor*, a wandering without goal, a pause for reflection, allows to unravel the problematic gendering of the notion of 'mobility' in film; *Vendredi soir* deepens the idea of inhabiting space as empowering through a haptic aesthetic that converts bodies into lived bodies, focuses on sensations and textures, and brings in the imaginative; *Wadjda* reveals the necessity for women to find their own space, and to sometimes put on a mask so as not to be identified as wilful; *Head-On* pushes the idea of masquerade and performance of gender to abjection, an erotic connection to one's bodily environment as an escape from norms and expectations.

The interdisciplinary models explored thus far go far beyond the critical theories that maintain men and women within gendered narratives of travel and mobility. By including feminist geography, feminism and gender theories, and theories of affect and phenomenology within film theory, this book considers spatial habitation as fluid and dynamic rather than 'static'. It posits women's subjectivities as bodily situations and spatial experiences, and extends beyond the 'grand (male) narratives' of travel by expanding representational analysis into an analysis of the forms of wilful affects and an affirmative rewriting of space, power, and bodies. Chapter 2 shows the limits of considering the mobility of women in the same terms as men's and reveals the need for other tools and vocabulary to consider women's relations to space. Through the close analysis of *Messidor* (Alain Tanner 1979), the chapter explores how the (male-dominated) road movie's conventional representation of mobility as transformative and as a repossession of the known (home, as *domesticated* space) does not work for women. Because of the obstacles women need to overcome before even leaving home, the transformative forces that generally emerge from the road movie genre through movement emerge here through the wilfulness to keep moving without aim and with the ability to pause, reflect, and inhabit space through lived affective experiences. The subversion of the genre creates affects of hope through inhabiting instead of travelling. The mise-en-scène of the film, with scenes often starting *in media res*, emphasises Jeanne and Marie's will to not stop moving: empowerment is about *becoming* mobile and embracing the road. If *Messidor* seems to critically condemn women characters to immobility, a micro-analysis of bodies and cinematic space reveals the film's affirmative aesthetic in face of the negativity present within the diegesis.

The following three chapters, which analyse *Vendredi soir, Wadjda,* and *Head-On*, are divided between the particular consideration of a space-time affected by the 'patriarchal gendering of space', namely the car, the house, and the street, respectively (as we will see, the habitation of these spaces prove to be intimately interrelated). These three films have in common the absence of a space that can be called 'home', and the difficulties that women face when roaming the streets (as observed in *Messidor*). Vehicles lose their aspect of possession of the land they travel through and instead enable women to fully inhabit spaces of intimacy (spaces of their own and of contact with others). In addition, 'home' becomes a liminal space that disrupts private/public boundaries, and the street is a space that one affectively embodies.

The third chapter, which analyses Claire Denis' film *Vendredi soir* (2002), delves deeper into the idea that affirmative aesthetics takes shape through micro-relations between bodies and space. The chapter anchors wilfulness into the lived habitation of space and the forming of a 'lived body' on screen. In the film, the car loses its dimension of travel and appraisal of the other through the windscreen and becomes a space of intimacy for the characters, a space in which the affectivity (the bodily experiences) of space manifests narratively and aesthetically. Whereas Sibel and Wadjda are overtly wilful within the narratives of *Head-On* and *Wadjda,* respectively, Laure, the woman protagonist of *Vendredi soir,* manifests as a timid woman inhabiting space through integrated gendered norms. Three aspects of the film's aesthetic, which become especially apparent when going beyond representational analysis, transform the negative affects of Laure's gendered situation into affirmative habitation of space. First, the magical aesthetic of the film creates a sensuous experience of the city, blurring the boundaries that separate diegetic 'real' from subjective imaginaries and allowing the 'virtual possibilities of the real' (in Deleuze's terms) to be actualised on screen. Second, through a haptic aesthetic that merges the bodies of the male and female protagonists, Denis blurs the gendered bodily binaries that regulate spatial habitation, as seen in the previous chapter. Finally, the film 'frees' space of its negative affects by building up 'spaces of intimacy' through representational and affective images, liminal spaces of encounter that (temporarily) suspend the patriarchal gendering of space. The film's blurring of the binary categories real/imaginary, male/female, and public/private becomes apparent through the analysis of bodies' micro-relations to space. The film's aesthetic creates an affirmative *passage* between virtual and actual, which counteracts the negative affects of power-geometries on women's habitation of space, and creates a transition to becoming a lived desiring body.

Chapter 4 reads for wilfulness as filmic forms in Haifaa Al-Mansour's *Wadjda* (2012) and shows how affirmative ethics is about understanding the limitations to our freedom. When the young protagonist Wadjda realises that she cannot have a bicycle because she is a girl, she begins to confront the unequal and gendered practices of space. As Wadjda claims 'what is simply given to others' (echoing here Sara Ahmed 2014, 147), her wilfulness to create an alternative future translates on screen as micro-instances of activism. If in cinema the traveller often takes central stage, the one who stays, like Wadjda, may also inhabit space in wilful ways and modify the power-geometries of space. As the chapter adopts the tools of phenomenology and explores how Wadjda and her mother inhabit different places, such as the street, the school, and the house, it shows how objects mediate wilfulness. Doors, veils, phones, and bicycles all produce wilful forms and *make space* for the protagonists to refuse docility. The recognition of one's limitations and the necessary masking of wilfulness take spatial shape; the roof of the house as such becomes a 'heterotopic' space (Foucault 2004 [1984]), at once contained within and opening beyond the structures of patriarchy—it is simultaneously a space subjected to unequal power-geometries and an affirmative space that accommodates and fosters wilfulness.

Chapter 5 focuses on the street as a contested diegetic space in Fatih Akin's film *Gegen die wand/Head-On* (2004), one that is gendered and requires negotiation. While the performance of gender appears as a spiral from which one cannot escape, it also appears as a means to disrupt established roles and the myth of subject identities governed by gender and racial categories. This chapter takes as point of departure Judith Butler's idea that gender is always a performance insofar as it figures as ideals that are *uninhabitable* (1993). It also follows Audre Lorde's idea of connecting to the erotic within one's body as a feminist approach to refuse conventions and require the best for oneself (1984). By examining the woman protagonist Sibel's body movements on screen (see also Kate Ince's phenomenological approach to film 2017), the chapter shows how dancing, walking in the streets, connecting to the erotic and abjecting one's body take affirmative forms; a suspension of the gendering and racialisation of space. While Sibel is punished for taking ownership of her body and sexuality several times in the diegesis, the affirmative aesthetic of the film becomes clear through her embodied habitation of everyday spaces as spheres of the possible.

In one way or another, *Messidor, Vendredi soir, Wadjda,* and *Head-On* engage in a process of transformation of space and of the affects of spatial habitation. While the films' narratives may (more or less overtly) confront and oppose the patriarchal gendering of space, it is their filmic aesthetics that transform negativity into affirmative forces. Desire manifests in different forms in each film, as lived, wilful, masquerading, and erotic bodies. The desiring bodies of the protagonists and of the films themselves experience a will to find and create spaces of intimacy, spaces of *belonging*, belonging then not to the current dichotomous conceptions of space but rather to affirmative fluid spaces.

While my approach, just as Braidotti's, is relational and geared towards alternative possibilities, it is anchored in visual culture and in finding concrete models of representation and affective forms that refuse to situate gender, sexuality, or race as valid categories of subject identities and spatial habitation. The affirmative in my view is a radical shift from binary models to recognising the deeply relational and complex dimension of existence. Rather than producing positive or negative affects, *Affirmative Aesthetics: and Wilful Women* modifies the reading of space and bodies as necessarily gendered, as found in the road movie genre or in numbers of films seen through the lens of feminist film theory. In this sense, the book follows the disobedience and disorientating dimension of Sara Ahmed's *Queer Phenomenology* (2006) and *Willful Subjects* (2014), the interruptions of the myth of the subject in Kristin Lené Hole's *Towards a Feminist Cinematic Aesthetic* (2016), and the radical ideality of José Esteban Muñoz's *Cruising Utopia* (2009). Unbalanced power-geometries spur a resistance that is collective and affective, an affirmative resistance that I argue manifests on screen as filmic forms that need to be read for.

Notes

1. As we will see throughout this book, though in road movies straying (female) wanderers are opposed to extensive (male) travellers, as the second chapter will explore, wandering off the prescribed path and inhabiting space without extensive movement become forms of affirmation of one's wilfulness.
2. Tanu Priya Uteng and Tim Cresswell observe how 'scientific schoolbooks [describe] the human reproductive process' in terms of the *passive* egg and the *travelling* sperm, and how touristic mobilities are still anchored in the masculinist concept of travel as 'exploration and conquest' (2008, 2–4). As they hope to depart from dichotomous gendered oppositions, Uteng and Cresswell advocate considering 'mobilities more generally' in a wider context and emerging from 'a variety of disciplinary backgrounds' to consider mobility through non-binary aspects: as at once 'physical movements', 'meanings associated with movement', and practice, 'embodied and experienced aspects of moving' (6).
3. Working-class women and prostitutes already had access to the public space, but were categorised as 'non-respectable'.
4. See also *Specters of Marx: the State of the Debt, the Work of Mourning, and the New International (Jacques* Derrida 1993*)*.
5. In fact, Wilson underlines the alienation of the male *flâneur* in the city, 'who represented not the triumph of masculine power, but its attenuation', a haunting figure, 'sexually insecure' and 'annihilated' by the anonymity of the urbanisation of the metropolis (Wilson 2001, 86–88). Walter Benjamin also emphasises that by roaming in the arcades filled with commodities 'arousing desires', the male *flâneur* too was part of the consumer mass (1999, 42). He was gazing at the world *around* him and was consuming its images as commodities, converting women themselves into commodities of his gaze and artistic production. In Benjamin's Marxist reading of the *flâneur* figure, not only is he a consumer but also a commodity of the capitalist society, whereby his strolls in the city were his necessary labour time for his artistic production (1999, 446–448). In this sense, the com-

modification and consumption to which the city appealed negatively affected both the *flâneur* and the *flâneuse*. However, if Baudelaire compared poets to prostitutes selling themselves through their art, female prostitutes had a much harder time for they had to be subjected to intimate medical controls and had increasingly been marginalised from other women.
6. Braidotti's 'cartography' resonates with Giuliana Bruno's idea of the map (in *Atlas of emotion*, 2002) and Moira Gatens' imaginaries (see *Imaginary bodies: Ethics, power and corporeality*, 1996), as I will explain later in this chapter. In fact, Bruno writes about film as 'a modern cartography: its haptic way of site-seeing turns pictures into architecture, transforming them into a geography of lived, and living, space' (2002, 9).
7. Before the rise of feminist geography at the beginning of the 1990s, in the writings of Doreen Massey, Gillian Rose, Linda McDowell, and Daphne Spain women's bodies had thus far been paired with childbirth, mothering, nurturing, and nature, and conflated with the domestic sphere, unproblematically shaping and legitimating gender roles and power relations. Gillian Rose explains that 'socially constituted relations and identities' have indeed become naturalised for claiming their source in the body (1993, 30). Rose describes how the public sphere became constructed around notions of 'rationality, individuality [and] self–control' associated with the 'masculine' standing in opposition to the female body and its naturalised 'interpersonal inclination' (35; 26).
8. In his book on gendered urban spatialities, *Les murs invisibles*, social geographer Guy Di Méo argues that *queering* our notions of space and gender is essential to reach an equal sense of spatial habitation in the city (2011, 317). Using Lefebvre's concept of the triplicity of space (lived–perceived–conceived), Di Méo interprets gender and space as evolutive processes, constituted by social behaviours and situations (313–314).
9. See the review articles by Kristyn Gorton (2007) and Pedwell and Whitehead (2012) for comparative accounts of affect theory from feminist perspectives.
10. Nigel Thrift similarly understands affect as a 'form of [indirect and nonreflective] thinking … [an] intelligence about the world' (175), 'transhuman … understood as effects of the events to which their body parts (broadly understood) respond and in which they participate' (2008, 175).
11. Translation mine. 'L'affect (affectus) 'c'est la variation continue de la force d'exister [ou de la puissance d'agir] de quelqu'un, en tant que cette variation est déterminée par les idées qu'il a' (Deleuze 1978–1981, 9).
12. Spinoza writes that 'the mind, as far as it can, endeavours to imagine whatever increases or assists the body's power of activity, that is those things it loves' (116), whereby love (as opposed to hate) is 'merely pleasure accompanied by the idea of an external cause' (113) and pleasure (as opposed to pain) is 'the passive transition of the mind to a state of greater perfection'

(1982 [1677], 111). For Spinoza, imagination leads the subject to attribute elements of pain or pleasure to an object (present or imagined) that they have previously regarded with love or hate (115–16), thereby the body can be affected by the sole imagination of the object. For Spinoza, one's affect constantly varies between two poles, of pleasure and pain, that is the increase or decrease of the power to act, or 'the will to exist' in Deleuze's words (1981).
13. Along the same line as Spinoza referring to the 'ideas of these affections' as fully contingent with affection itself, Margaret Wetherell writes that 'core affects… are simultaneously perceived, organised, categorised, labelled and communicated becoming socially recognisable 'emotions'. Any initial bodily hit, in other words, is always already occurring within an ongoing stream of meaning-making or semiosis' (2013, 355).
14. While Ahmed uses the American spelling 'willfulness', which will be preserved when quoting her work, this book uses the British spelling 'wilfulness', for both coherence and integrating the idea that the will does not emanate from an individual subject, but that wilfulness rather figures as collective affect that take shape through filmic forms on screen.
15. Part of 'the whole of matter', each object contains endless *virtualities* (in Deleuze's words), potentialities that it can become, but it first 'needs to unbecome, undo its actuality as fixed givenness' (Grosz 2005, 10). See also *Le Bergsonisme* (Deleuze 1966).
16. 'L'affect, c'est la variation continue ou le passage d'un degré de réalité à un autre' (Deleuze 1978–1981, 10).
17. For more on the geographies of hope, see David Harvey's *Spaces of hope* (2000).

References

Ahmed, Sara. 2004. *The Cultural Politics of Emotion*. Edinburgh: Edinburgh University Press.
———. 2006. *Queer Phenomenology: Orientations, Objects, Others*. Durham/London: Duke University Press.
———. 2010. *The Promise of Happiness*. Durham/London: Duke University Press.
———. 2014. *Willful Subjects*. Durham: Duke University Press.
Akerman, Chantal. 1978. *Les Rendez-Vous d'Anna*. DVD. France/Belgium/West Germany: Paradise Films.
Akin, Fatih. 2004. *Gegen Die Wand [Head-On]*. DVD. Germany/Turkey: Strand Releasing.
Al-Mansour, Haifaa. 2012. *Wadjda*. DVD. Saudi Arabia/Germany: Sony Pictures Home Entertainment.
Appadurai, Arjun. 2002. The Right to Participate in the Work of the Imagination. In *Transurbanism*, ed. Arjen Mulder. Rotterdam: NAi Publishers.

Bachelard, Gaston. 1961. *La Poétique de l'espace*. 1st edition in 1957. Paris: Presses Universitaires de France.
Barker, Jennifer M. 2009. *The Tactile Eye: Touch and Cinematic Experience*. Berkeley/Los Angeles/London: University of California Press.
Benjamin, Walter. 1999 [1927–1940]. *The Arcades Project*. Cambridge, MA: Belknap Press.
Berlant, Lauren. 1997. *The Queen of America Goes to Washington City: Essays on Sex and Citizenship*. Durham: Duke University Press.
Berlant, Lauren Gail. 2011. *Cruel Optimism*. Durham: Duke University Press.
Bersani, Leo, and Ulysse Dutoit. 2004. *Forms of Being: Cinema, Aesthetics, Subjectivity*. London: BFI Publishing.
Bolton, Lucy. 2011. *Film and Female Consciousness: Irigaray, Cinema and Thinking Women*. Hampshire/New York: Palgrave Macmillan.
Boutant, Juliette, and Thomas Mathieu. 2013. *Projet Crocodiles*. Comics Online. https://projetcrocodiles.tumblr.com
Bovenschen, Silvia. 1977. Is There a Feminine Aesthetic? *New German Critique* 10: 111–137.
Braidotti, Rosi. 2011a. *Nomadic Theory: The Portable Rosi Braidotti*. Chichester: Columbia University Press.
———. 2011b. The New Activism: A Plea for Affirmative Ethics. In *Art and Activism in the Age of Globalization*, ed. L. De Cauter, R. De Roo, and K. Vanhaesebrouk, 264–270. Rotterdam: NAi Publishers.
Brennan, Teresa. 2004. *Transmission of Affect*. London: Continuum.
Brinkema, Eugenie. 2014. *The Forms of the Affects*. Durham/London: Duke University Press.
Bruno, Giuliana. 2002. *Atlas of emotion: Journeys in art, architecture, and film*. London/New York: Verso Books.
Butler, Judith. 1993. Critically Queer. *GLQ: A Journal of Lesbian and Gay Studies* 1 (1): 17–32.
———. 1997. *Excitable Speech: A Politics of the Performative*. New York: Routledge.
Colebrook, Claire. 2000. From Radical Representations to Corporeal Becomings: The Feminist Philosophy of Lloyd, Grosz and Gatens. *Hypatia* 15 (2): 76.
Cresswell, Tim. 2000. Falling Down: Resistance as Diagnostic. In *Entanglements of Power: Geographies of Domination/Resistance*, ed. Joanne P. Sharp, Paul Routledge, Chris Philo, and Ronan Paddison, 256–268. London/New York: Routledge.
de Certeau, Michel. 1984. *The Practice of Everyday Life*. Berkeley: University of California Press.
De Lauretis, Teresa. 1984. *Alice Doesn't: Feminism, Semiotics, Cinema*. Bloomington/Indianapolis: Indiana University Press.
Del Río, Elena. 2008. *Deleuze and the Cinemas of Performance: Powers of Affection*. Edinburgh: Edinburgh University Press.
Deleuze, Gilles. 1966. *Le Bergsonisme*. Paris: Presses Universitaires de France.

———. 1976. *Différence et répétition*. Paris: Presses Universitaires de France.
———. 1978–1981. Cours Vincennes: Intégralité du cours 1978–1981, cours du 02/12/1977 (Spinoza). Retrieved on 9 Oct 2019 from https://www.webdeleuze.com/textes/188
———. 1985. *Cinéma 2: L'image-temps*. Paris: Editions de minuit.
Denis, Claire. 2002. *Vendredi Soir*. DVD. France: Bac Films.
Derrida, Jacques. 1993. *Spectres de Marx: l'état de la dette, le travail du deuil et la nouvelle internationale*. Paris: Editions Galilée.
Di Méo, Guy. 2011. *Les murs invisibles: femmes, genre et géographie sociale*. Paris: Armand Colin.
Diab, Mohamed. 2010. *678*. DVD. Egypt: Audio Visual Entertainment.
Duff, Cameron. 2010. On the Role of Affect and Practice in the Production of Place. *Environment and Planning D: Society and Space* 28: 881–895.
Dyer, Richard. 2002 [1992]. *Only Entertainment*. London/New York: Routledge.
Fanon, Frantz. 1967 [1952]. *Black Skin, White Masks*. New York: Grove Press.
Foreman, Aricka, and Mimi Wong. 2016. Except, all of us: Women and the myth of safety, February 2. Essay Online. Retrieved on 9 Oct. 2019 from https://theoffingmag.com/enumerate/except-all-of-us
Foucault, Michel. 2004 [1984]. Des espaces autres. *Empan* 2 (54): 12–19.
Fullwood, Natalie. 2015. *Cinema, Gender, and Everyday Space: Comedy, Italian Style*. New York: Palgrave Macmillan.
Gorton, Kristyn. 2007. Theorizing Emotion and Affect: Feminist Engagements. *Feminist Theory* 8 (3): 333–348.
Grosz, Elizabeth. 2005. Bergson, Deleuze and the Becoming of Unbecoming. *Parallax* 11 (2): 4–13.
Harvey, David. 2000. *Spaces of Hope*. Edinburgh: Taylor & Francis.
Haynes, Todd. 2002. *Far from Heaven*. DVD. USA/France: Focus Features and Vulcan Productions.
Hemmings, Clare. 2005. Invoking Affect. *Cultural Studies* 19 (5): 548–567.
Hole, Kristin Lené. 2016. *Towards a Feminist Cinematic Ethics: Claire Denis, Emmanuel Levinas and Jean-Luc Nancy*. Edinburgh: Edinburgh University Press.
hooks, bell. 2009. *Belonging: A Culture of Place*. New York: Routledge.
Ince, Kate. 2017. *The Body and the Screen: Female Subjectivities in Contemporary Women's Cinema*. London/Oxford: Bloomsbury.
Irigaray, Luce. 1977. *This Sex Which Is Not One [Ce sexe qui n'en est pas un]*. Ithaca: Cornell University Press.
Johnston, Claire. 2000 [1973]. Women's Cinema as Counter-Cinema. In *Feminism and Film*, ed. E. Ann Kaplan, 22–33. Oxford: Oxford University Press.
Jordan, Neil. 2002 [1984]. *The Company of Wolves*. DVD. United Kingdom: Hen's Tooth Video.
Lefebvre, Henri. 1974. *La production de l'espace*. Paris: Anthropos.

Loden, Barbara. 2006 [1970]. *Wanda*. DVD. USA: Parlour Pictures.
Lorde, Audre. 1984. *Sister Outsider: Essays and Speeches*. Berkeley: Crossing Press.
Massey, Doreen B. 1994. *Space, Place, and Gender*. Minneapolis: University of Minnesota Press.
Massey, Doreen. 2000. Entanglements of Power: Reflections. In *Entanglements of Power: Geographies of Domination/Resistance*, ed. Joanne P. Sharp, Paul Routledge, Chris Philo, and Ronan Paddison, 279–286. London/New York: Routledge.
Massumi, Brian. 2002. Navigating Movements. *21C Magazine* 2: 210–243.
McDowell, Linda. 1999. *Gender, Identity and Place: Understanding Feminist Geographies*. Minneapolis: University of Minnesota Press.
Mehta, Deepa. 1996. *Fire*. DVD. India/Canada: Seville Pictures.
Merleau-Ponty, Maurice. 2012 [1962]. *Phenomenology of Perception*. London/New York: Routledge.
Meshkini, Marzieh. 2000. *Roozi ke zan shodam [The Day I Became a Woman]*. DVD. Iran: Makhmalbaf Productions.
Mulvey, Laura. 1975. Visual Pleasure and Narrative Cinema. *Screen* 16 (3): 6–18.
Muñoz, José Esteban. 2009. *Cruising Utopia: The Then and There of Queer Futurity*. New York: New York University Press.
Muscato, Danielle. 2018. *Ladies, What Would You Do if All Men Had a 9pm Curfew?*, September 26. Retrieved on 27 Sep 2018 from https://twitter.com/DanielleMuscato/status/1044686450028163074
Neshat, Shirin. 2009. *Zanan-e bedun-e mardan [Women without Men]*. DVD. Iran: Essential Filmproduktion.
Panahi, Jafar. 2000. *Dayereh [The Circle]*. DVD. Iran: Winstar TV and Video.
———. 2006. *Offside*. DVD. Iran: Artificial Eye.
Pedwell, Carolyn, and Anne Whitehead. 2012. Affecting Feminism: Questions of Feeling in Feminist Theory. *Feminist Theory* 13 (2): 115–129.
Peeters, Sofie. 2012. *Femmes de la rue*, July 26. Video Online. Retrieved on 3 Mar 2013 from https://www.dailymotion.com/video/x3fb4sp
Pidduck, Julianne. 1997. Travels with Sally Potter's *Orlando*: Gender, Narrative, Movement. *Screen* 38 (2): 172–189.
———. 1998. Of Windows and Country Walks: Frames of Space and Movement in 1990s Austen Adaptations. *Screen* 39 (4): 381–400.
Radner, Hilary. 2010. *Neo-Feminist Cinema: Girly Films, Chick Flicks, and Consumer Culture*. New York: Routledge.
Rob Bliss Creative. 2014. *10 Hours of Walking in NYC as a Woman*. YouTube. Posted on 28 Oct 2014. https://youtu.be/b1XGPvbWn0A
Rose, G. 1993. *Feminism and Geography: The Limits of Geographical Knowledge*. Cambridge: Polity Press.
Sana, Eros. 2015. *Sexual Harassment in the Subway*. Photography Online. http://eros-sana.com/auteur/france/sexual-harassment

Sanders-Brahms, Helma. 2008 [1980]. *Deutschland Bleiche Mutter [Germany, Pale Mother]*. DVD. West Germany: Facets Video.
Sedgwick, Eve Kosofsky. 2003. *Touching Feeling: Affect, Pedagogy, Performativity*. Durham: Duke University Press.
Sharp, Joanne P., Paul Routledge, Chris Philo, and Ronan Paddison, eds. 2000. *Entanglements of Power: Geographies of Domination/Resistance*. London/New York: Routledge.
Shaviro, Steven. 2010. *Post-cinematic Affect*. Winchester/Washington, DC: 0 [zero] Books.
Sheller, Mimi, and John Urry. 2000. The City and the Car. *International Journal of Urban and Regional Research* 24 (4): 737–757.
Sobchack, Vivian. 1992. *The Address of the Eye: A Phenomenology of Film Experience*. Princeton: Princeton University Press.
———. 2004. *Carnal Thoughts: Embodiment and Moving Image Culture*. Berkeley/Los Angeles/London: University of California Press.
Solnit, Rebecca. 2001. *Wanderlust: A History of Walking*. London: Penguin Books.
Spain, Daphne. 1992. *Gendered Spaces*. Chapel Hill: University of North Carolina Press.
Spinoza, Baruch. 1982 [1677]. *The Ethics and Selected Letters*. Indianapolis/Cambridge: Hackett.
Stewart, Kathleen. 2007. *Ordinary Affects*. Durham: Duke University Press.
Tanner, Alain. 1995 [1979]. *Messidor*. VHS. Switzerland: Citel Films.
Thornham, Sue. 2012. *What If I Had Been the Hero?: Investigating Women's Cinema*. Basingstoke: Palgrave Macmillan.
———. 2019. *Spaces of Women's Cinema: Space, Place and Genre in Contemporary Women's Filmmaking*. London: The British Film Institute.
Thrift, N.J. 2008. *Non-representational Theory: Space, Politics, Affect*. New York: Routledge.
Uteng, Tanu Priya, and Tim Cresswell. 2008. *Gendered Mobilities*. Farnham: Ashgate Publishing.
Loon, Tinne Van, and Colette Ghunim. 2014. *Creepers on the Bridge*, August 30. Vimeo. Retrieved on 9 Oct 2019 from https://vimeo.com/104798581
Varda, Agnès. 1985. *Sans toit ni loi* [Vagabond]. VHS. France: Ciné Tamaris.
Wetherell, M. 2013. Affect and Discourse – What's the Problem? From Affect as Excess to Affective/Discursive Practice. *Subjectivity* 6: 349–368.
Wilson, Elizabeth. 1991. *The Sphinx in the City: Urban Life, the Control of Disorder, and Women*. Berkeley: University of California Press.
———. 2001. *The Contradictions of Culture: Cities, Culture, Women*. London: SAGE.
Wolff, Janet. 1985. The Invisible flâneuse: Women and the Literature of Modernity. *Theory, Culture and Society* 2 (3): 37–46.

———. 2006. Gender and the Haunting of the Cities (or, the Retirement of the flâneur). In *The Invisible Flâneuse?: Gender, Public Space, and Visual Culture in Nineteenth-Century Paris,* ed. Aruna D'Souza and Tom McDonough, 18–31. Manchester: Manchester University Press.

Woolf, Virginia. 1942. *The Death of the Moth, and Other Essays.* London: Hogarth Press.

Open Access This chapter is licensed under the terms of the Creative Commons Attribution 4.0 International License (http://creativecommons.org/licenses/by/4.0/), which permits use, sharing, adaptation, distribution and reproduction in any medium or format, as long as you give appropriate credit to the original author(s) and the source, provide a link to the Creative Commons licence and indicate if changes were made.

The images or other third party material in this chapter are included in the chapter's Creative Commons license, unless indicated otherwise in a credit line to the material. If material is not included in the chapter's Creative Commons licence and your intended use is not permitted by statutory regulation or exceeds the permitted use, you will need to obtain permission directly from the copyright holder.

CHAPTER 2

Women's Road Movies and Affirmative Wandering: *Messidor*

> *For the* voyageuse *to exist as nomadic subject, a different idea of voyage and different housing of gender is to be sought: travel that is not a conquest, dwelling that is not domination. A place where nostalgia is replaced by* transito—*a mobile map.*
> (Giuliana Bruno 2002, 86)

Giuliana Bruno's words resonate with the idea behind this book that both subjects and places are in continual transformation. Whether traveling through or dwelling in a place, mobility and habitation are about constant change; power relations, subjects, and places are never fixed. While patriarchal structures negatively affect women's movement and travel, affirmative forces arise from these forms of oppression, which appear particularly clearly when analysing women in the road movie genre. As we will discover through this chapter, this analysis suggests that women's mobility cannot and should not be compared to men's. In critiques of road movies involving women protagonists, the mobility of the characters is often seen as a non-mobility and a lack of achievement when compared to men's mobility in the traditional road movie. The bitterness that arises from these films often arises from the many economic and social obstacles women encounter on the road, as well as from a much-too-common dependency on men to achieve mobility, such as in

© The Author(s) 2020
M. Ceuterick, *Affirmative Aesthetics and Wilful Women*,
https://doi.org/10.1007/978-3-030-37039-8_2

Wanda (Barbara Loden 2006 [1970]), *Germany, Pale Mother* (Helma Sanders-Brahms 2008 [1980]), *Mortelle randonnée* (Claude Miller 1983), *Sans toit ni loi* (Agnès Varda 1985), *Thelma and Louise* (Ridley Scott 2002 [1991]), *Butterfly Kiss* (Michael Winterbottom 1995), *Monster* (Patty Jenkins 2003), *Morvern Callar* (Lynne Ramsay 2003), *In July* (Fatih Akin 2004), *Marseille* (Angela Schanelec 2004), *Transylvania* (Tony Gatlif 2006), *My Blueberry Nights* (Wong Kar-Wai 2007), *Yella* (Christian Petzold 2007), *Wendy and Lucy* (Kelly Reichardt 2008), and *American Honey* (Andrea Arnold 2016). Rather than placing women's (non-)achievement against men's, this chapter will use an affirmative lens to explore how women's wilful habitation of space manifests on screen in the road movie *Messidor* (Alain Tanner 1995 [1979]), a film made in continuation of the feminist movements of the 1970s.

As many film scholars have noted, the road movie is generally dominated by male protagonists, while examples of 'women road movies' are scarce (Cohan and Hark 1997; Corrigan 1992; Eyerman and Löfgren 1995; Gott and Schilt 2013; Laderman 2002; Mazierska and Rascaroli 2006; Mills 2006; Orgeron 2008; Pérez 2011). The road movie is traditionally recognised by a male protagonist who undertakes a self-reflective quest away from home, with the home often representing a conservative lifestyle that he hopes to escape. Timothy Corrigan describes road movies in the following manner:

> the heroes of these travelogues embark on a learning experience that becomes most historically determined in bildungsroman tradition: the familiar is left behind or transformed through the protagonist's movement through space and time, and the confrontations that he encounters generally lead, in most cases, to a wiser individual and often a more stable spiritual or social state. (1992, 144)

Through physical mobility, the protagonist hopes to find the freedom that being on the road promises and, if possible, even achieve social mobility (Eyerman and Löfgren 1995, 56–57). The familiar, or 'home', appears in opposition to travel. In *The Road Movie Book*, editors Steve Cohan and Ina Rae Hark write that 'the road movie promotes a male escapist fantasy linking masculinity to technology and defining the road as a space that is at once resistant while ultimately contained by the responsibility of domesticity: home life, marriage, employment' (1997, 3). Home becomes at once a space of conventions and one of lost intimacy that the protagonist hopes to regain on the road. The road thus becomes an alternative to 'home', where the main character searches for a more 'authentic' space of intimate relations.

In contemporary cinema, and in road movies in particular, the notion of home often signifies a familiar domestic space associated with women and in opposition to mobility and the 'masculine' (see Blum-Reid 2016; Bruno 2002; De Lauretis 1984; Fullwood 2015; Frederick and Hyde 1993; Mazierska and Rascaroli 2006; Robertson 1997; Rollet 2003; Royer 2011). Giuliana Bruno describes how the notion of home, of one's origin, of *domus*—domesticity, domestication—in male narratives of travel 'continues to be confused and gendered feminine' (2002, 86). As such, home has acquired a meaning of 'the womb from which one originates and to which one wishes to return' and has become 'the very site of the production of sexual difference' (Bruno 2002, 86). In travel narratives, returning and 'repossessing' home often emerge as repossessing the female subject or 're-housing gender'. Instead, Bruno argues for rewriting home as a sphere of the possible, emphasising it as a space that is always in *transito*, in writing, constantly made and remade through time and social relations.

Road movies with women protagonists are often considered to be a rewriting of the male genre, in the same way that European road movies 'seem a reaction to, or reformulation of, the American genre' (Laderman 2002, 247). Accordingly, scholars have relegated both European and 'women's road movies' to the last chapter of their works (see Cohan and Hark 1997; Corrigan 1992; Eyerman and Löfgren 1995; Laderman 2002; Orgeron 2008; Pérez 2011). With the exception of the recent collection of essays *Open Roads, Closed Borders: The Contemporary French-Language Road Movie*, edited by Gott and Schilt (2013), women's road movies are treated separately from other road movies and are typically cast as an *alternative* to the male genre. If both the European and women's road movies appear at the margins of the generic definition of the road movie, on-screen 'appropriations' of the genre by women characters have not been as successful as the European ones. As mentioned, women have to overcome many obstacles before even starting their journey, including a lack of a means of mobility (transport, economic independence) and limited agency in the public sphere when compared to their male counterparts. Women's journeys also tend to end in more troublesome predicaments than the journeys men undertake on screen. A handful of scholars have looked for fruitful feminist models for mobility throughout the road movie genre (see Blum-Reid 2016; Mazierska and Rascaroli 2006; Rollet 2003; Royer 2011; Tarr and Rollet 2001). To give one example: In their analysis of the film *Morvern Callar* (Lynne Ramsay 2003), Ewa Mazierska and Laura Rascaroli suggest that 'the best way of travelling is not travelling', as the protagonist only finds satisfaction in relative immobility (2006, 197)—in other words, it is difficult for women to inhabit and belong to 'public' places. Mazierska and Rascaroli rightly conclude their chapter on women's mobility in *Crossing New Europe: Postmodern Travel and the European Road Movie* by underlining the many social and economic conditions that women need to fulfil, as opposed to men, before they can even begin their travels or become (successful) travellers (2006, 198). The above studies have noted how women tend to move in a less expansive manner as male protagonists; instead, women seem to be spatially limited by gender roles and expectations: first, to get out of the house and then second, onto the road itself. They often wander aimlessly, disempowered or dependent on other (male) characters to achieve mobility. I share the conclusions of a number of these scholars that women's mobility might not be identifiable through the male narratives of travel (see Bruno 2002; Frederick and Hyde 1993; Mazierska and Rascaroli 2006; Pratt 2012; Uteng and Cresswell 2008). Significantly, few of these scholars provide alternative models, with a recent exception in the work of Kate Ince (2017), who turns to phenomenology to consider women's mobility through body movements.

By offering a detailed examination of women's bodily relations to space, this chapter aims to put into practice what the previous chapter suggested theoretically. Whereas the gendered dimension of women's bodies conditions their access to and control over their mobility and habitation of space, a micro-analysis of space and bodies on screen allows us to see how *Messidor* produces affirmative forms. The film aesthetically transgresses and transforms the traditional road movie genre and its representation of space as immutably gendered and inflected by established (that is, seemingly fixed) power-geometries. While Tanner's film exemplifies the obstacles to women's mobility, it also critiques the concept of mobility itself, by which women and men are opposed in terms of stasis and transformation (see Uteng and Cresswell 2008). Rather than emerging through extensive travel, the affirmative forces of *Messidor* take shape at a micro-level. It is through the characters' affective relations to space that the film aesthetically untangles mobility from masculinity, power, and the possession of home.

As the opening credits unroll, a series of forward and lateral tracking shots filmed from a helicopter establishes the setting for *Messidor*. Travelling across countryside and peripheral highways, and ending its course in the mountains, the camera sets the landscapes for the protagonists' journey. The sudden changes of directions of the filming, with the camera filming ahead or completely tilted towards the ground, create a disjointed scene. The lateral tracking shots from right to left, opposite to the Western direction of reading, evoke the desolation and fatalism contained in Schubert's song 'Gute Nacht', part of his 'Winterreise', that plays during the scene. In the music and the cinematography of this sequence, and in the film as a whole, Alain Tanner alternates moments of hope and hopelessness. The music's lyrics and variations between major and minor tones, and the contrast between its title 'Winterreise' (meaning 'winter travel') and the film's title *Messidor* (referring to the first summer month in the old French Republican calendar), foreground the uneven adventures of the protagonists, Jeanne and Marie. If the path of Jeanne and Marie is 'covered in snow'—or obstacles—like in the beginning of Schubert's song ('Der Weg gehüllt in Schnee'), they will still 'roam on the road rather than linger in the master's house' ('Lass irre Hunde heulen; Vor Ihres Herren Haus!; Die Liebe liebt das Wandern'): both Jeanne and Marie were living with a man who had some power over the house before going on their journey. Reading *Messidor* through an affirmative lens brings attention to the film's critical perspective upon women's difficulties in travelling, as well as to the aesthetic shaping of the protagonists' wilful habitation of space.

The transgressive intentions of *Messidor* are evident from the beginning of the film, when Jeanne rebels against a misogynist man who picks her and Marie up. Marie, another woman hitchhiker. Marie soon abandons her plan to return home to her mother and unpalatable stepfather, and joins Jeanne to wander around the countryside. As they travel together around Switzerland without aim or money, Jeanne and Marie have to rely on others, predominantly on men, to provide them with transport, food, and accommodation. After resisting a sexual assault, they steal a policeman's gun out of his glove box and as a result are pursued as 'criminals'. Their portrayal as *dangerous women* on national television limits their ability to move around freely. At the conclusion of the film, they mistakenly kill a man in a café and are arrested.

Comparing *Messidor* briefly with another European road movie produced three years prior, *Kings of the Road* (Wim Wenders 1976), involving two male strangers bonding on the road, pinpoints the extra difficulties Jeanne and Marie encounter on their journey because of their gender. Three main differences emerge. First, in *Kings of the Road*, the male protagonists, Bruno and Robert, have a vehicle (a truck) and economic means to travel, while Jeanne and Marie lack transport and money, and thus are restricted and dependent (mostly on men) for access to mobility (generally understood as long travel in road movies). Whereas Bruno and Robert's ownership of a vehicle allows them unproblematic access to the social spaces,[1] which is also granted by their bodies gendered as masculine, Jeanne and Marie's lack of a car positions them in a vulnerable situation, also created by a patriarchal society which portrays their female bodies as *problematic*. Second, while Bruno and Robert's truck provides them with a space of intimacy, a space to bond and express their desires, Jeanne and Marie are vulnerable and in danger because of the absence of any kind of dwelling space. Unlike Bruno and Robert, Jeanne and Marie are unable to return to the domestic space and repossess it, nor are they able to find a 'home' on the road, it being a constraining space for women. Third, through their bonding and mobility, the two men appraise the road as a space that they can fully inhabit, and experience a journey of self-transformation. In contrast, Jeanne and Marie lose their independence on the road as their bonding becomes necessary for their survival. They seem trapped in an image of themselves as dangerous women, threatening to a patriarchy that strives to maintain their wilful bodies in a hierarchical, dichotomous situation as gendered bodies.

While gendered identities and expectations determine Jeanne and Marie's journey and fate, their wilfulness brings up affirmative forms on screen. Jeanne and Marie's lack of money, means of transport, and inadequacy in social spaces foreground the way in which space is gendered, preventing them from dwelling and moving with ease. From the beginning of the film, Tanner makes clear that the road does not offer the same 'freedom' to women as it does to men. On their journey, Jeanne and Marie meet numerous bourgeois men who display a paternalistic attitude towards them, advising them on life, economy, and travel. However, Jeanne and Marie are portrayed as disobedient and wilful to fully inhabit space, and as better educated than most of the male characters they meet on the road, whose actions and discourses appear petty, reactionary, and absurd. By performing a micro-analysis of how the two women inhabit the three contested spaces of the road movie genre, the car, the road and home, it becomes clear that the wilfulness of the protagonists take affirmative forms on screen, which need to be read for and made visible.

While the first scene uniting Jeanne and Marie narratively sets the negative tone for the entire film, emphasising the difficulties the two women will encounter on the road, the scene also takes affirmative forms that a micro-analysis can reveal. The first man to give them a ride is a misogynist neoliberal man who complains about 'working his ass off' for other people to study and is especially critical of the fact that 'all girls go to university now'. Jeanne, herself a student, responds to this critique, answering in a manner far superior to that of the driver, her eloquent intervention resulting in the women being left on the side of the road. The tight close-up framing of the misogynist man from a slight low angle (see Fig. 2.1) characterises him as an overtly ridiculous, pedantic voice. The shallow focus of the filming of the man's head, blurring the road in the background, displaces his voice, making its discourse look out of time and space, somewhat universally (or widely) accepted, though harmful. The dissonant violin chords that resonate during the scene, and are then heard again repeatedly during the film, help to create a hostile atmosphere, suggesting that the road is dangerous for the two women. The camera, however, frames Jeanne and Marie together in the backseat in a medium shot that makes the passing road visible in the back window (see Fig. 2.2). Their visual situatedness in time and

Fig. 2.1 *Messidor*: First misogynist driver

Fig. 2.2 *Messidor*: Jeanne answers back

space, and the eloquence of Jeanne's response compared to the man's simplistic speech, place them in an affirmative situation. Whereas the film diegetically points to the pessimistic conclusion that subversion of the patriarchal and capitalist Swiss society as a whole is insurmountable, wilful affects are aesthetically visible from the start. Rather than on encounters and self-transformation, the focus of this unconventional road movie is on the process, albeit a struggle doomed to fail, of inhabiting and moving through space as unaccommodated bodies.

As opposed to traditional road movies, which involve the mobility of characters in their car or another personal vehicle, *Messidor* shows how the absence of a car implies an absence of a space of intimacy. The protagonists' lack of economic resources and means of transport of their own leads to their alienation from society. Cars in fact figure as impersonal objects, metaphors for the capitalist patriarchal society as a whole, which is unaccommodating to characters such as Jeanne and Marie. When the voices of the male drivers are heard or part of their faces are shown, it is to emphasise their paternalistic, at times racist, speech as obstacles to the women's intention of mobility. As if seeing from another passenger's perspective, the camera often films the road ahead rather than the driver, as would be expected in a road movie. Such a disembodiment of the male characters, contrasting with the deeply embodied Jeanne and Marie, shows how little the negativity emanating from these characters affects the wilfulness of the protagonists to travel. Similarly, as two men assault Jeanne, the camera remains distant and fixed during the whole scene and only changes to a closer shot when Marie grabs a rock to knock out the attackers. Even if they lack a vehicle of transport and protection, Jeanne and Marie appear as empowered, wilful women instead of passive victims, who put their bodies in the way of patriarchy and gender expectations.

An analysis of *Messidor* within the framework of the road movie genre would only lead to the negative statements formulated earlier: of the impossibility of the women to become *flâneuses* because of their constant sexualisation through the male gazes they encounter. In contrast with the traditional road movie involving men travellers, *Messidor* does not focus on self-transformation or finding the meaning of home on the road, but instead on the wilfulness to become mobile and on the institutionalised sexism that limits Jeanne and Marie's full habitation of space. Jeanne and Marie's view of travel resonates with Frederick and Hyde's observation of women's travel in travel-writing literature:

> Movement becomes a way to combat a feeling of homelessness that has nothing to do with the physical site of home. (xxi) ... Whatever the reasons for embarking on a journey, women travellers both accept and embrace risk. ... no danger means no freedom. ... when the journeyer exults in danger and celebrates her survival, she is glorying in the *freedom* to be in danger. (1993, xxii)

As Jeanne and Marie also affirm 'if you don't take risks, you go nowhere' ('si on ne risque rien, on a rien'), the risks they take by venturing into a space dominated by men become the risks necessary to combat their feeling of homelessness. The protagonists find affirmation through the recognition of the 'limitations to their freedom' and their liberation from the 'burden of negativity' (in Braidotti's words).

Wilful affects translate as persistence in moving, incessant movement on screen. Jeanne and Marie mock their own representation as dangerous women on television and the injunctions that the road is dangerous for women 'alone' (read: without men), similarly to the women protagonists of later films such as Thelma and Louise (Ridley Scott, 1991), Butterfly Kiss (Michael Winterbottom, 1995), Monster (Patty Jenkins, 2003), and

Frozen River (Coutney Hunt, 2008). To keep moving is their weapon against the unjust power-geometries that define the road and other 'public' spaces, to go on a journey whose only goal is not to go *home*—a journey that began with Jeanne's desire to leave her apartment and Marie's refusal to go back to her mother's house. While the car appears as a masculine space *par excellence* where they only are passengers—no woman is shown driving in the whole film—houses and interior spaces such as cafés and restaurants epitomise the bourgeoisie that Jeanne and Marie's journey protests against. Jeanne expresses how she hates the 'cute little houses' that they see in the small town of Aarberg. The dialogue emphasises how home is a space of domesticity and conventions, as opposed to the playful aspect of the road and the 'freedom' that movement brings. Despite their lack of economic resources, the women agree to continue travelling, with Jeanne stating, 'either we act conventionally and go home like everyone else, or we can play a game… we go on… until we find out. I'm not sure what, but that's beside the point'. As in *Head-On*, as the last chapter will explore, the possibility of transforming the power-geometries of space takes shape in *Messidor* through its aesthetic forming of space and subjects as fluid, rather than in its diegesis. Just as in *Vendredi soir* or in *Wadjda*, 'finding out' may mean finding another kind of home, one that is in transit and one that they inhabit affectively.

The Swiss landscape becomes their home, a space of both liberation and boredom. The film leaves behind a messy cartography, as Jeanne and Marie cross linguistic boundaries and go around in circles, up the mountain and back down again, to the city and back to the countryside, as it becomes increasingly clear that the road is the protagonists' real home. As Jeanne and Marie become increasingly alienated from social spaces—dominated by middle-aged, middle-class men—the mountains become their new dwelling. It is where they take refuge, their safe space, albeit one that is hostile to habitation because of the lack of food. The almost constant sunny weather in *Messidor* (also expressed through the title) provides the road journey with an optimism that the general sociality of its space lacks. When the two women first head to the mountains, with the goal to 'go up and even further, to the point of no return', they are shown in an extremely long shot in high angle as they walk up the mountain. They are seen as tiny bodies only made visible by their movement through the monotonous gray rock and small patches of snow; they inhabit a space that absorbs them, an environment into which they visually merge (see Fig. 2.3). The silence, length, and fixity of the take, along with the faint, occasional bird song, constitute a peaceful atmosphere. After the two women have climbed the

Fig. 2.3 *Messidor*: Long shot of Jeanne and Marie walking up the mountain

ridge and emerge onto a grassy plateau, fixed medium shots situate them in an environment that they fully inhabit. Jeanne opens her arms in a V-shape towards the sky (see Fig. 2.4), and in a seamless movement slowly lets herself slide onto the rock behind her, adapting her body to its shape. Jeanne's silent exclamation, in spite of her open mouth, echoes the silence of the environment. Her standing body reiterates the mountain lines, instead of disturbing the cinematic space.

Similarly, the camera, Marie's body and the rock behind her form a perfect line. The visual and aural representation of Jeanne and Marie in the mountains give affirmative shape to their habitation of space. These moments of affirmative aesthetics indicate the optimism that emerges from the film—Jeanne's cheerful body is also featured on the cover of the released video—despite the abundance of obstacles that the two women confront in the urban space. Rather than offering the 'possibilities of resistance' that Elizabeth Wilson identified for the *flâneuse* in the modern city (1991, 8), the city in *Messidor* is hostile. The film instead adopts the trope of finding oneself in nature, in the great outdoors—a trope that may appear somehow *cliché* in its usual association with femininity, but that in Tanner's film connotes rebellion against capitalism (a foundation of 1970s social movements).

Fig. 2.4 *Messidor*: Jeanne and Marie seamlessly inhabit their spatial environment

Fig. 2.3 *Messidor*: Long shot of Jeanne and Marie walking up the mountain-Fig. 2.4 *Messidor*: Jeanne and Marie seamlessly inhabit their spatial environment-While a narrative reading of *Messidor* may hinder its optimism by setting excessive attention on the women's failure to travel expansively and become *flâneuses* as men are able, the micro-analysis of cinematic spaces unveils how the film displaces the centre rather than marginalising its protagonists from the urban space. If cities and cars appear as the shelter of capitalism and the bourgeoisie, the mountains and lakesides become the homeland of the rebellious youth, the youth at the centre of the May 68 movement and the youth that appear as the protagonist of Tanner's film *Jonas qui aura 25 ans en l'an 2000* (Tanner 1992 [1976]). The only overtly joyful music in *Messidor*, an oriental score during which Jeanne and Marie dance in a moment of affirmation, symptomatically resonates on the border of a lake in the mountains. As in the next scene, when Jeanne and Marie decide not to cross the Swiss border into Italy after being publicly portrayed as criminals, the deep silence, majestic landscape, and high surrounding mountains give form to an immense space that is in constant transformation, both accommodating, giving rise to affirmative affects, and persistently unwelcoming, the sign of the loneliness of resistance to the status

Fig. 2.5 *Messidor*: The road forms a social border difficult to cross for Jeanne and Marie

quo. The sudden heavy sound of traffic interrupts the silence of the mountains and situates the two hitchhiking women on the side of a busy road (see Fig. 2.5). The dissonant score in a minor key and the long take of the two small bodies framed in a long shot immobile on the side of the road—in opposition to the movement of the cars in the centre of the frame—produce a sense of entrapment, an entrapment into a sexist system, which the urban space embodies and from which it is difficult to escape. Whereas the road forms a visual border on screen, maintaining the women in stasis and on the margins of the public sphere, the mountains become their home on the road, a 'room for themselves'. As we will see in the following chapters, affirmation of wilful women often coincides with establishing and inhabiting one's own space, which manifest both diegetically and aesthetically.

Movement figures as a remedy for the homelessness of the protagonists. The protagonists' persistence in the face of adversity—their constant sexual commodification and paternalistic belittling—takes shape as they take the road and keep moving without stopping. The movement of the camera and of the bodies on screen give form both to the duration and the disobedience involved in their resistance. The slow rhythm of the film, its lack of frequent action, and numerous ellipses emphasise the long-lasting persistence of the protagonists against the power-geometries they have to face. Scenes often start *in medias res* (such as in Homer's *The Odyssey*): in the middle of conversations, with a response to an unheard question, or by framing a landscape in a fixed shot that the moving bodies of the protagonists interrupt. The lack of chronology and cartography of the women's journey creates a sense of affective duration, not limited by time and space but expandable across times and spaces through how one is affected and affects others. The wilful affects of the protagonists are demonstrated on screen as disobedience, going against the flow, and occupying space. When Jeanne and Marie walk on the side of the road, the camera films them in tracking shots from right to left, walking against the traffic that flows in a conventionally forward direction from left to right on the screen. As they philosophically reflect on their own movement 'in empty space… [becoming] interesting', their paused bodies and their voices take the foreground while the passing cars and the sounds of traffic are relegated to the background (see Fig. 2.6). Their bodies taking space on screen give form to wilful affects, as a refusal to go with the flow of the patriarchal capitalist system. The aesthetic choices of this scene show how their paused

Fig. 2.6 *Messidor*: 'We're moving through empty space'

reflection empowers them and affirmatively turns them into the Greek *idiotes* in opposition to the pedantic rhetoric of the men they cross paths with (see Chris Ingraham's book *Gestures of Concern* (2020) on the empowered concern of *idiotes*). If, as Ingraham writes, it is the *idiotes*' ability to pause that allows them to reflect and thoughtfully express political or social concern, Jeanne and Marie's ability to stop is what also enables them to move through the unaccommodating spaces they encounter.

The empowerment of the two women manifests aesthetically as an ability to pause and keep moving. According to Naila Kabeer, empowerment is inextricably linked to agency and choice: 'the expansion in people's ability to make strategic life choices' thanks to a combination of three interrelated dimensions: resources (material, human, and social preconditions), agency (process), and achievements (outcomes), whereby agency is the 'people's capacity to define their own life-choices and to pursue their own goals, even in the face of opposition from others' (1999, 437–438). For Sarah Banet-Weiser, however, there is an urgent need to debunk the harmful opposition between agent and victim, and the association of agency with individual choice, which fail to recognise the institutional sexism that *keeps women in their place* outside of the public sphere (2019). If the two women apparently lack the material and social resources to achieve their goals and become empowered, Jeanne and Marie are far from being depicted as victims. The persistence of the protagonists to move and fully inhabit space are represented aesthetically in the film as bodies that come *in front* or *in the way* of the patriarchy that negatively affects their freedom of movement. As the two women resist sexual assault, throw themselves in front of cars to get a ride, enter uninvited into sheds for a place to sleep, and sit at other people's tables in cafés, their bodies visually interrupt the fixity of the frame and give a physical and tangible shape to wilfulness. While several men in the film perceive Jeanne and Marie as prostitutes, thus reproducing the frequent commodification of women in public places, the gun the women steal becomes an extension of their body, the penis they lack in order to move as freely as men do (see Fig. 2.7). The gesture of Jeanne holding the gun as a penis constitutes a queering of gender, reducing it (and men's domination) to an inanimate object, one that others can possess and control. This wilful gesture debunks the myth of the subject as a fixed set of identities, and the gendered dichotomy opposing agents and victims. Rather than as an individual decision, however, this gesture emerges as an affective experience of collective negative affects. As explained in the previous chapter the gendered dichotomy

Fig. 2.7 *Messidor*: A weapon is a penis and vice versa

opposing agents and victims, while also counteracting the gendering of space and myth of the subject as a fixed set of identities.. As explained in the previous chapter, it is the accumulation of being negatively affected in their habitation of 'public' spaces that spurs women's wilful acts. In *A Question of Silence* (Marleen Gorris 1982), wilfulness is borne out of a casual encounter between women who have suffered from institutionalised forms of sexism and misogyny, which have barred them from inhabiting public spaces as freely as men do. The accentuated sound of the wheels of one woman's shopping trolley and another's pushchair stroller as the two women enter a clothing shop, soon to become a crime scene, brings to the fore the everyday duty they are charged with. The coincidental murder that they commit together in spite of not knowing each other, and the complicit silence of the other women in the shop, points to a societal abuse of women as a collective that eventually results in affirmative resistance. In *Messidor*, it is also a lack of resources (not having access to their own car) that brings the protagonists together. It is a tiredness of abuse, of not being accommodated—a general accumulation of negative affects—that brings women together and leads to their bonding over wilful acts, which is emphasised in these two films as well as in *Butterfly Kiss, Monster*, and *Frozen River* among others.

In *Messidor*, it is in fact when the two women decide to thoroughly stop, not as a pause for reflection but to abandon their resistance, that the two characters get caught and are visually cornered at the table of a café. I disagree with Marsha Kinder, who qualifies *Messidor* as lacking the 'exuberant energy and good humor' of *Thelma and Louise*, which is seemingly, for Kinder, necessary to empowerment and feminist politics (1991, 30). While she writes that Ridley Scott's film begins where Tanner's ends, I would say that *Thelma and Louise* (1991) parallels the narrative of *Messidor* two decades later. Thelma and Louise's leap into the Grand Canyon has ambiguously come across both as death or as a new movement, a desperate motion out of a patriarchal space pushed by those who represent it. Jeanne and Marie stop because of a similar gendering of space and make their last move by killing someone who they mistakenly suspect called the police and who they thereby perceive as someone who represents the oppressive system. Their leap happens by remaining in place, by wilfully stopping their movement, and calmly inhabiting a space that does not accommodate them. The film closes with a police car driving Jeanne and Marie through an open landscape across the countryside, suggesting an ending that may arguably appear more open than the final scene of *Thelma and Louise*, if the death of Thelma and Louise suggests a forced end to movement and the possibility of travel. However, both the car driving Jeanne and Marie and the car leaping into the Grand Canyon leave a trace on screen, a trace that aesthetically gives form to the virtual present within the real, the affirmative beyond the negativity of the films' diegeses.

What emerges from this chapter is the importance to look at space and bodies from an analytical lens that does not obscure instances of affirmative aesthetics. As a rewriting of the traditionally men-dominated road movie genre, *Messidor* portrays men as both enablers of and obstacles to women's journeys. In opposition to the quest of self-discovery of the usual male protagonists, the ability of the women protagonists to pause and reflect allows them to move farther and further. The camera places emphasis on Jeanne and Marie's will not to stop moving, on the long-lasting persistence of their journey, on their slow mobility that leaves a trace. The film and my affirmative approach to the film are critical of the additional obstacles women encounter on the road compared to their male counterparts. While *Messidor* emphasises how the road movie does not work for women's empowerment and full habitation of space, the film's aesthetic creates glimpses of future possibilities: transformations of the binary schemes of men and women, mobility and stasis, road and home.

Note

1. I deliberately use the term 'social' instead of 'public' spaces in order to signal the problem of naming social spaces 'public' when these are not freely available to all.

References

Akin, Fatih. 2004. *Gegen Die Wand [Head-On]*. DVD. Germany/Turkey: Strand Releasing.
Arnold, Andrea. 2016. *American Honey*. DVD. UK/USA: Film4.
Banet-Weiser, Sarah. 2019. *Rewriting Female Victimhood*. Conference Paper Presented at the *International Symposium Keeping Up with Empowerment and Popular Misogyny*, May 17, Universitat Jaume I, Spain.
Blum-Reid, Sylvie. 2016. *Traveling in French Cinema*. Hampshire/New York: Palgrave Macmillan.
Bruno, Giuliana. 2002. *Atlas of Emotion: Journeys in Art, Architecture, and Film*. London/New York: Verso.
Cohan, Steven, and Ina Rae Hark. 1997. *The Road Movie Book*. London: Routledge.
Corrigan, Timothy. 1992. *A Cinema without Walls: Movies and Culture after Vietnam*. London: Routledge.
De Lauretis, Teresa. 1984. *Alice Doesn't: Feminism, Semiotics, Cinema*. Bloomington/Indianapolis: Indiana University Press.
Eyerman, Ron, and Orvar Löfgren. 1995. Romancing the Road: Road Movies and Images of Mobility. *Theory, Culture and Society* 12 (1): 53–79.
Frederick, Bonnie, and Virginia Hyde. 1993. Introduction. In *Women and the Journey: The Female Travel Experience*, ed. Bonnie Frederick and Susan H. McLeod, xvii–xxxiii. Washington, DC: Washington University Press.
Fullwood, Natalie. 2015. *Cinema, Gender, and Everyday Space: Comedy, Italian Style*. New York: Palgrave Macmillan.
Gatlif, Tony. 2006. *Transylvania*. DVD. France: Mongrel Media.
Gorris, Marleen. 1982. *De stilte rond Christine M. [A Question of Silence]*. DVD. Netherlands: Sigma Film Productions.
Gott, Michael, and Thibaut Schilt. 2013. *Open Roads, Closed Borders: The Contemporary French-Language Road Movie*. Bristol: Intellect.
Hunt, Courtney. 2008. *Frozen River*. DVD. USA: Cohen Media Group.
Ince, Kate. 2017. *The Body and the Screen: Female Subjectivities in Contemporary Women's Cinema*. London/Oxford: Bloomsbury.

Ingraham, Chris. 2020. (forthcoming). *Gestures of Concern*. Durham: Duke University Press.
Jenkins, Patty. 2003. *Monster*. DVD. USA/Germany: Media 8 Entertainment.
Kabeer, Naila. 1999. Resources, Agency, Achievements: Reflections on the Measurement of Women's Empowerment. *Development and Change* 30 (3): 435–464.
Kar-Wai, Wong. 2007. *My Blueberry Nights*. DVD. Hong Kong: Roadshow Entertainment.
Kinder, Marsha. 1991. The Many Faces of *Thelma & Louise*: *Thelma & Louise* and *Messidor* as Feminist Road Movies. *Film Quarterly* 45 (2): 20–31.
Laderman, David. 2002. *Driving Visions: Exploring the Road Movie*. Austin: University of Texas Press.
Loden, Barbara. 2006 [1970]. *Wanda*. DVD. USA: Parlour Pictures.
Mazierska, Ewa, and Laura Rascaroli. 2006. *Crossing New Europe: Postmodern Travel and the European Road Movie*. London/New York: Wallflower Press.
Miller, Claude. 1983. *Mortelle randonnée*. VHS. France: TF1 Films Production.
Mills, Katie. 2006. *The Road Story and the Rebel: Moving Through Film, Fiction, and Television*. Carbondale: Southern Illinois University Press.
Orgeron, D. 2008. *Road Movies: From Muybridge and Melies to Lynch and Kiarostami*. New York: Palgrave Macmillan.
Pérez, Jorge. 2011. *Cultural Roundabouts: Spanish Film and Novel on the Road*. Lewisburg: Bucknell University Press.
Petzold, Christian. 2007. *Yella*. DVD. Germany: Cinema Guild.
Pratt, Mary-Louise. 2012. On Staying. Conference Paper Presented at the *Travel Ideals: Engaging with Spaces of Mobility*, July 18, University of Melbourne, Australia.
Ramsay, Lynne. 2003. *Morvern Callar*. DVD. UK/Canada: Palm Pictures.
Reichardt, Kelly. 2008. *Wendy and Lucy*. DVD. USA: Madman Entertainment.
Robertson, Pamela. 1997. Home and Away: Friends with Dorothy on the Road in Oz. In *The Road Movie Book*, ed. Steven Cohan and Ina Rae Hark, 271–286. London: Routledge.
Rollet, Brigitte. 2003. Women Directors and Genre Films in France. In *Women Filmmakers: Refocusing*, ed. Judith Plessis Jacqueline Levitin and Valérie Raoul, 127–137. UBC Press.
Royer, Michelle. 2011. The Hijacking of a Genre: French Female Film-Makers and the Road Movie. In *Parcours De femmes: Twenty years of women in French*, Modern French Identities, ed. Maggie Allison and Angela Kershaw, 243–256. Oxford: Peter Lang.
Sanders-Brahms, Helma. 2008 [1980]. *Deutschland Bleiche Mutter [Germany, Pale Mother]*. DVD. West Germany: Facets Video.
Schanelec, Angela. 2004. *Marseille*. DVD. Germany: Filmgalerie 451.

Scott, Ridley. 2002 [1991]. *Thelma and Louise*. DVD. USA: MGM Home Entertainment.
Tanner, Alain. 1992 [1976]. *Jonas qui aura 25 ans en l'an 2000*. VHS. Switzerland; France: New Yorker Video.
———. 1995 [1979]. *Messidor*. VHS. Switzerland: Citel Films.
Tarr, Carrie, and Brigitte Rollet. 2001. *Cinema and the Second Sex: Women's Filmmaking in France in the 1980s and 1990s*. New York: Continuum.
Uteng, Tanu Priya, and Tim Cresswell. 2008. *Gendered Mobilities*. Farnham: Ashgate Publishing.
Varda, Agnès. 1985. *Sans toit ni loi [Vagabond]*. VHS. France: Ciné Tamaris.
Wenders, Wim. 1976. *Kings of the Road*. VHS. West Germany: Wim Wenders Productions.
Wilson, Elizabeth. 1991. *The Sphinx in the City: Urban Life, the Control of Disorder, and Women*. Berkeley: University of California Press.
Winterbottom, Michael. 1995. *Butterfly Kiss*. DVD. United Kingdom: First Run Features.

Open Access This chapter is licensed under the terms of the Creative Commons Attribution 4.0 International License (http://creativecommons.org/licenses/by/4.0/), which permits use, sharing, adaptation, distribution and reproduction in any medium or format, as long as you give appropriate credit to the original author(s) and the source, provide a link to the Creative Commons licence and indicate if changes were made.

The images or other third party material in this chapter are included in the chapter's Creative Commons licence, unless indicated otherwise in a credit line to the material. If material is not included in the chapter's Creative Commons licence and your intended use is not permitted by statutory regulation or exceeds the permitted use, you will need to obtain permission directly from the copyright holder.

CHAPTER 3

Cars: A Micro-analysis of Space and Bodies in *Vendredi soir*

> *I describe the imagination as something more than a kind of individual faculty, and something other than a mechanism for escaping the real. It's actually a collective tool for the transformation of the real, for the creation of multiple horizons of possibility.*
> (Arjun Appadurai 2002, 34)

In an interview on his book *Modernity at Large: Cultural Dimensions of Globalization,* Arjun Appadurai explains that a 'locality' is as much a structure of feeling as a tangible construction. Imagination plays a central role in the making of a locality and of social changes; the imagination of artists, architects, urban planners, geographers, and social scientists all participate in the making of space as a structure of feeling (in Raymond Williams' words). Appadurai's emphasis on imagination as a social practice resonates through this chapter's analysis of Claire Denis' film *Vendredi soir* (2002), which illustrates how imagination takes urban space beyond gendered and power relations.

In the previous chapter, we saw how patriarchal cultures negatively affect women's freedom of movement.[1] Jeanne and Marie, the protagonists in the road movie *Messidor,* react to the constraints upon their mobility with wilfulness. In turn, such wilfulness changes the way they inhabit social spaces. *Messidor* portrays its women characters as wilfully—albeit with difficulties—inhabiting the public sphere as their male counterparts do. These women wish to benefit from the 'democratic "right" … to disrupt public space … and to undermine proper politics' (Sheller and Urry 2000, 741). My analysis of *Messidor* demonstrates that Mimi Sheller and John Urry's definition of mobility as a 'democratic right' does not apply to women.[2] Women are denied access to the public sphere that Habermas describes as 'a sphere of personal freedom, leisure, and freedom of movement' (Habermas 1989 [1962], 129). By contrast, in *Messidor*, Jeanne and Marie's lack of a car and money, coupled with their representation as 'dangerous women', leads to immobility: they cannot undertake the same journey of self-discovery as their male counterparts.

In this chapter I argue that Denis' subversion of the road movie genre in *Vendredi soir* modifies the patriarchal structures of social spaces (so-called 'public' spaces) and the concept of mobility by bringing Paris to a standstill. The stalling of 'traffic' reduces both men and women to a state of immobility. In this exceptional static state (or crisis of mobility), the commonly gendered narrative of mobility is suspended or rendered valueless. We shall see how, for example, the car that is ordinarily an index of 'masculine' power within the logic of mobility transforms into a space in need of re-appropriation and re-definition. Although the car reproduces current inequalities of class, race, and gender, Sheller and Urry note that the automobile participates in the 'great transformation of modern civil societies', 'collapsing the distinction between what is private and what is public' and putting auto-mobility at the core of civic and political existence in cities (2000, 741). *Vendredi Soir*, therefore, proposes a situation in which space is open to new relations of gender and power.

Claire Denis challenges the idea that the road quester finds a space for oneself through his or her mobility and assimilates it instead to the 'domestication' of space. If *Vendredi soir* echoes Jean-Luc Godard's *Weekend* (1967) in the absurd immobility and strangeness of human contacts, the cars stuck in traffic do not epitomise the purposelessness and meaninglessness of human existence. On the contrary, Denis' camera affirmatively converts the modern apocalyptic imaginary about immobilised cars into an opportunity for embracing one's desires and transforming the power-geometries of space.

Several recent filmic examples also convert the car into a space of dwelling whose 'inhabitants' somehow challenge gender binaries, such as *Night on Earth* (Jim Jarmusch 1991), *No Sex Last Night* (Sophie Calle and Greg Shephard 1996), *Crash* (David Cronenberg 1996), *Ten* (Abbas Kiarostami 2002), *Lluvia* (Paula Hernández 2008), *Wendy and Lucy* (Kelly Reichardt 2008),

Drive (Nicholas Refn 2011), and *Locke* (Steven Knight 2013). In *Vendredi Soir*, the car becomes a 'poetic' vehicle—a medium of *poiesis*, or else 'story-making', in which intimacy and connections are generated. Domesticating space emerges as inhabiting space through one's senses, through a body that affects and is affected.

Laure, the female protagonist of *Vendredi soir*, fully inhabits space through bodily sensations and affects. This is evinced through the aesthetic representation of the spaces she traverses as fluid, as space-times. She constructs spaces of intimacy for herself through a wilful, desiring body and through objects that *expand her intimacy* (echoing Bachelard's words). In Denis' film, Laure fully inhabits three spaces: her apartment, her car, and a motel room. If these spaces are embedded within gendered sociocultural norms and thus restrict the protagonist's fully embodied and empowered habitation, in the film the very same spaces also appear aesthetically as spaces of intimacy in continual transformation. This chapter analyses how Laure's habitation of these three spaces blur the boundaries that make up the binaries of mobility/immobility, subjective/objective reality, and male/female.

In *Vendredi soir*, the car expands Laure's intimacy beyond the domesticity of the house. In particular, the car and the motel room allow her to affirmatively rewrite her habitation of space as a subject of desire rather than as a gendered subject. When the film begins, Laure (interpreted by the famous French actress Valérie Lemercier) is packing up boxes: she is moving, we find out, to her (male) partner's house the following morning. In short, she is leaving her apartment, her own affective space, to live with her partner in his apartment, which she has not yet learned to call 'home'. She washes her hair in the bathroom and then drives to her friend Marie's house for dinner. As soon as she leaves her street, Laure is caught in a gigantic traffic jam, due to a public-transport strike that has blocked the roads of the entire city of Paris. Shivering pedestrians bundled up in winter jackets overrun the pathways and swarm onto the road in between motionless cars, while a woman's voice on the radio suggests drivers should welcome cold, stranded pedestrians into the warm safety of their cars.

While Laure's car is stuck in traffic, a man, Jean, gets in (played by another star of French cinema, Vincent Lindon). As Laure starts feeling desire for him, she steps out of the car to call Marie and cancel their dinner. When she returns to her car, Jean has taken the wheel and magically manoeuvres through the traffic jam. Laure panics and asks him to stop the car and get out, but soon after looks for him, until she finds him in a café.

They then go to a motel where they have sex, and have dinner at an Italian restaurant, along with several other couples who are also stranded. They spend the night together in the motel room, and very early in the morning, while Jean is still asleep, Laure leaves the room and runs onto the street with a smile on her face.

This chapter explores three key spaces: the apartment, the car, and the motel. In spite of her gendered 'situation', Laure fully inhabits each space through a lived body, a body of sensations. I argue that the interweaving of representational, haptic, and magical-realist elements in the film contributes to the film's affirmative and affective aesthetic, which I explore through Laure's habitation of space. On the one hand, the film portrays houses, cars, streets, and social spaces as '[housings] of gender' (Bruno 2002, 86), informed by heteronormative patriarchal norms. By focusing on Laure's move from her own apartment to her (male) partner's apartment, the film places emphasis on the gendered power relations of the household. On the other hand, Massey argues that any place—the household, the workplace, the street—is an 'ever-shifting geometry of social/power relations' (1994, 4). Laure rediscovers her spatial environment through bodily sensations and affective relations, and she extends her *spaces of intimacy*—and her power—into other spaces, namely her car and a motel room. The textures of the film and its focus on Laure's sense of touch create haptic spaces marked by affects and sensations. Whereas diegetic elements of the film constantly threaten to reposition the woman protagonist within gendered discourses, the haptic conveys the character's embodiment of space and spaces as ever-changing space-times. In a first instance, Laure is made to feel out of place, and moves through Paris with the fear of violence. However, when a giant traffic jam immobilises the whole city, micro-relations between bodies and space on screen give mobility another signification that is playful, affirmative, and goes beyond gender.

While films may produce and reinforce social and spatial dichotomies, Denis' haptic aesthetic contributes to dismantling them. I refer to haptic aesthetic as textures of images and sounds that create spaces of affects and sensations. Following the work of Laura U. Marks, Vivian Sobchack, and Jennifer Barker, I argue that by creating a 'habitable world' (in Sobchack's words, 2004, 151) emphasising the *lived*, textural, and affective dimensions of space, the film invites the viewers to *touch* and *experience* what is being shown. As Marks writes in *The Skin of Film* 'haptic images can give the impression of seeing for the first time, gradually discovering what is in the image rather than coming to the image already knowing what it is' (2000, 178). The haptic aesthetic of *Vendredi soir* functions as a political strategy that takes viewers beyond what they already know of gender, mobility, and the domestic space. More than solely through physical sensations or *visceral* affects, the film impacts on the viewer's affect in its sociocultural dimension. Laura U. Marks notes that 'perception is already informed by culture, and so even illegible images are (cultural) perceptions, not raw sensations' (145):

> embodied responses to cinema vary not only individually but also collectively. The cinematic encounter takes place not only between my body and the film's body, but my sensorium and the film's sensorium. We bring our own personal and cultural organisation of the senses to cinema, and cinema brings a particular organisation of the senses to us. (Marks 2000, 153)

Similarly, in her book *Cinema and Sensation: French Film and the Art of Transgression,* Martine Beugnet studies the haptic images of *Vendredi soir.* She examines how films 'affect us viscerally as well as intellectually' and investigates how film can be approached as a 'form of embodied thinking' (2007, 7, 8). The embodied thinking that cinema offers also comes through in Jennifer Barker's description of the haptic, which particularly resonates within Claire Denis' film:

> [The haptic] is a clever kind of political activism, in that it invites us not only to consider from a distance the film's feminist celebration of female desire but also, and more important, to partake in it, to experience this desire for ourselves in the act of watching the film. The power of the film's feminist political statement is thus not merely rhetorical, but profoundly tactile. (2009, 24)

Beugnet expands on Steven Shaviro's (2004) study of cinematic affect to explore film as 'primarily material, sensory phenomena' (2007, 11). She adds that insisting on affect does not mean cutting off all processes of critical analysis. On the contrary, a focus on affect complements the analysis of film as 'narrative process, system of representation, or articulation of an ideological discourse' (Beugnet, 11; 14). As explained in the introductory chapter, I understand affect as having forms on screen instead of being sensations transmitted to the spectator. Rather than focusing on what the spectator *feels* or *lives through* while experiencing the film as Sobchack or

Barker do, I wish to concentrate on the textures, objects, and rhythms that make up the cinematic spaces of *Vendredi soir* and give form to a haptic form of political activism. The film is well-suited for a micro-analysis: looking at the micro-movements of bodies and the 'scratches' of the screen's surface, and examining how the film 'breathes' (in Barker's words, 2009, 3)[3] and creates rhythm, while also considering the characters' habitation of diegetic spaces (houses, cars, streets, and hotel rooms).

Vendredi soir creates a tension between haptic and representational images, through which 'passages' of affects take place, from the patriarchal discourses that negatively affect the female protagonist's spatialities to her desiring body wilfully inhabiting space. On screen, such transformations are especially visible through thresholds, liminal spaces, and the magical realism of the film. Just as in *Head-On* and *Wadjda*, liminal spaces, in particular windows, function as thresholds between spaces of intimacy and outside spaces. In *Vendredi soir*, the affirmative transformation of space occurs in the passage between the film's realist elements, which convey the negative effects of navigating 'patriarchal spaces', and the haptic and 'magical' images that activate an affirmative imaginary of spatial habitation beyond gender norms.

Windows, Wandering Camera, and Magical Realism

Laure's dwelling (in her apartment, car, and the motel room) questions the power-geometries and the gendered norms that determine the habitation of space. The first space appearing on screen, Laure's apartment, aesthetically conveys her heteronormative situation: she is moving into her (male) partner's apartment. For Laure, her apartment is a space of intimacy. Three aspects in the apartment sequence highlight the film's affirmative aesthetic: the cinematography, the sound, and the mise-en-scène and objects filmed. Each aspect helps to show space as complex and in continual transformation rather than fixed, unchangeable, or 'stuck' in gendered sociocultural discourse. These aspects contribute to the tension between representing 'home' as the 'housing of gender' (in the words of Giuliana Bruno 2002, 86)—that is, Laure's potential containment in a seemingly fixed sociocultural situation (moving in with her partner)—and *haptically* evoking the affirmative transformation of negative sensations into the embodiment of space as possibility, unfolding in the present through Laure's sensations.

As we will see in the analysis of *Head-On*, the window in *Vendredi soir* appears throughout the film as a trope of containment, but also of spatial transformation and imaginary possibilities. A series of static long shots of the roofs of Paris opens the film. First, the shots show roofs visible from Laure's windows, and then, as the sun sets and the city sinks deeper into the night, the camera wanders further and shows some of the city's iconic monuments, such as the Eiffel Tower and Montmartre, likely not visible from Laure's apartment. While these images establish the diegetic environment of the film, they also disturb its temporality and narrative point of view, through the use of a 'wandering camera' (which we will discuss later). When the camera returns to Laure's apartment, the light coming from outside of her window suggests that it is in fact an earlier stage of the day than in the previous images. The magical and lyrical chords, scored by Dickon Hinchliffe, that resonate during these establishing shots point to the film's forthcoming magical realism and the possibilities offered by the imaginary (and also establishes the film itself as an imaginary space). When the camera enters the apartment and films Laure while she packs and looks out of the window at the surrounding rooftops, the music takes a dissonant turn and becomes more complex, richer, and sombre.

The soundtrack of the opening sequence creates an affective atmosphere, in between intimacy, nostalgia, and insecurity. Squeaking sounds of Laure's permanent marker and packing tape interrupt the non-diegetic, sombre music and give *affective texture* to the space that Laure is leaving, thereby reinforcing the distress that the music conveys. When Laure looks out of the window and admires the view one last time, the soundtrack changes to a more peaceful classical score—which will become a recurrent leitmotiv of Laure and Jean's intimate encounter. The magical-sounding score that resonates again and the point-of-view shots of lit windows that pierce the darkness of the night confer intimate and fanciful affects, and point to the multiple possibilities of people's lives in the comfort of their apartment.

Magical realism becomes a way to express the many possibilities of the real, including Laure's rewriting of her habitation of the apartment with her partner, possibly outside of the rules of gendered living. As will become clear, the blending between narrative elements and Laure's lived sensations affectively conveys spatial imaginary. The intense focus on textures, the soundtrack, and the cinematography lead the viewer into an imaginary world. Departing from Laure's apartment window, the camera 'wanders' beyond Laure's actual vision of the city. The director edits together a series of bird's-eye views of Paris. The camera's gaze allows us to 'travel' meta-cinematically into the sphere of the possible: possibly, the sphere of Laure's imagination as the camera's wanderings are edited through an eye-line match of Laure looking out the window (see Fig. 3.1).

The window sheds light on how a woman is locked in away from the outside world of men and also allows her a vision on the world essential to creativity. About this scene that multiplies views of the city, Beugnet writes that it evokes the 'vertiginous choice of stories that the city contains' (2004, 186). The window of her apartment magically allows Laure to wander, to look at other people while remaining in a 'space of her own'. Later in the film, the car windows push this spatial liminality and imaginative wandering further, allowing Laure to enter into contact with others from a semi-private space. Windows in the film give form to the frames of patriarchy that contain Laure within a gendered role and open up the outcomes of moving in with her partner to different possible stories.

What I call a 'wandering camera' introduces the magical into the realism of the film and positions Laure on the threshold of mobility. It does so by drawing a parallel between the illuminated windows and Laure's immobility, and also by emphasising the mobility of the outside world through

Fig. 3.1 *Vendredi soir.* Laure looking out from the window of her apartment

the passing of time and a high-angle establishing shot of fast-forwarded cars piling up at a traffic light. In the apartment sequence, the wandering camera and the visual contrast between the fast-moving editing and the cars ceasing to move forward figures as the first magical realist elements of the film. The wandering camera converts Laure's apartment—and even more obviously her car—into what Giuliana Bruno calls a 'mobile-house', a 'space of *transito*' (2002). The camera 'magically' offers Laure the wandering gaze that cinema offers to women. Laure meta-cinematically becomes empowered to look without being looked at, without her female body being identified as a problem for 'public' spaces. As we will see, this empowerment is similar to that of Wadjda and her mother who 'hide' behind their veils and on the roof of their house, and of Sibel's appropriation of domestic spaces as spaces of transit in *Head-On*. By bringing magical elements into *Vendredi soir,* Claire Denis introduces a critique of the patriarchal rules that govern urban spaces.

The early scenes of the film point to the difficulty Laure has leaving her apartment and moving in with her partner. Her move is problematic because it represents a move towards dependency, and the film suggests that she may not be able to fully commit to this space. As she is moving into François' apartment, rather than him moving into hers, she risks not being able to find Woolf's 'space of her own', a space of creative production, imagination, and self-transformation (insofar as it has a window) (1945 [1929], 22–23). When the film begins, the sun is setting as Laure says goodbye to her apartment. She has packed numerous boxes (suggesting she has lived there for a long time). As she is leaving a space that she fully inhabits, Laure is *jumping into* an unknowable future, a space which may be shaped by patriarchal dynamics as a result of the heteronormative relation with her partner.[4] As she leaves her apartment to go to her friend's house for dinner, Laure's hand is filmed in a close-up; she pauses for a moment while holding her car keys, highlighting two sets of keys next to each other: her car keys and François' apartment keys, which are labeled 'chez nous' ('our place'). As she grabs her car keys and leaves, François' keys are shown in a close-up, sitting alone on a table in the dark, empty apartment. The pause in Laure's gesture emphasises her choice to grab her own car keys *rather than* François' keys and conveys her doubts about moving in with him. Once she is in the street, Laure calls François from a public phone box. During their conversation she refers to the apartment as 'his' before correcting herself and saying 'ours'. She remarks, 'I need to train myself to say "at ours"'. As if to cement this momentous occasion, she repeats 'chez nous' ('our place') several times to herself.

Fig. 3.2 *Vendredi soir*: Laure looking towards or imagining lit windows that pierce the darkness of the night

A close-up superimposes Laure's inexpressive face over lit apartment windows with their light orange curtains and black bars and frames (see Fig. 3.2).[5] The use of a telephoto lens flattens the windows, reducing them to faded coloured shapes in the darkness of the night, which gives form to affects of entrapment. The shot of the windows merging on Laure's face, and the Parisian rooftops and windows seen at the beginning of the film, evoke the character's imaginary of houses as spaces of both intimacy and containment.[6] On the one hand, the windows merging with Laure's face evoke the domestic space as a place of intimacy and protection, which is reinforced by the warm orange colours. On the other hand, the dark frames dividing the screen and visually cutting up Laure's face, as they merge with her image, reveal her mixed feelings about moving into her partner's apartment.

Laure's habitation of the apartment, the car, and the motel always appears in continual transformation through how she affects and is affected by social relations. Laure's sensory habitation of space always functions as an *affective passage* depending on how the relational and contagious impacts of other bodies on hers increase or decrease her ability to act. Laure's extension of her spaces of intimacy originates in (re-)connecting to the erotic, whereby she transforms her negative affects towards patriarchal spaces into embodied 'generative desires'. While at the beginning of the film, the window locks the woman character in a geometrical space of piled-up boxes, it also allows for an imagination of a sphere of possibilities. If balconies, balustrades, and windows appear as boundaries separating 'feminine domesticity' from 'the masculine spheres of production' (in the words of Mary Ann Doane 1987, 288), they also function as 'soft screens' that allow these boundaries to be crossed and binaries to be transformed.

A Space of Intimacy: Recollection Objects and Haptic Cinematic Space

Throughout the film, haptic images, cinematography, and sounds liberate spaces from their seeming 'fixity' in discourse and gendered narratives. As Laure touches and sorts objects more attentively in her apartment a handheld camera films her gestures in closer shots and the musical score goes silent: there is silence, punctuated only by sounds of the objects that Laure moves and packs (along with some murmurs to herself and the throbbing noise of the electric heater). These sounds give *texture* to the space, which Laure inhabits through bodily sensations that transcend any pre-given gendered narrative. The aural texture given to the space and Laure's relation to objects in this sequence indicates a constant passage of affect: she moves from inhabiting space that is seemingly fixed in her sociocultural and gendered situation (a single, middle-aged, middle-class woman, which becomes evident as the film progresses) to inhabiting space through bodily sensations. The apartment and her car function as 'spaces of her own'. Laure fully inhabits these spaces of intimacy through 'sense-memories', the affective past that objects contain. For Laure, these objects are those that she handles: the objects she selects to take with her to her partner's apartment, and those that she discards and leaves behind.

Objects in *Vendredi soir* correspond to what Laura U. Marks calls 'recollection-objects': objects that carry collective and personal memory and 'condens[e] time within themselves' (2000, 77). Deleuze's 'recollection-images' (himself following Bergson's idea of duration, as touched upon in the first chapter of this book) are 'floating, dream-like images' that cannot be directly connected to history (Marks 2000, 37). Like any object, they enclose both virtual and actual affects; objects embody endless potentialities based on the multiple forms that they can take, as well as an actualised present form, which makes objects appear (mistakenly) fixed and immutable (see Deleuze 1966). In one respect, recollection-objects may appear to fix Laure's apartment in time, creating a site of apparently 'fixed' meaning, containment, and immobility in opposition to the 'mobility' of the city outside, which Laure explores later in the film. As Marks writes, objects that 'condens[e] time within themselves' may appear fossil-like in an 'infinitely contracted past' that they bring into the present (77–78). In another respect, Laure's affective relation to these objects is further enhanced by the fact that they condense her sense memories and provide possible ways to act and react to her present situation. The objects that Laure handles with care, as the haptic shots suggest, function as potential *traitsdunion* between the past, the present, and the future (in the new apartment). The 'recollection-objects' are invested with the power to transform the new apartment into a space of Laure's own.

The recollection-objects of the apartment sequence function as sites of meaning for Laure. For instance, the red skirt that she decides to keep (and in fact puts on in the book by Emmanuèle Bernheim from which the film was adapted, 1998) carries a sense of the erotic, a forgotten sexuality. The objects seem to entrap social situations and past affects, which they relocate in other, new, spaces. A red lampshade that Laure discards also represents her petit bourgeois sense of domesticity (before becoming an object of 'intimacy' when it reappears in the motel room). In the midst of scenes of Laure packing, the films cuts to the basement of Laure's building and shows the concierge rescuing the red lampshade from the rubbish bin. As the only scene in which a character other than Laure or Jean appears on screen without being in their presence, it clearly expresses the object's function as a 'carrier' of Laure's intimacy while also expressing her bourgeois situation in comparison to that of the concierge, portrayed as a poorer immigrant (which is evident through the character's accent), who cannot afford to throw away well functioning objects.[7]

Laure's recollection-objects evoke the 'fixed' appearance that places can take, fixed into gendered, patriarchal, and capitalist structures. While recollection-objects such as Laure's red lampshade enclose in themselves her socioeconomic ability to inhabit a cosy, warm house or motel room, they also convey past affects and the comfort and intimacy of domestic spaces. They contain the potential to affirmatively transform a space that Laure fears is already bound to be ruled by gender laws; they are able to connect her to her senses and embodiment of space, which is transmitted through haptic images.

When the red lampshade that Laure throws out 'magically' reappears in the motel room, it converts her habitation of this space with Jean (through potentially heteronormative spatialities) into a 'space of her own', a space in constant transformation through affective relations and social relations.

The haptic framing of recollection-objects turn the apartment, the car, and the motel room into spaces of intimacy, confirming Doreen Massey's idea that spaces always exist through social relations and in continual transformation. Compared to the white, gray, and beige tones of her now empty apartment, the orange and red colours of recollection-objects (the lampshade, electric heater, curtains, and the skirt) evoke for Laure the intimate dimension of the apartment: its value as 'inhabited space'. In particular, the bright orange light of the electric heater and its throbbing noise provide a consistency to the otherwise silent and disembodied apartment; the heater contains within itself Laure's sense-memories and her affective habitation of space, reinforced by the winter weather outside. As Bachelard points out, the aesthetic evocation of winter time increases the dwelling aspect of the house (1961, 66).[8] The mise-en-scène of the film makes the winter time setting of the diegesis visible; the dialogue of the characters references the cold, the characters wear winter clothes, steam comes out of characters' mouths when they speak and from the exhaust pipes of cars, and the crisp winter light of the day unfolds outside the window of the apartment.[9] Each of these elements reinforces the 'intimate value' of inhabited spaces.

If the recollection-objects *of Vendredi Soir* do not quite express the intercultural dimension of displacement that Laura U. Marks describes (2000, 77), they nonetheless contain Laure's personal history, connecting her to her past and expressing a kind of 'social displacement' between her life as a single woman and her affective (and necessarily sociocultural) knowledge of the potential gendered restrictions associated with moving to her male partner's apartment. As Laure packs up her apartment into boxes, the camera films her in close-ups or in tight, obstructed medium shots. We see how Laure carefully handles objects, tries on clothes, and tests the springs of her mattress. Such images transmit Laure's lived sensations, the sense-memories of her life as a single woman. Through extreme close-ups and long takes in which Laure manipulates her curtains, for instance, Denis forces the viewer to focus on the texture of objects and thereby give shape to the affectivity of Laure's apartment. The mise-en-scène create a sensory atmosphere of intimacy: her apartment is a space that she can fully inhabit in opposition to an outside world dominated by men who look at her female body as a problem, as I will explore further later in this chapter. As 'haptic' images show Laure handling objects in close-up or extreme close-up, they create textures and make space, 'as part of the fabric of cinematic space' (on textures and creation of space on screen, see Lucy Life Donaldson 2014, 81–111). The lighting and colours of the scene haptically create a 'texture' or an affective atmosphere (in Ben Anderson's term, 2009): a space of intimacy.

The haptic layer of the film gives shape to the micro-transformations of Laure's affective habitation of space. When Laure takes the sexy red skirt out of her wardrobe (a piece of clothing that she has not worn in a long time and had almost forgotten) and tries it on, it puts her in touch with the erotic again. The tight close-ups convey the haptic 'effect' of the dress on Laure's leg, the intensity of its red colour, and its deep split as she tries the skirt on with high heels. These shots surpass the discursive dimensions of the scene and convey Laure's submerged awareness of, and possibly fear or resistance to, the fact that she is about to give up the erotic in exchange for a 'domesticated' body.

By connecting spatial habitation to objects and to the body, these images disrupt the apparent fixity of the sociocultural dictates on which Laure's gendered situation relies. These haptic images, which linger on Laure's touch, on colours, and on texture, delay the narrative and interrupt the storyline—namely, the beginning of her conjugal life. They also open up a time of memories and sensations that interfere with and ultimately derail the 'happy ending'. These images expand the moments of transition (packing, moving, and time on the road) into times of lived experience, of sensual coming to oneself. At home these images aesthetically morph the apartment into a lived space, one of imagination in continual transformation, through the sense-memories of its inhabitants.

THE CAR, A VEHICLE OF (IM)MOBILITY

This section explores in detail three main ideas of *Vendredi soir* that the analysis of the apartment space has already suggested. First, if Laure is shown as reluctant to leave her apartment, it is because of the seemingly unchangeable patriarchal structures that condition her spatial habitation, according to the binary logic of gender. The limitations to Laure's movement, ensuing from such a logic, return once again when Laure moves from her apartment to the car. Second, the film's haptic transmission of

Laure's affects and sense-memories construes her habitation of space as an affective and fluid present in continual transformation. Third, the film's magical realism merges the seemingly simple and straightforward story of Laure's shift from one place (her home) to another (her 'new home' with her partner) with Laure's spatial imaginary, emphasising that space is inseparable from affects, and affects in turn are rooted—at least to an extent—in sense-memories. Below, I explore how the car provides Laure with yet another space for experiencing intimacy. As I argue, this is a space that the film sets up over and against the city—the patriarchal space the car traverses. As we will see, in *Wadjda* the bike and the roof become 'vehicles' for the girl's (and her mother's) escape from, and wilful transformation of, the gendering of social spaces; likewise, in *Vendredi soir*, Laure's car offers her both protection from the male-dominated city and the opportunity to make contact with others.

As suggested earlier, in a great number of classical and popular films the car functions as an object of man's desire, violence, and freedom; in short, it is a symbol of man's mobility. In *Vendredi soir*, the car complicates the road movie genre's association of 'freedom' and self-discovery with mobility. The semi-mobile car quite literally morphs into a space of transit between a 'home' seemingly fixed into past affects (Laure's apartment) and a space of intimacy (the motel room and potentially her new apartment with François). By immobilising the car, Denis challenges the idea that the transformation of the subject arises from his or her mobility and situates it instead in the expansion of one's spaces of intimacy. Jean-Luc Godard also dealt with the theme of immobility in his film *Weekend* (1967). One could argue that the cars stuck in traffic in *Weekend* epitomise the absurdity (or purposelessness and meaninglessness) of human existence. In contrast, Denis' camera affirmatively transforms the modern apocalyptic imaginary about immobilised cars into an opportunity to embrace one's desires. As I demonstrate below, Laure's car becomes a domestic space first, a liminal one second, and finally, a space of intimate contact.

More than being simply a means of transport, Laure's car fulfils the role of a *home* that is no longer to be found in her old apartment or indeed in her new one with her partner. The car provides her with refuge (in a moment of homelessness) and protects her from the patriarchal city that negatively affects her full habitation of space. The car also provides Laure with the self-confidence that was denied to Jeanne and Marie in *Messidor*. In the first instance, Laure's car still figures as a necessary vehicle for her to move about in a 'sphere of men',[10] the city that she observed from the safety of her apartment. Interestingly, Denis continually subverts the very notion of the city being a sphere of mobility and 'masculinity'.[11] As Laure leaves her safe domestic space, from where she could observe the city unobserved, she is immediately confronted with the 'dangers' that the urban space represents for a woman who is on her own at night (as is also seen in *Head-On*). Soon after Laure enters her car, a man bangs his palm on her window, startling her. Only slightly lit by street lights, the white face of the man contrasts with his dark outfit and the darkness of the street, both elements that endow him with a frightening look. Instead of opening the car, as the man wanted, Laure locks the doors and starts the engine. However, the man starts walking behind Laure's car and is obviously annoyed. Even though we come to understand that the man was in fact only asking for a lift (because of the general transport strike), the mise-en-scène still portrays him as 'frightening', aesthetically conveying how much the patriarchy of the urban space has negatively affected Laure (see Fig. 3.3).

The mise-en-scène of the first scenes of Laure in her car, much like the scenes in her apartment, convey her affective relation to the city space that is, in this case, expressed by her (socially induced) unease as a woman

Fig. 3.3 *Vendredi soir*: Frightening man mockingly waves to Laure

travelling alone in the urban space at night.[12] Although these images are not point-of-view shots and remain unattributed—filmed by a wandering camera—the framing of Laure and other characters stuck in their cars successfully renders Laure's subjective perception of the city. As Elizabeth Wilson (2001) notes and as I highlighted in my analysis of *Messidor*, Laure appears fearful in her (restricted) habitation of the city. The chiaroscuro lighting and the claustrophobic close-ups of other people behind their windows give them a frightening and ghostly appearance. This emphasises both the stressful dimension of the urban space (especially in its congested state) and Laure's spatial imaginaries, conditioned by being negatively affected in her habitation of the urban space previously (as illustrated by her reaction to the 'frightening' man). Rather than thresholds of mobility, windows now appear as openings to the *other* (whether frightening or desiring, just as Jean will be for Laure later in the film).

Much as she locks her car door in response to the 'frightening' man, Laure responds to the ghostly presence of others by fashioning her car as an intimate space of protection that ultimately contains her. Her habitation of the space of the car is evident in its habitual aspect. When Laure gets into her car, she dries her wet hair, an act which 'domesticates' the car. Immobilised in the traffic jam, Laure sits at the back and goes through her boxes; she starts rereading her books out loud and sorts her things while talking to herself. It is a continuation of the scene in her apartment, except now all of her activities reinforce the 'homeliness' of her car.[13] After she has emptied and left her apartment, the car remains the only 'space of her own', an object *into which* Laure extends her intimacy.

Laure's car enables her to inhabit the city, while at the same time it contains her. When seen from the outside of the car, Laure often appears 'locked in', trapped inside, due to the window frames. The car's space seems to enclose Laure. The cinematography of these car scenes portrays Laure's body as *belonging* to the car (see Fig. 3.4), which also echoes the real spatial restrictions of the car during filming. After Laure has dried her hair, the next image, an extreme close-up of the fumes coming out of the car, cut together in a Eisensteinian montage, reinforces the idea that Laure's body is united with her car. Laure converts her apartment into a space of her own, or into *her own self*, through recollection-objects; the

Fig. 3.4 *Vendredi soir*: Close-ups and frames within the frame contain Laure in her car, which drives forward without Laure watching

car, likewise, 'entraps' Laure into a fixed idea of space, while also opening her to the outside and therefore potentially facilitating intimate contacts and spatial transformation through affective situations. This is *in opposition to* the seemingly fixed gendered structures of the male-dominated street located just outside of her car. The immobilised car is, before Laure's encounter with Jean, a space of entrapment and containment due to the threatening presence of the masculine other outside. While Laure also becomes a body-machine, like all of the other drivers and passengers sitting in their cars, the fact that cars are depicted as immobile allows for their transformation into liminal spaces, spaces that stand on the threshold between an inside and an outside. If Laure's car protects her from the world outside, it is also a 'leaking' space that opens onto the outside.

Affirmative Wandering

Rather than her car, it is the 'wandering camera' that provides Laure with mobility, a 'magical' or meta-cinematic mobility. The magical realism of the film converts the car into a poetic 'gaseous' object: a space existing through social contact and affective relations. Unlike the windows of the house, which appeared more 'solid' because they were situated "above" the city and did not provide intimate contact, the windows of the car appear as 'soft screens', at once marking the boundary of the domestic space and facilitating Laure's imaginative 'travel' through the city as the camera wanders off from her car and explores the surroundings.

While the car provides a 'mobile habitation of space', 'a dominant way of dwelling in contemporary experience', it also becomes a form of 'sensing the world through [a] screen' (Sheller and Urry 2000, 747). In opposition to the close-ups and frames within the frame that contain Laure inside the car, at various times the camera leaves Laure's car. In short, the camera acts like a bored passenger who explores the city while everyone is stuck in traffic. A pedestrian's point of view replaces the bird's-eye view of the beginning of the film, though it still remains unattributable. By rupturing the 'authority' of the gaze and blurring the boundaries of subjectivity, the wandering camera 'frees' Laure spatially, converting her into a *disembodied flâneuse* '[flourishing] in the interstices of the city' (Wilson 1991, 8). When the camera leaves the car, it seems to take Laure along in its meandering by intermittently coming back to Laure in the car, who is filmed using claustrophobic close-ups or extreme close-ups. At times the camera escapes the confines of Laure's car to film other passengers and cars in a range of medium to close-up shots. While 'visiting' other cars, the camera connects Laure with a collectivity of car-bodies similarly affected by the traffic jam; it also positions her on one of the many 'virtual lines' present within the real, so we see the way in which others inhabit space. Through the introducion of 'magical' elements into the realism of the film and the conversion of cars into poetic objects, images from the wandering camera and the soundtrack of the sequence 'free' the city and cars from their negative affects as male-dominated and frightening spaces.

The wandering camera ensures Laure's 'magical' mobility through which she surpasses the negativity of women's exclusion from the mobile 'public' sphere. As the camera films cars, roofs, bright lights, smoking hoods, sleeping passengers, and drivers, the characters merge with their cars, which become characters themselves that take their passengers with them (see Fig. 3.4).[14] Hinchliffe's classical score and the wandering camera interweave the car body with the human body and create a lyrical city in which cars appear to move by themselves, as if they were dancing (see Fig. 3.5). In this sequence, fixed a little above the ground, the wandering

Fig. 3.5 *Vendredi soir*: Claire Denis' ballet of cars

camera films the lights of slowly moving cars in a close-up with a telephoto lens, which reduces the depth of field and creates a surreal, ethereal atmosphere—non-anchored in real space. The classical music, tight shots, shallow depth of field, and very slow movements (of the camera and the cars themselves) portray a *ballet of cars*, transforming modern purposeful objects of transport into poetic abstractions. By recurrently filming smoke and steam in close-ups, Denis reinforces the magical dimension of the scene by giving cars a 'poetic' texture.

Elements of magical realism merge the 'diegetic reality' and Laure's imaginary, both visually and aurally. Stuck in the traffic jam, Laure sings along to the popular 1979 French hit 'Manureva'. In this scene, subjective shots are edited together with 'authorial' shots. While the camera alternates from handheld (when filming Laure's [imaginative] vision) to fixed (when filming Laure from outside of the car), the sound inconsistently (albeit discreetly so) changes volume and source. From being diegetic, the sound becomes a soundtrack: the volume of the song lowers when the camera leaves Laure's car and films her through the driver's lateral window. As the camera wanders, the song surprisingly remains at the same volume, as if outside Laure's window. The soundtrack confuses and disturbs the subjectivity of the shots and the realist aesthetic.

The magical realist aesthetic blurs inside and outside spaces, the 'diegetic real' and Laure's imaginary, and activates the *virtualities* of the real. It is a 'magical' moment that brings out the liminality of the car space. Laure turns on the radio and a woman's voice announces, 'You all know that by now... Paris is at a complete standstill due to the public-transport strike'. The radio announcer seems to address Laure personally, who has been packing up all day and is probably 'the only one who did not know' ('Y en a peut-être encore deux qui sont pas au courant') about the strike. This is reinforced by the announcer's intimate-sounding voice, almost a sensual whisper, characteristic of the (exclusively) female announcers of FIP radio (such as Jane Villenet, who is cast as the radio announcer in the film).[15] While the voice 'talking to Laure' suggests offering a lift to cold, stranded pedestrians, the magical-realist aspect of this address is reinforced when Jean (Vincent Lindon) enters the car as if he himself heard the radio announcement (however unlikely).

It is the wandering camera, exiting Laure's car, that in fact stumbles over Jean and 'magically' brings him to her car. The soft voice of the radio announcer and Jean's first appearance on screen introduce a dream-like dimension to the car, giving it an aspect of a 'space of intimacy'. According to Bachelard, 'the house' (and, as such, any *inhabited space*) 'provides a shelter to the dream' ('la maison abrite la rêverie' (1961, 34)). Laure falls asleep almost immediately after Jean has entered her car, which adds to the blurring of 'diegetic reality' and Laure's imaginary. While the diegetic veracity of Laure and Jean's night together is not important, the imaginary dimension granted to the film underlines the many paths that Laure's life and her affective habitation of space can take. Oscillating between living as a single woman and living as part of a couple, Laure's habitation of space is challenged in its everyday appearance as fixed and monotonous, which is epitomised in the car space when Jean enters. The car as a space of intimacy, a 'shelter to the dream', becomes a space of *expansion* of the virtual into the real.

Jean's presence emphasises the liminal aspect of the car, on the border between Laure's own space, protected from the hostility of the city, and a social space-time in which power dynamics and intimacy are to be negotiated. As soon as Jean steps into the car, the car appears as a space of passage, a space of transit. When Laure asks him where he wants to go, Jean answers with a soft, calm voice, 'Vous n'aurez qu'à me laisser là où vous voulez' ('You can leave me wherever you wish'), suggesting that he diegetically exists to help Laure on her journey towards the erotic, towards her deep self and her refusal of conventions. Jean makes himself available to

Laure's desire, thereby at once penetrating and transforming Laure's space of intimacy.

By continually blurring the boundaries between the 'real' and the imaginary, Denis destroys the gendered binaries that still permeate films 'with' cars, where cars are typically imagined as a male domain. The car window also figures as a threshold, as a direct opening to the other, onto the 'spaces of men' (for Laure, connoting both fear and excitement, as per Elizabeth Wilson's description of the city, 2001). Rather than protecting or containing Laure inside, the car window *connects* her to the outside; it shapes the car as a space of transitions and transformations. Jean's body seems to activate Laure's desire and imagination; at once she *feels* his physical closeness while also relating to the heterosocial aspects of his 'intimidating and protective' male presence.[16]

Gendered Contacts, Affective Contacts

As seen in the previous section, the magical realism of *Vendredi soir* converts the car into a liminal space. Jean's presence in the car *brings in* the gendered, patriarchal aspects of the city to Laure's personal 'domestic' space; it both converts the car into a 'housing of gender' (in Bruno's terms) and *suspends gender* as the two characters relate at the micro-level of affects, which allows Laure to reconnect to a long-forgotten desiring body. It is by constantly oscillating between patriarchy and embodiment of space that *Vendredi soir* manifests its *affirmative political intentions*, transforming the gendering of space into fluid relational habitation.

Jean climbs into Laure's car uninvited, asking a rhetorical question ('Can I come in?'), an act which demonstrates his sense of entitlement: as a man he feels it is legitimate to enter this woman's space as if it were his own. Once in the car, his masculine body occupies more space than that of Laure, evinced in his few, smooth movements as well as in his gaze, straight ahead and beyond the windshield. While he only looks towards her a few times, with steady movements of the head, Laure repetitively glances at him in jerky movements. As opposed to the long takes that compose the first part of the film, short takes characterise the first interactions between Laure and Jean. Jean's male presence affords him a position of spatial power over Laure's female body, which, as Iris Marion Young (1980) would write, inhibits women's spatial movement. The characters' mutual desire and the contagiousness of affects that arise from their bodily presence in an intimate space, however, overshadow Laure's nervousness at having a (male) stranger in her car. Laure's connection to the erotic grants her the capability to rewrite her own story and her habitation of social spaces through sensations, instead of through the gender norms that govern them.[17]

As Jean steps into her car—Laure's space of her own—his presence changes it, at a micro bodily level. This change takes place through contact between the characters, which the film chooses to convey haptically to the viewer. Upon entering the car, Laure instantly *feels* his presence; as Martine Beugnet writes, she can smell him, and his body comes with its weight (2004, 194). The silence of the scene is punctuated by diegetic sounds that give a materiality to the space (on textures in film, see also Donaldson 2014). The door opening and closing, Laure turning off the inside light, Jean closing the window, Jean's movement on the seat, and Jean's clearing of his throat all create a silence with consistency, a space of contact and intimacy. As he enters the car, he immediately lowers the passenger seat so that he can lie down comfortably. He says to Laure, 'Il fait bon dans votre voiture' ('It's warm in here'), which reinforces the 'space of intimacy' that the car offers. Through this familiar gesture, he 'makes himself at home'. Jean could be perceived as Laure's partner François, a confusion that is reinforced later in the motel scenes, since François never directly appears on screen. A dreamy-sounding score interrupts the silence and creates an atmosphere of *rêverie*, an affective and imaginative habitation of space.

On the one hand, the gendered power-geometries that Jean brings with him into Laure's car culminates when Jean takes the wheel for a brief moment, and in his doing so the car regains its gendered aspects of 'masculinity', speed, and travel (Sheller and Urry 2000, 738). The aesthetic of the scene conveys Laure's affective transformation. As a sombre score plays, a long take shows multiple dark window frames filmed from Laure's point of view out of the passenger window in a low-angled, fast tracking shot. The reflection of these windows and shop signs then become abstract trails of light that superimpose over Laure's bewildered face, filmed in a close-up through the lateral window that at times mask or erase her image. These scenes echo the window frames superimposed over Laure's face earlier in the film when she was apprehensively thinking about her move to François' apartment. The rhythm of the film, thus far slow and dream-like, becomes fast and object-driven as soon as Jean takes the wheel—as if the traffic jam had suddenly disappeared and the car had been relocated into a 'masculine' narrative of travel. The cinematography and editing of the scene, as well as the score- which introduces urgent violin music suggestive of the thriller genre- synesthetically produce the sensation of the car's rapid motion and give shape to affects of anxiety.[18] In an affective reaction to the motion that Jean imposes upon her, Laure becomes panicked and asks Jean to let her exit the vehicle, though the car is hers—it is as if she is conditioned by a gendered and normative spatiality that generally situates women as passengers rather than drivers (as *Messidor* also shows). This scene highlights the constant tension between a gendered spatial economy and an affective one that is in continual transformation, through the relational aspect of space and the contagiousness of affect.

On the other hand, the haptic aesthetic of the scenes with Jean in the car transmits Laure's rewriting of her habitation of space through the erotic; hers is a body of affects and desire rather than a gendered body. It is by expanding Laure's spaces of intimacy (her intimate contacts with other human and non-human bodies) in her car and in the motel room that the film suspends her habitation of space through gender and situates her within a 'lived' body. This is created through the exceptional (almost absurd and 'magical') traffic jam that brings the car to an unusual immobility and therefore facilitates affective contacts. By losing its speed, the car invites connections with others, affirming the subject's embodied habitation of space. Through haptic images, Claire Denis transforms the traditional and seemingly fixed power-geometries of 'public' space into fluid micro-relations to space. She does so by closely filming Laure's affective connections and blurring her bodily limits. This blurring will be increasingly apparent in the analysis of the motel room that follows.

Laure and Jean inhabit space affectively through their connection with each other. This becomes clearer during the course of the film, and especially so in the motel room. When Jean smokes, extreme close-ups show him inhaling and exhaling through his mouth and nose, while other extreme close-ups portray Laure physically reacting to the smell of the cigarette, lightly inhaling and exhaling the smoke of Jean's cigarettes as she recalls an old habit. These haptic images create a space of intimacy, an 'embodied' cinematic space that 'transcends' Laure and Jean's interactions as everyday performances of gender norms and situates them within the affective dimension of spatial habitation. In a point-of-view shot from Laure's perspective, an extreme close-up shows Jean's hand entering the opening of his shirt and making contact with his own skin (see Fig. 3.6), which reveals the texture of his bare skin and thus creates a haptic cinematic space, one that has a certain texture. Likewise, in the scene when

Fig. 3.6 *Vendredi soir*: Laure watches Jean passing his hand inside the collar of his shirt

Jean enters the car, the accumulation of haptic images creates an atmosphere, a space that continually changes through affective exchanges. When Laure watches Jean extend his legs, putting himself at ease, an extreme close-up shows her feet rubbing against each other, her knees extending, and her hands lightly stroking the steering wheel. The film's focus on textures accentuates the intimacy of the car, wherein the characters develop desire for each other and inhabit space affectively, suspending their gendered identities. If one can never fully transcend gendered power relations within the current configuration of society, the haptic aesthetic of the film creates temporal and intermittent interruptions of power-geometries.

There is no relation of subject-object anymore; no one 'possesses' the other with their gaze, but the characters look at each other just as they are touching themselves and being touched. Denis places much emphasis on hands touching each other or one another. For philosopher Merleau-Ponty, there is always a *reversibility* of the touching experience; as he explains, two hands of one's body always simultaneously touch and are being touched, and this is also true with another's body (Merleau-Ponty 1964, 183).[19] I argue that if the power structures of social spaces are to be transformed, this can only occur through *inhabiting space affectively*, which means recognising the reversibility of experience. According to

Merleau-Ponty, when experience is shared, it 'reverts, transfers and reconverts' one's private world into a world 'levied off' from the world of all others (1968, 142). The haptic aesthetic opens up a world of relations and potentialities, one that puts into question binaries and power structures.

If at first the car seems to contain Laure in a comfortable space of domesticity or accommodate her where the patriarchal city does not, the wandering camera and magical-realist elements convert the car into a 'leaking', liminal space. On the border between inside and outside, mobility and immobility, the car becomes a space of intimate contacts. The magical realism of the film blurs the 'diegetic real' and allows for the re-writing of the gendered habitation of space along imaginative lines. The haptic aesthetic reinforces the idea that space is not fixed within sociocultural norms, but is instead 'lived' and in continual transformation, as a result of affective connections. It is the combination of representational elements and magical and haptic aspects that shape the affirmative aesthetic of the film. The negative affects of Laure's habitation of the city morph into a rewriting of spatial habitation through bodily senses.

Desiring Bodies

In reaction to how the male domination of social spaces has negatively affected Laure's spatial imaginary, Laure—just like Sibel in *Head-On* and the title character of *Wadjda*—experiences wilfulness to fully inhabit space in an unconscious, embodied way and at the micro-level of the skin. Laure's habitation of the third space of the motel room (the first two spaces being her apartment and car) where she spends the night with Jean, takes form as a haptic cinematic space. As the previous section has already suggested, it is by haptically conveying the characters' embodiment of space that *Vendredi soir* subverts the seemingly fixed gendering of space. As the characters are shown inhabiting space through their physical sensations, they are portrayed as lived bodies mutually affecting each other, creating an affective 'atmosphere' (see also Anderson 2009), thereby producing space itself.

It is the combination of the representational with haptic and recollection-images that brings out the affirmative aesthetic of the film. Let us for example, consider the café scene (described in more detail below) and the moment when Jean starts driving Laure's car: the characters' dialogue and the mise-en-scène depict Jean as leading their movements.[20] On a haptic level, however the characters' desire appears mutual, as does their decision to act on it. While the representational level reaffirms gender norms—stereotypically, men make decisions, women approve—, the haptic level give shape to Laure's wilfulness and connection to the erotic.

Whereas Sibel and Wadjda are overtly wilful, as we will see, perhaps by acquiring a cultural distance from their own selves (a diasporic distance and a 'mediated' one through television, respectively), Laure is still caught within the compulsory performativity of gender that Judith Butler describes (1990, 1993). Thus, arguably, her wilfulness happens at a micro-level (in this case, through skin contact), as is the case with Wadjda's mother (albeit differently). It is the haptic aesthetic of *Vendredi soir* that conveys Laure's micro-instances of wilfulness, thereby affirming her habitation of space.

As opposed to Butler, who argues that there is no escape from gender other than through its reiteration, I maintain that considering the body as a 'lived body' and gender as a situation which is dynamic and constantly being negotiated (Beauvoir 1949; Moi 2001) allows for transformations at the level of both spatial habitation and gender discourse.[21] Laure's performance of 'femininity' clearly appears three times in the film.[22] Each time, Laure's habitation of space is conveyed through sensory experiences and a 'lived body' that represents 'the radical uninhabitability' of gender (Butler 1993, 25). For Butler, gender is uninhabitable insofar as it sets roles and expectations that are ideals, which can thus not be reached. Since gender is a social construction rather than something that arises from the body or the subject, it cannot be fully integrated but always remains a performance (from which one cannot escape, according to Butler). While Laure performs femininity (unconsciously and inescapably so), the aesthetic of the film reveals a body that is lived, and thereby suspends gender.

Visual exchanges between Laure and other women in the film emphasise the 'uninhabitability' of gender. After Jean has left her car, Laure finds him again in a café where she sees him (from outside through the window) interacting with a younger woman. The café scene illustrates the power dynamics that dictate heterosexual interactions, the habitation of heterosocial spaces, and how spatial imaginaries are gendered. The sound and haptic images reveal the subjectivity of the scene. From the outside, Laure looks at the young woman and Jean playing pinball through the café's window; their voices are muffled, but as Laure enters the café, the sounds of the pinball machine grow louder and Jean's words become clearer. The young woman appraises Laure, looking her up and down (see Fig. 3.7). An extreme close-up of Jean slightly touching Laure's hand with intention

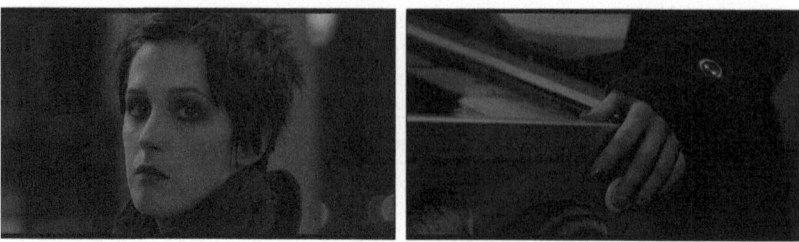

Fig. 3.7 *Vendredi soir*. Focus on a younger woman's gaze and hands in a café

highlights the desire between them. The camera films the young woman's gaze towards their hands and then shows her own hand on the pinball machine in a close-up that blurs her uncovered belly in the background (see Fig. 3.7). The editing of these two images underlines the women's internalisation of sexual norms and their play of power to get to *touch* Jean. Like many scenes in the film, this one mingles representational and haptic images; it requires the viewer's critical vision of the heteronormative habitation of space and Laure's performativity of gender, while inviting them to experience Laure's embodied habitation of space.[23]

In Laure and Jean's first embrace in the street *en route* to the motel, the haptic images of their intimate connections blur the individuality of their bodies and therefore their gendered identification. When Laure and Jean kiss for the first time, they appear in chiaroscuro: they are blurred and appear 'strangely and terribly flat' in the way they are lit (in Deleuze's words regarding chiaroscuros). This lighting constructs what Deleuze would call an *any-space-whatever* (1986, 111), which 'universalises' the story, extending it to a specific sociocultural collectivity. It also emphasises the banality of the moment and creates a 'sphere of the possible' (Deleuze 1986, 111), an oneiric atmosphere created by quiet, tinkling piano notes. This atmosphere allows for different conceptions of space outside of the patriarchal status quo. The camera remains filming in extreme close-up during the whole scene, with a warm light illuminating the characters' faces and leaving everything around them in utter darkness, thereby reinforcing its 'magical' appearance. Meanwhile, the direct sounds of the scene convey the characters' embodiment of space, in this case, the street. The rustling of their clothes is foregrounded, while traffic can be heard in the background. Hearing the rustling sounds of clothes and the faint sounds of their kisses synesthetically brings us to *feel* the textures of their skin and their warm wool jackets. As the sounds of the traffic become a constant hum, the viewer becomes increasingly immersed in the lovers' embrace.

The extreme close-ups of the intimate scene in the street convey the reversibility of their touch; they are simultaneously kissing and being kissed (see Fig. 3.8). The hands that continually invade the frame meta-cinematically emphasise the 'tactile gaze of the camera' (Beugnet 2004, 192), and the haptic images the camera creates, such as the long take in extreme close-up that shows one of Laure's gloves on the ground. The glove recalls Laure's lamp; it too is a recollection-object able to crystallise her sense-memories, having appeared earlier in the film. The texture of the glove conveys the warmth of the embrace and situates the habitation of space as embodied.

When Laure and Jean decide to act on their mutual desire and go to a motel together, they both initiate the movement, thus showing equality in the decision-making process. The fast editing of extreme close-ups and the unattributable diegetic sounds synesthetically transmit the impatience of Laure and Jean's embrace. The haptic aesthetic of the kissing scene extends to the images in the motel room and blurs the identity of the characters. Instead of filming the characters' faces during intercourse, Denis's camera shatters the cinematic conventions of erotic-sexual encounters by filming

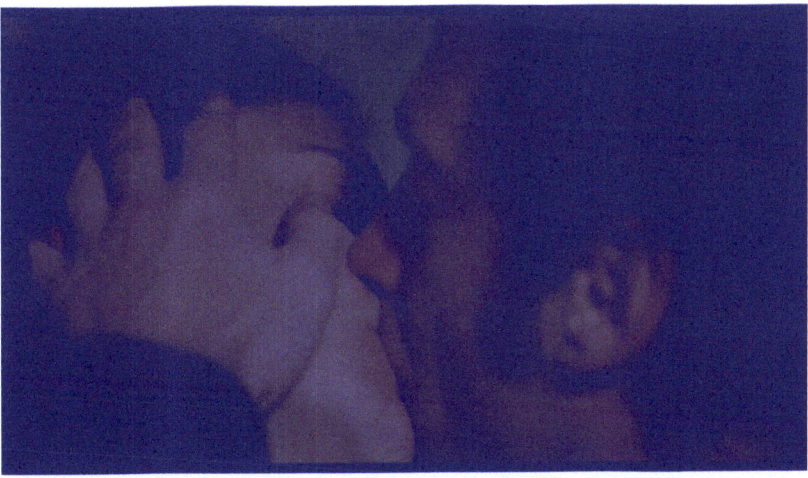

Fig. 3.8 *Vendredi soir*: Laure's and Jean's faces become almost indistinguishable as they kiss

hands in extreme close-ups and by moving with the rhythm of the bodies. A shaky handheld camera films body parts in extreme close-up: a hand on a knee and on a back, upper and inner thighs, parts of a leg, a hand removing underwear. The camera finds its way under winter clothes and gets lost in the characters' hair and the caresses of unidentifiable thighs, bellies, and backs (see Fig. 3.9). Extreme close-ups and chiaroscuro lighting merge bodies into one, disrupting the attributability of body parts to one specific sexed body. Both Laure and Jean have dark brown hair, dark clothes, very similar complexions, and body proportions, all of which facilitates their appearance as one androgynous body. As the characters' bodies merge, so too do the boundaries of gender, thereby challenging traditional power structures.

In addition to the haptic images that blur the limits of their bodies, the actors playing Laure and Jean have a queer appearance, one that refuses the binaries of femininity and masculinity. Laure appears on screen without 'feminine' attributes, wearing androgynous clothes (with the exception of the token appearance of the red sexy skirt), and no makeup. She is filmed from the back when showering. The actress who plays Laure, Valérie Lemercier, has also acted the part of a transgender person in one of the few films she herself directed, *Le derrière* (Lemercier 1999), and has appeared as a transgender on the cover of the gay magazine *Têtu*.[24] While

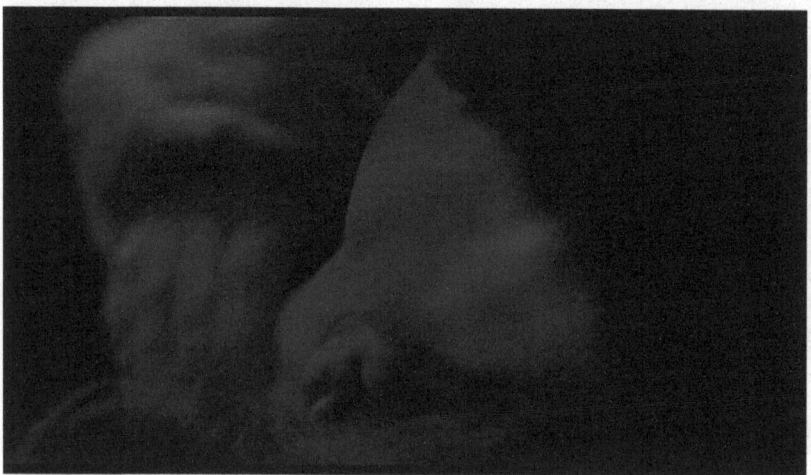

Fig. 3.9 *Vendredi soir*: Body parts in extreme close-up in the motel room

Jean (Vincent Lindon) embodies, at least in part, the heterosocial dynamics of power, his masculine appearance is queered (or 'disorientated', as Sara Ahmed would put it, 2010) by his soft voice, his androgynous look, his availability as Laure's fantasy, and his 'in-betweenness' as a 'real' character or as a product of the imagination. Both the characters' costumes and characterisation on screen, and the aesthetic representation of their erotic encounter in the motel room, confound the limits of bodies and create a 'passage' between and beyond gender.

Rewriting Spatial Habitation: A Place Called Home?

As a result of her night in the motel, Laure comes to live fully and inhabit affirmatively the spaces outside her apartment. The film's aesthetic expands Laure's 'spaces of intimacy' (the spaces she fully inhabits) from her private apartment to semi-public social spaces. While the motel room is first marked in the film as 'neutral' (as an impersonal space, waiting to be inhabited), the mise-en-scène transforms it into a space of intimacy; the objects and the bodies' marks on each other, on the bed, and on pieces of furniture charge the room affectively, and create an erotic connection. The film once again adopts poignant haptic shots to give form to both Laure's immersion in the space of the motel room and the depiction of the motel room as an intimate space. For example, just like the scenes in the car, the scenes in the hotel room show the characters' alertness to their 'proximal senses'—smell and touch in particular. 'Recollection-objects' also return in the motel scenes, rooting the characters even further through their senses. Compared to the car that Laure had come to construct as a space of her own before Jean's intrusion, the motel room already figures as a space-time of transit, thoroughly open to the virtualities of the real. The room is a genuine *any-space-whatever*: a 'pure locus of the possible', a singular space which has 'lost its homogeneity… so that the linkages can be made in an infinite number of ways' (Deleuze 1986, 109). The possibility of 'writing' this space anew increases, because—as the concierge declares—the motel is empty, uninhabited (because of the transport strike).

This new space gives Laure the opportunity to appropriate it as her own space, and to imagine that Jean, not she, is the one moving in to the space. The paratextual elements of the film support this interpretation. For example, the film's DVD menu is entitled 'Back home'; additionally, the novel on which the film is based makes it very clear that Laure fantasises about the motel room as her home ('Laure locked the door. That was it. They were at home' [Bernheim 1998, 61, translation mine]). This occurs in the book when the omniscient narrator compares the motel room to Laure's own apartment: 'Small, square and with a low ceiling, this room looked like hers. Laure stopped. It was hers. She was at her place with Frédéric. And just as every night, before going to bed, he would turn down the heating. Because together at night, they would never get cold' (92–93, translation mine).[25] Through Laure and Jean's habitation of the space in the film, the motel room is transformed from being dark, coldly lit, and blue-hued (similar to Laure's empty apartment), to a warm, inviting space (it becomes golden-hued). The change in colour enhances the sense of 'intimacy', the constant affective exchange between (human and non-human) bodies, which results in spatial transformation.

Objects from Laure's apartment magically resurface in the motel room, such as the red lamp, and somewhat facilitate the merging of the two spaces. When the characters come back to the motel room after having had dinner, images from both Laure's apartment and the motel room are edited together in a parallel montage, united through a red-orange tone that contrasts with the chiaroscuro of the sequence as a whole. The red lampshade that floats around the room, the bright light of the electric heater, the red bedsheets, and the orange tip of Jean's cigarette all bathe the dark space in a warm orange light. The close-ups on these objects separate them from their actual spatial environment and create intimate affects. This montage appears as a 'recollection-sequence', an imaginative rewriting of *home*; not as fixed in time or as 'housing of gender', but rather as a space that is always in transit, one that (human and non-human) bodies always affectively make and remake.

The haptic aesthetic (the emphasis on touch, colours, and textures) and magical realism of the film situate space on two simultaneous and contingent levels: of affects and fluid collective power-geometries. The film's aesthetic 'magically' converts Jean into an 'any-man-whatever'. We know very little about him—he could even pass for François, since François never appears in the film.[26] Multiple times in the motel room Jean's head is out of shot or is captured using extreme close-ups that somewhat blur his face, making him indistinguishable from any other man. This reinforces the 'collective' (or 'universal' yet socioculturally specific and heterosexual) dimension of their encounter and brings spatial habitation to the micro-level of bodily affects. In a close-up, Jean takes off his coat and places it on a hanger, and as he exits the frame, Laure enters it in the same continuous shot—underscoring the intimate relationship they have, or better yet, its familiar domestic character. When she hangs her coat next to his, a tighter shot in slow motion shows her hand touching both coats. The scene's chiaroscuro lighting and focus on textures and sensations rather than on Jean as an individual seems to stop time and give form to a space with texture; in this scene personal identity matters less than the affects of social relations and spatial experience. The scene rehearses Laure's move into her partner François' apartment in a different light: as a lived body rather than through gendered spatial norms.

If recollection-objects may appear to fix the motel room as a type of domestic space, the scenes when Laure visits other empty motel rooms and runs down the street at the end of the film point to a genuine fluidity of space-time. Instead of recreating another home with walls and borders that protects Laure from the outside social world, the motel room figures as a space of intimacy in continual transformation and open to the outside. Windows and balconies provide ideal liminal spaces—similar to the roof and balcony in *Wadjda* and *Head-On*, respectively—in between public/ private, social/pre-social, *any-space-whatever/space* of intimacy. The balcony, which belongs to one of the empty motel rooms that Laure visits while Jean is sleeping—not to the room that she inhabits together with Jean—gives shape to the virtualities of spatial habitation: the possibilities beyond yet still within heteronormative patriarchal culture. On the balcony and later in the streets, Laure fully and 'freely' inhabits space from an embodied affirmative position, as a desiring body rather than solely imprisoned by gender norms. This intimates the possibility that spatial relations (and Laure and Francois' future together) may not necessarily involve women's 'sacrifice' of their own space or subjectivity, even from within a heterosexual norm.

Filming Laure as she stands on the balcony, the camera alternates between extreme close-ups of her hair moving in the chilly winter breeze, and medium shots of the transparent curtains similarly moving in the light wind. This scene contrasts with an earlier scene, when Laure steps into the street and blows her hair dry with the car's air vents, a gesture edited in parallel with the exhaust fumes coming out of her car. Now on the balcony, the wind penetrates Laure's hair directly, without the car as a mediator and a protector from the outside world. Likewise, the wind stirring the curtains suggests a material, embodied space that contrasts with the 'immateriality' of the car's exhaust fumes dissipating in the city air. In opposition to her first 'magical haunting' experience of the city, seen through the wandering camera, Laure now inhabits space through and with her body.

Fig. 3.10 *Vendredi soir*: Laure runs through the street towards the camera

In the last image of the film, Laure runs joyfully through the early-morning street towards the camera (see Fig. 3.10). A wide shot situates her in the immediate environment. Several aspects of the mise-en-scène are significant. Narratively, Laure has just left the room where Jean is still sleeping. Laure lives her fantasy, and she is empowered by it—this constitutes quite a contrast in the cinema, where women are so frequently demeaned or 'exploited' as objects of male fantasy.

Aesthetically, this scene is the first in which Laure's body appears uncut and in daylight. Compared to the general languid pace of the film, Laure's action now initiates a rapid movement. While the slow motion of Laure's movement towards the camera embeds her embodied habitation of space, the faster rhythm of Hinchliffe's light and harmonious music increases the impression of her mobility. By rediscovering her body as an empowered, desiring body, Laure has gained self-confidence, and thus social and spatial power that allows her to affirmatively inhabit space and interact with the other.

Vendredi soir affirms the woman protagonist's habitation of space through micro-instances. Laure is in the precarious situation of losing her own space. By moving into her partner's apartment, she risks being assigned a domestic role dictated by gender norms and expectations. The film conveys the negative affects of her situation, while simultaneously providing an image of alternative spatial habitation. While it highlights the patriarchal nature of space and Laure's insecure habitation of 'public' spaces, it also activates the virtual within the real. By adopting a haptic aesthetic and focusing on colours and textures, the film reveals a virtual reality, where both men and women are free to follow their desires. Claire Denis' film thus displays 'affirmative aesthetics': aesthetically establishing affirmative ethics whereby negativity figures as 'a productive moment in the dialectical scheme, which fundamentally aims at overturning the conditions that produced it in the first place' (Braidotti 2011, 285). Whether the imaginative layer represents 'true' diegetic events is irrelevant; what matters is that it opens up possibilities for Laure and other women to inhabit space affirmatively.

Just as in *Wadjda* and *Head-On*, as we will see, *Vendredi soir* suggests that social and spatial transformation occurs at the threshold of mobility by inhabiting space affectively. Instead of embarking on a journey of self-discovery that travel promises in classical narratives, all three protagonists, Laure, Wadjda, and Sibel, are able to transform spaces of '(im)mobility' into spaces of intimate connections. Laure's expansion of her spaces of intimacy originates in a connection to the erotic (as the last chapter on *Head-On* will explore further), whereby women transform the negative affects of patriarchal spaces into embodied generative desires. *Vendredi soir, Wadjda,* and *Head-On* (and to a certain extent *Messidor*) show how women create spaces of self-confidence for themselves in spite of the patriarchal structures that negatively affect their mobility. Most importantly, these films suggest—mostly through their aesthetic choices—that spaces are not fixed within these oppressive structures and that other affirmative possibilities exist.

Notes

1. Some parts of this chapter already appear in Baschiera, Stefano and Miriam De Rosa (eds.), Film and Domestic Space: Architectures, Representaions, Dispositif, Edinburg: Edinburg University Press, 2020.
2. For a critique of Habermas' claim that the public sphere is open and available to all, see Nancy Fraser (1990).

3. For Jennifer Barker, drawing on Sobchack's work, the film's body is a lived-body (not a human one) that exists:

   haptically, at the screen's surface, with the caress of shimmering nitrate and the scratch of dust and fiber on celluloid; kinaesthetically, through the contours of on- and off-screen space and of the bodies, both human and mechanical, that inhabit or escape those spaces; and viscerally, with the film's rush through a projector's gate and the "breathing" of lenses. (2009, 3)

4. Laure's apprehension regarding heteronormative habitation of the home space is evident when she imagines bringing Jean to Marie's dinner. She imagines a scene in which she and Jean sit on the couch while Marie rocks her newborn. The faded colour of the scene, its old-fashioned editing through an iris transition (the only instance in the film), and the fixed camera filming Laure and Jean standing 'front on' in a medium shot all convey Laure's bleak image of heteronormative habitation of the home space.
5. Lemercier's acting in this film is particularly sober, in contrast with her most famous roles in French family comedies such as in *Les visiteurs* (Jean-Marie Poiré 1993).
6. This night scene, which occurs immediately after establishing the city as a threatening masculine environment (as will be explored in the next section), reminds one of the colourful windows from which Ariane sings in *La Captive* (Chantal Akerman 2000), which allows for the breaking the spatial boundary of her room in which she is contained by her male partner.
7. This scene clearly appears as a comment on social inequalities in the French capital, which is reiterated with the cold man in the streets asking for a ride that Laure refuses to give. The other characters appear to be middle class, as demonstrated through their costumes, attitudes, and oral expressions (starting with Laure and Jean themselves). Although I do not discuss it here, this is particularly visible in the restaurant where Laure and Jean have dinner, which mocks the Parisian bourgeoisie through stereotypical characters.
8. 'A reminder of winter strengthens the happiness of inhabiting. In the reign of the imagination alone, a reminder of winter increases the house's value as a place to live in' (Bachelard 1994 [1964], 40).
9. Claire Denis explains that it was crucial to film in winter so as to accurately capture the sensations of a winter's night (Beugnet 2004).
10. Just as Sibel's glasses somewhat protect her from the masculine gaze in the last part of *Head-On*, when Laure leaves her apartment above the city her car functions as her own passport to be mobile; a vehicle for her habitation of the city and protection from the frightening and overwhelming presence of the male other.

11. Through absurd elements that invade the realism of the film, Denis ridicules the machismo of the city and the space of the car itself. In a scene in which Laure witnesses an accident, Denis mocks how men's voices often emerge as voices of authority in the urban space, especially in relation to cars. The theatricality of the scene, with its cheesy dialogue and mise-en-scène, recalls the opening accident scenes of Jean-Luc Godard's film *Weekend* (1967), which also crosses the borders of realism and imaginary as it denounces the heteronormativity of space.
12. In his research on Marseilles, another French metropolis, social geographer Guy Di Méo (2011) notes the many social dimensions and negative affects of women's habitation of Marseilles at different times of the day.
13. The film *Lluvia* (Paula Hernández 2008) conveys the same aspect, as the protagonist actually lives in her car after leaving her partner's apartment. The story line echoes *Vendredi soir* insofar as the protagonist escapes to her car to have a space of her own which she does not have at her partner's.
14. Sheller and Urry write that 'the driver's body is itself fragmented and disciplined to the machine, with eyes, cars, hands and feet all trained to respond instantaneously, while the desire to stretch, to change position, or to look around must be suppressed. The car becomes an extension of the driver's body, creating new urban subjectivities' (2000, 747).
15. Jane Villenet made a short video titled 'How to deliver traffic info on radio in a *fipette's* way?', in which *fipette* refers to the exclusively female announcers of *France Inter Paris (FIP)* radio: http://www.dailymoyion.com/video/xp3100jane-villenet-radio-france-comment-faire-un-bulletin-trafic-a-la-maniere-d-une-fipettecreation
16. Later, in the restaurant scene (which I do not discuss here), Laure voices the idea of protection as a 'masculine' characteristic: After a woman has been in the bathroom for a long moment, and Jean tells Laure that they should check if something happened to her, she replies that 'il ne peut rien lui arriver, son mari est là' ('her husband is there, nothing can happen to her').
17. While the entire car sequence draws attention to cars as male-dominated objects, absurd elements denounce the patriarchal heteronormativity of spatial habitation. Laure takes advantage of the greater immobility caused by the accident and leaves her car to make a quick phone call to her friend Marie; however, when she returns, she cannot find her car. Echoing the rude and aggressive behaviour of the fighting men, the male driver whom she asks if he has seen her car answers childishly and with disdain that it probably 'flew off'. Jean too demonstrates a patronising attitude towards Laure, denoting the gendered power-geometries of space, when he finds Laure looking for her car, which he himself moved, and tells her not to leave her car in the middle of the street (an absurd comment since the car behind Laure is still in the same place as when she left). His gesture also

points to traditional male control over women's bodies and habitation of space: he takes her by the arm, physically guiding her back to the car, and sits in the driver seat without hesitation, even though the car belongs to Laure.
18. Merleau-Ponty describes the synesthesia of cinema: 'the ambiguity of experience is such that an auditory rhythm fuses cinematic images together and gives rise to a perception of movement whereas, without an auditory contribution, the same succession of images would be too slow to provoke the stroboscopic movement' (Merleau-Ponty 2012 [1962], 237).
19. In Merleau-Ponty's words: 'while each monocular vision, each touching with one sole hand has its own visible, its tactile, each is bound to every other vision, to every other touch; it is bound in such a way as to make up with them the experience of one sole body before one sole world, through a possibility for reversion, reconversion of its language into theirs, transfer, and reversal' (1968, 142). Thinking about Laure and Jean's reversibility of experience in political terms, it seems that the 'reconversion of one's language into another's' can benefit an affirmative politics that, Rosi Braidotti asserts, requires the bonding of its actors, the recognition that '"we" are in this together. This is a collective activity, a group project that connects active, conscious, and desiring citizens... [which may be] a painful experience, given that identifications constitute an inner scaffolding that supports one's sense of identity' (2011, 294).
20. In the book from which the film was adapted, Emmanuèle Bernheim describes with precision the movement of the characters, which emphasise Laure's lack of power in decision-making and her spatial subordination to Frédéric (Jean, in the film). Like Jean, Frédéric takes Laure by the arm several times during the film to direct her steps and precedes her in the streets as they arrive at the motel, 'Ils montèrent [les escaliers], lui devant elle derrière' ('They went up [the stairs], he in front, she behind', 60), he dictates when they leave: 'On s'en va... marchons' ('We are leaving ... let's walk ', 54–55), or again when they go out for dinner, 'Viens, on va dîner. J'ai faim' ('Let's go for dinner. I'm hungry', 73). On a representational level, the characters' spatiality indeed denotes their compulsory performances of 'masculinity' and 'femininity', as is also evident in *Head-On*.
21. Whereas for Butler the subject does not prefigure gender but is already born in gender, for de Beauvoir and Toril Moi, drawing on de Beauvoir's work, the lived body is a process rather than linked to sexual anatomy, the 'ongoing interaction between the subject and the world' (Moi 2001, 63).
22. Three women in the film, the blonde woman in the car, a young woman at a café, and a bourgeois woman at the restaurant where Laure and Jean have dinner together, function as a gauge of Laure's own habitation of gender and heterosexual desirability.

23. While noting that she is exaggerating the dichotomy between the terms, Marks opposes what she calls 'optical' and 'haptic' visuality. Whereas 'in optical visuality … the viewer isolates and comprehends the object of vision' in a relation of 'mastery' to the image, 'haptic visuality … closes the distance and implicates the viewer in the viewed … losing [him or herself] in the intensified relation with an other that cannot be possessed' (Marks 2000, 184).
24. As Judith Mayne indicates, 'given her unconventional looks, as well as her reputation as a gay icon and a gender-blending performer, [Lemercier] brings to the film as much emphasis on how the character is transformed as on the sexual experience' (2005, 122).
25. Original text: 'Petite, carrée et basse de plafond, cette chambre ressemblait à la sienne. Laure s'immobilisa. C'était la sienne. Elle était chez elle avec Frédéric. Et comme tous les soirs, avant de se coucher, il baissait le chauffage. Car la nuit, ensemble, ils n'avaient jamais froid' (Bernheim 1998, 92–93).
26. In Bernheim's book, the stranger Laure meets (Jean) is called Frédéric, sharing thus the first two letters of his name with Laure's partner François. Laure also compares the two men in inner monologues. She wonders why François does not dress the way Frédéric does and imagines moving in with Frédéric just as she will (we suppose) with François.

References

Ahmed, Sara. 2010. *The Promise of Happiness*. Durham/London: Duke University Press.
Akerman, Chantal. 2000. *La Captive*. DVD. Belgium; France: Paradise Films.
Anderson, Ben. 2009. Affective Atmospheres. *Emotion, Space and Society* 2: 77–81.
Appadurai, Arjun. 2002. The Right to Participate in the Work of the Imagination. In *Transurbanism*, ed. Joke Brouwer and Arjen Mulder. Rotterdam: NAi Publishers.
Bachelard, Gaston. 1961. *La Poétique de l'espace*. 1st edition in 1957. Paris: Presses Universitaires de France.
———. 1994 [1964]. *The Poetics of Space*. Boston: Beacon Press.
Barker, Jennifer M. 2009. *The Tactile Eye: Touch and Cinematic Experience*. Berkeley/Los Angeles/London: University of California Press.
Bernheim, Emmanuèle. 1998. *Vendredi Soir*. Paris: Gallimard.
Beugnet, Martine. 2004. *Claire Denis and the Cinema of the Senses*. Manchester: Manchester University Press.
———. 2007. *Cinema and Sensation: French Film and the Art of Transgression*. Edinburgh: Edinburgh University Press.

Braidotti, Rosi. 2011. *Nomadic Theory: The Portable Rosi Braidotti*. Chichester: Columbia University Press.
Bruno, Giuliana. 2002. *Atlas of Emotion: Journeys in Art, Architecture, and Film*. London/New York: Verso.
Butler, J. 1990. *Gender trouble: Feminism and the subversion of identity*. New York; London: Routledge.
Butler, J. 1993. Critically Queer. *GLQ: A Journal of Lesbian and Gay Studies* 1 (1): 17–32.
———. 1997. *Excitable Speech: A Politics of the Performative*. New York: Routledge.
Calle, Sophie, and Greg Shephard. 1996. *No Sex Last Night*. DVD. USA: Gemini Films.
Cronenberg, David. 1996. *Crash*. DVD. Adaptation of the novel of the same name by J. G. Ballard, Canada/UK: Alliance Communications Corporation.
de Beauvoir, Simone. 1949. *Le deuxime sexe I: les faits et les mythes*. Paris: Gallimard.
Deleuze, Gilles. 1966. *Le Bergsonisme*. Paris: Presses Universitaires de France.
———. 1986. *Cinema 1: The Movement-Image*. Minneapolis: University of Minnesota Press.
Denis, Claire. 2002. *Vendredi Soir*. DVD. France: Bac Films.
Di Méo, Guy. 2011. *Les murs invisibles: femmes, genre et géographie sociale*. Paris: Armand Colin.
Doane, Mary Ann. 1987. The 'Woman's Film': Possession and Address. In *Home Is Where the Heart Is: Studies in Melodrama and the Woman's Film*, ed. Christine Gledhill, 283–298. London: British Film Institute.
Donaldson, Lucy Fife. 2014. *Texture in Film*. Hampshire/New York: Palgrave Macmillan.
Fraser, Nancy. 1990. Rethinking the Public Sphere: A Contribution to the Critique of Actually Existing Democracy. *Social Text* 25 (26): 56–80.
Friedberg, Anne. 1993. *Window Shopping: Cinema and the Postmodern*. Berkeley: University of California Press.
Godard, Jean-Luc. 2012 [1967]. *Weekend*. DVD. France: Criterion Collection.
Habermas, Jürgen. 1989 [1962]. *The Structural Transformation of the Public Sphere: An Inquiry into a Category of Bourgeois Society*. Malden: Polity Press.
Hernández, Paula. 2008. *Lluvia*. DVD. Argentina: Buena Vista International.
Jarmusch, Jim. 1991. *Night on Earth*. DVD. France/UK/Germany/USA/Japan: Pyramide.
Kiarostami, Abbas. 2002. *Ten*. DVD. France/Iran: MK2 Productions.
Knight, Steven. 2013. *Locke*. DVD. UK/USA: Lionsgate Home Entertainment.
Lemercier, Valérie. 1999. *Le Derrière*. DVD. France: TF1 Films Production.
Marks, Laura U. 2000. *The Skin of the Film: Intercultural Cinema, Embodiment, and the Senses*. Durham/London: Duke University Press.
Massey, Doreen B. 1994. *Space, Place, and Gender*. Minneapolis: University of Minnesota Press.
Mayne, Judith. 2005. *Claire Denis*. Urbana/Chicago: University of Illinois Press.

Merleau-Ponty, Maurice. 1964. *Le visible et l'invisible; suivi de notes de travail*. Paris: Gallimard.
———. 1968. *The Visible and the Invisible*. Evanston: Northwestern University Press.
Merleau-Ponty, Maurice. 2012 [1962]. *Phenomenology of Perception*. London/New York: Routledge.
Moi, Toril. 2001. *What Is a Woman?: And Other Essays*. New York: Oxford University Press.
Poiré, Jean-Marie. 1993. *Les Visiteurs*. VHS. France: Gaumont.
Refn, Nicolas Winding. 2011. *Drive*. DVD. USA: FilmDistrict.
Reichardt, Kelly. 2008. *Wendy and Lucy*. DVD. USA: Madman Entertainment.
Shaviro, Steven. 2004. *The Cinematic Body*. 4th ed. Minneapolis: University of Minnesota Press.
Sheller, Mimi, and John Urry. 2000. The City and the Car. *International Journal of Urban and Regional Research* 24 (4): 737–757.
Sobchack, Vivian. 2004. *Carnal Thoughts: Embodiment and Moving Image Culture*. Berkeley/Los Angeles/London: University of California Press.
Wilson, Elizabeth. 1991. *The Sphinx in the City: Urban Life, the Control of Disorder, and Women*. Berkeley: University of California Press.
———. 2001. *The Contradictions of Culture: Cities, Culture, Women*. London: SAGE Publications.
Woolf, Virginia. 1945 [1929]. *A Room of One's Own*. London: Penguin Books.
Young, Iris Marion. 1980. Throwing Like a Girl: A Phenomenology of Feminine Body Comportment Motility and Spatiality. *Human Studies* 3 (1): 137–156.

Open Access This chapter is licensed under the terms of the Creative Commons Attribution 4.0 International License (http://creativecommons.org/licenses/by/4.0/), which permits use, sharing, adaptation, distribution and reproduction in any medium or format, as long as you give appropriate credit to the original author(s) and the source, provide a link to the Creative Commons licence and indicate if changes were made.

The images or other third party material in this chapter are included in the chapter's Creative Commons license, unless indicated otherwise in a credit line to the material. If material is not included in the chapter's Creative Commons licence and your intended use is not permitted by statutory regulation or exceeds the permitted use, you will need to obtain permission directly from the copyright holder.

CHAPTER 4

Houses and Wilful Women: *Wadjda*

My pain is not fences around the pond but to live amongst fish that cannot imagine the ocean.
Mohammad Mosaddegh, as cited in *Sepideh* (Madsen 2013)

Prime Minister Mohammad Mosaddegh uttered the above sentence when he was overthrown in the 1953 coup and jailed. The coup orchestrated by the U.S. Central Intelligence Agency was meant to prevent the nationalisation of Iranian oil and the government's move toward a communist political system (Merica and Hanna 2013). The coup also shut down Mosaddegh's wilfulness to prevent foreign supremacy in his country. Mosaddegh's statement seems to encapsulate the failure of his opponents to imagine the future otherwise, to imagine a world besides Western capitalism. At times wilfulness needs to be concealed in order to become stronger, to affect deeper. The previous chapter has revealed that wilful women and wilful forms challenge the status quo at a micro-level. The aesthetic of *Vendredi soir* unveils spaces of activism, a wilfulness that persists beyond the gendered norms that the character has integrated over time. If Laure embodies gender as an unconscious performance, the young girl in Haifaa Al-Mansour's film *Wadjda* (2012) learns how to manage expectations imposed on her because of her female body. Her relative ignorance of norms and regulations takes form as both a wilful, mobile habitation of space and a necessity of *appearing with*, of masking wilfulness. This chapter explores how the characters' predicament and the visual

© The Author(s) 2020
M. Ceuterick, *Affirmative Aesthetics and Wilful Women*,
https://doi.org/10.1007/978-3-030-37039-8_4

forms of *Wadjda* reveal a need for insistence and strategies of persistence when patriarchy acts as an obstacle to wilfulness; such insistence and persistence finds refuge in the house, a liminal space in between public scrutiny and affirmative resistance.

The spaces of *Wadjda*—namely, streets, a school, and a house—give shape to ever-changing power-geometries, which modify relations of gender. First, I consider how heteronormative patriarchal rules regulate street spaces and how wilfulness changes filmic forms. Second, though the power-geometries at play in Wadjda's school reduce the 'loudness' of her free will, that free will persists. Third, the protagonists' wilfulness remains particularly visible as micro-relations in and around the house. This chapter will demonstrate how both the aesthetic construction of space and the bodies of the protagonists take wilful forms. By developing her bodily capabilities (through learning to ride a bicycle), the young protagonist Wadjda challenges 'naturalised' social roles and spatial existence as determined by sex. The film thereby transforms the gendered and deterministic narratives of 'feminine' spatiality theorised by Iris Marion Young (1980) into a phenomenological account of bodies as lived bodies. Accordingly, gender appears as a *background* to, rather than a *source* of, a subject's spatiality, and the body becomes a 'capable body' through training and intention (Diane Chisholm 2008).[1] This capable body and its movements, along with the forms of the film, transform the power-geometries of space by making it fluid and open to modifications.

Cinema, in particular Middle Eastern contemporary cinema directed by women, is full of examples of women's will being silenced; however, that will persists, is built up between the walls of houses, and erupts through movement. Examples of such films include *Silences of the Palace* (Moufida Tlatli 1994), *The Apple* (Samira Makhmalbaf 1998), *The Day I Became a Woman* (Marzieh Meshkini 2000), *The Circle* (Jafar Panahi 2000), *Women without Men* (Shirin Neshat 2009), *678* (Mohamed Diab 2010), and *Circumstance* (Maryam Keshavarz 2011). Wilfulness, as seen in the introductory chapter, is about making space for oneself when spaces are not naturally accommodating. The women protagonists of these films are willing 'not to go with the flow', as Sara Ahmed would put it. They are willing not to follow a path that has been instructed by others—even while they often have to 'pass as willing [to follow the prescribed path] in order to be willful' (Ahmed 2014, 11; 152). While wilfulness appears as 'an act of disobedience', it also is an act of persisting and 'appearing with' the general will in order to not be dismissed (2; 151). In this chapter we will see how wilfulness produces micro-instances of affirmation through filmic forms and characters' movements. Such forms and movements give shape to the spaces of *Wadjda*. As the first feature film directed by a Saudi woman, and one that required the director's wilful insistence to be produced (Al-Mansour directed the film from the back of a van in order not to appear in public with the men of the crew), *Wadjda* offers an excellent example of how wilfulness manifests as being both 'against' and 'appearing with' the patriarchal flow.

Wadjda challenges some well-established sexist social norms in Saudi Arabia. By choosing a child protagonist, Al-Mansour was able to expose gender inequalities without seeming polemical. In interviews, the director asserts that telling the story from a child's, Wadjda's, perspective was a deliberate choice: the child's innocence and greater mobility allow her to comment on cultural issues without appearing to overtly criticise the culture (Pape 2013). Akin with Al-Mansour's statement, Fatima Mernissi writes that girls and elderly women benefit from greater freedom of movement in heterosocial spaces, in contrast with young adult women who are regarded as 'sexual beings' (1975, 83–84). Al-Mansour notes that it is important not to appear angry or confrontational, so as 'to be accepted back home' (Premiere Scene 2013). Recognising her own limitations to 'freedom', and the importance of not appearing 'against', Al-Mansour explains that she chose a bicycle as Wadjda's mode of transportation because it is 'not frightening, it is a toy' (Pape 2013), and it is only slightly subversive. The bicycle also functions as an analogy: it advocates for the right of women to drive cars in Saudi Arabia. Rather than focusing on the patriarchal norms that negatively affect women's mobility and habitation of the public space, the film takes wilful forms through Wadjda's lived body and the spaces she inhabits.

Wadjda in Context

Before reading for wilfulness in *Wadjda*, a brief note needs to be made on the context of the film and women's habitation of heterosocial spaces in Saudi culture. In heterosocial (that is, mixed-sex) spaces such as the streets, women (and men, but with less emphasis) are required to dress modestly and obey the Shari'a laws of chastity when in contact with the opposite sex who are not family. In one of the rare books on gender in Saudi Arabia, *A Most Masculine State: Gender, Politics and Religion in Saudi Arabia,* Madawi Al-Rasheed writes that the 1970s were a time of wealth and growing education for women, as well as the beginning of foreign domestic labour. These factors contributed to the freeing of Saudi middle-class women from their household duties and to the creation of a new class of educated (but unemployed) women increasingly present in urban spaces (2013, 103–104).

According to Al-Rasheed, the rapid changes of the 1970s transformed urban space into 'an arena for flirtation, challenging many social and religious taboos', which in turn led to an increase of harassment in the streets; the streets were thought of as 'male' space and hence were not accommodating to women (2013, 105). As Fatima Mernissi points out, in traditional Islam, women were encouraged to go out accompanied by a male family member or an older woman, since elderly women were not regarded as sexual beings (1975, 84). The Mecca mosque siege in 1979, along with the Iranian revolution (known as the 'Islamic revival' in the Muslim world), led the Saudi state to hand over more power to Islamic scholars, who campaigned for a return to more traditional gender views and roles, which included the exclusion of women from public spaces, the control of women's behaviour, and the establishment of a dress code for women (Al-Rasheed 2013, 131). Al-Rasheed writes that the state gave more and more power to religious guardians, making 'monitoring women's conduct [especially in the public sphere]... a collective male responsibility to be upheld by all Saudi men' (2013, 105). While men are likely to be punished for harassing women in urban spaces, women are reprimanded for not covering their face or arms while wearing their *abaya* (a loose garment which covers most of the body, except for the face, hands, and feet).

Not only are the injunctions for women to wear the veil practical strategies to maintain the 'piety of the nation', they are also political strategies, in which men are given control over women's social and spatial actions. In her book *Politics of Piety*, Saba Mahmood explains that:

> the juristic Islamic tradition assumes that women are the objects of sexual desire and men the desiring subjects, an assumption that has come to justify the injunction that women should 'hide their charms' when in public so as to not excite the libidinal energies of men who are not their immediate kin. ... As a number of feminist scholars have pointed out, these kinds of arguments assign the burden of maintaining a community's purity and integrity to women, a task that necessitates their subordination to men, who are entrusted to oversee and control women's sexuality and mobility, as well as their access to a community's symbolic and material resources. In a system

of inequality predicated on this view of male-female sexuality, differential gender roles are rooted in the naturalized topography of female and male nature in which the former is regarded as passive and the latter as agentival. (2005, 110; 112)

In Saudi Arabia, selective verses of the Qur'an and the Prophet's *hadiths* (his sayings and deeds) have been interpreted as religious heritage and now dictate social norms and the rights of women, even if they are not inscribed in the law. In the essay collection *The New Voices of Islam*, Amina Wadud observes that the foundations of Islam were developed exclusively by (misogynistic) male scholars and thinkers who:

> moved away from the Qur'an's ethical codes for female autonomy, to advocate instead women's *subservience, silence and seclusion*. If women's agency was taken into consideration, it was with regard to service to men, family and community. Women came to be discussed in law in the same terms as material objects and possessions. (2002, 203, emphasis mine)

Women's seclusion and silencing emerged as a reaction to the perception of women as objects of desire, which has a continuous impact on their habitation of heterosocial spaces.

Since 9/11, local demands and the international image of Saudi Arabia have led to the withdrawal of some religious and political advisors. There have been some efforts to reform current views on women and attempts to emancipate women (Al-Rasheed 2013, 153). Al-Rasheed notes that new public debates have led to fierce divisions in the religious community and Saudi society as a whole. Issues of *ikhtilat* (permitted mixing between the sexes in certain spatial environments) and women's legitimacy in public places traditionally reserved for men have been particularly controversial (159). In the current global capitalist system, women are increasingly encouraged to work, although opportunities to become economically independent remain limited. In *Feminism and Islam*, Mai Yamani explains that in the conservative Najd region, where Riyadh is located (and where *Wadjda* was filmed), only a few professions are currently available to women: teaching in women's schools or in university branches for women, working in women-only shops, or working as a nurse or doctor in a hospital (both of which are considered as 'virtuous professions' because they involve caring for the community) (Yamani 1996, 262). Similarly, there are no film theatres in Saudi Arabia (nor is there a proper film industry), and women are not encouraged to work as filmmakers, as Haifaa

Al-Mansour explains: 'Saudi Arabia is a conservative place and a lot of people are against women making films and voicing their opinion' (Pape 2013).

IN THE STREETS OF RIYADH

In Al-Mansour's film, like the films I have examined in the previous chapters, wilfulness stems from being made to feel 'out of place'. When Massey describes the *power-geometries* of space, she contends that it is how women are made to feel 'out of place' when suffering from physical or mental abuse, or when they are 'ogled at' in the streets, that affect their spatial behaviour and their mobility (Massey 1994, 148). As such, power-geometries originate in and constantly change through social interactions, thus forming and transforming space. The film's aesthetic reflects this constant transformation of power-geometries and space. The protagonist, Wadjda, is at once innocent as a child can be and constantly annoyed by the spatial and social norms that negatively affect her movement and behaviour. After she loses a race against her male friend Abdullah, he on a bicycle and she on foot, she sets out to fight the injustice of not having access to a bike. Wadjda lives with her mother while her father visits them from time to time. In spite of social practices that prohibit women from riding bicycles, Wadjda decides she must have one. As her mother refuses to buy her a bicycle, Wadjda enters the Qur'an competition at school in the hope of winning the prize money to buy one for herself. However, when Wadjda wins the competition and reveals her intention to buy a bike with the money, the head of the school refuses to give her the prize. At the end of the film, Wadjda's mother decides to buy her the green bicycle she wanted.

As a result of the incident, Wadjda becomes increasingly aware that heterosocial spaces do not accommodate her in the same way as they do boys of her own age. Wadjda's lack of mobility and spatial power become obstacles that she is willing to overcome. Wilfulness is not a personality trait but a characteristic that the subject 'experiences as having'; it is '*a matter of how we are affected*' (Ahmed 2014, 24; 76, emphasis in original). Wilfulness in fact manifests both through the characters' bodies and in the form it takes shape on screen.

As heterosocial and dominated by men, the street is where women's mobility is most visibly affected. In the film's first scene in the streets, Wadjda is walking to school. Her friend Abdullah steals her sandwich as he passes by her and starts running. From the other side of the street, a fixed camera follows Wadjda and Abdullah in a panning movement as they run side by side on the pathway, while the leitmotiv music of the film resonates. On the one hand, passing cars obstructing the shot place the characters within society and daily life, in which women have to fight for their rights, and nothing is given to them. On the other hand, the ambient and playful music establishes the characters' innocent and thus-far unproblematic friendship. However, when Abdullah returns with his bicycle and steals the headscarf from the head of Wadjda, who then drops her sandwich on the ground in surprise, the music stops and a handheld camera begins a panning movement around Wadjda as her friend imposes his masculine privilege on her (the privilege of not having the physical restriction of wearing a veil and of having access to a bike). The movement and high angle of the camera close-up on Wadjda as she picks up her sandwich from the ground emphasises her immobility and creates uneasiness about the inequality that the gendered situation conveys. As Wadjda runs again in pursuit of her veil, the camera stays behind for a bit longer—the characters become smaller in the frame—before cutting to Abdullah, who drops the veil on the dusty ground with disdain. Still on his bicycle, he then says patronisingly: 'Did you really think you could catch up with me?' The delay of the camera to 'react' and follow the characters introduces an affect of powerlessness, reinforced by the absence of music, which adds seriousness to the scene and a sense that power-geometries sometimes appear immutable. However, the absence of external elements, such as the passing cars of the previous scene, removes the characters from their daily lives and opens future possibilities. The scene calls for what is not yet present: the bike and the right to move that Wadjda wishes she had.

The characters' unequal access to mobility and the wilfulness to transform power-geometries produce the cinematic spaces of this sequence in the streets. In the shot/reverse shot that closes the sequence, the two characters part ways. Wadjda picks up her veil from the ground proudly and continues walking. She then turns and watches Abdullah leave with his male friends and says, 'If I had a bike, you'd see'; she then turns around again and leaves in the other direction (see Fig. 4.1). Abdullah and his friends (who have suddenly appeared on their bicycles) take up the entire frame as they are filmed from behind, glorified by a low angle—this angle, however, appears ironic and creates a wilful form as it over-venerates their social position compared to Wadjda's. The sudden return to a crowded frame also conjures again the present situation, whereby the boys' mobility is privileged over that of a girl. Rather than depicting

Fig. 4.1 Closing a street sequence in *Wadjda*: Shots of Abdullah and Wadjda

Wadjda as powerless by filming her from afar, as earlier, the camera places her in a medium shot in the middle of the frame as she turns her back on the boys. As her body occupies the frame, it creates wilful affects that change the power-geometry of the street space. If change for now occurs in an empty space that only Wadjda inhabits, this points to the further unfolding of the narrative: Wadjda will not go with the flow and will instead buy a bicycle despite the injunctions against her riding one. The mise-en-scène, sound, and cinematography of the sequence create spaces of affirmation beyond the narrative, which aesthetically challenge and transform existing power-geometries.

The affirmative forms of this street sequence take shape at a micro- and bodily level. In her work on 'affirmative ethics', Rosi Braidotti writes that 'the material that damages is also that which engenders positive resistance, counteraction, or transcendence' (Braidotti 2011, 285). It is out of negative bodily affects, of injustice, that affirmative forms emerge. A micro-analysis of filmic forms and of Wadjda's body as filmic form allows us to read for wilfulness, and how wilfulness creates space. Wadjda's movement within the frame requires a phenomenological approach that looks at Wadjda's body as capable, not determined by gender but living through gender as a situation and *making* space. Since the realism of the film 'forces' it to convey the gendering of space and power-geometries, which may appear fixed, representation alone fails to thoroughly encompass women's wilfulness to divert from the patriarchal path. Wilfulness in fact takes form as affects, as 'structures that work through formal means, as consisting in their formal dimensions (as line, light, color, rhythm, and so on) of passionate structures' (Brinkema 2014, 37). The possibility of wilfulness to modify space and bring the new into the present comes through at a micro-level, through aesthetic choices. This is, this book argues, what gives shape to affirmative aesthetics.

A Passport to Be Mobile

In *Wadjda*, the veil becomes central to the persistence and concealment of wilfulness. As explained in my brief contextualisation of the film, the veil hides women's bodies as 'desired objects', and it also acquires wilful forms, becomes a disguise, a passport, a vehicle of belonging, and an index of sexuality. When Abdullah strips Wadjda of her veil, he essentially steals her *passport to be mobile* while also emphasising her lack of a bicycle. He is thus reaffirming his dominating male position and her lack of power as a young woman in the street. The veil is a 'screen' that allows women to venture into 'public spaces, which are, by definition, male spaces' (Mernissi 1975, 81). With the veil, Mernissi writes, women are considered invisible while trespassing in male spaces—so-called public spaces (1975, 84). Without the veil, however, women are considered exhibitionists or *aryana* (translated both as 'nude' and 'a woman who is not veiled' in Moroccan Arabic) (Mernissi 1975, 84–85). The principal of the school repeatedly scolds Wadjda for not covering her face as the other girls do, or for not behaving piously as a woman should in the presence of men. Mostly unconsciously, out of ignorance, and because she is still a child, Wadjda disobeys the precepts for women to hide their bodies, remain silent, or stay secluded.

The fact that the veil is only strongly recommended—rather than compulsory—for young women (who are neither children nor old women) establishes a direct link between the veil and a woman's sexuality. When Wadjda tells her mother that the principal asked her to wear *abaya* in the streets on her way to school, the mother jokes that it is maybe time to marry her daughter off. When Wadjda is walking back home after school, a builder perched on scaffolding calls out an obscene comment. While he is *above* the street in a spatial position of power, he is also removed from it and thus not on the same spatial plane as Wadjda. The man's comment both identifies and stigmatises Wadjda as a sexual being (in spite of her wearing her headscarf) and participates in deeper and wider sexist structures of power that make women feel like they do not belong on the street. In this instance, and many others, the film places emphasis on the power-geometries of streets, whereby men have power and control over their movements and habitation of 'public' spaces while women do not. However, this does not deter Wadjda from pursuing her project of riding a bike in spite of the fact that bicycles are not considered appropriate for girls. If the builder's comment provokes a mix of contempt, disgust, and bewilderment, Wadjda resumes her life as a child immediately: she plays with Abdullah and chases a bicycle being delivered down the street until she reaches the shop where she will be able to buy it. The veil that she wears does not 'protect' her from the gaze of unrelated men, as it promised, but it does prevent her from running as fast as she would like to.

As a wilful child, Wadjda does not take the *abaya* seriously and in fact plays with it, imitating a thief, as she tells her mother with a sceptical expression that '"a thief" jumped over the principal Ms. Hussa's fence to see' Ms. Hussa. Through her playful gestures, not only does Wadjda challenge the veracity of the account that it was a thief who entered Ms. Hussa's house and not Ms. Hussa's lover (which would be prohibited by the Shari'a, as they are not married), she also subverts the *abaya* as a potential disguise for women to hide things from social control in heterosocial situations. When an older schoolmate of Wadjda's asks her to take a note to her lover (whom she calls her brother) waiting outside the school, the film places much emphasis on the schoolmate partly covering her gestures with her veil while acting 'unlawfully' (see Fig. 4.2). The veil acts like a screen (to use Mernissi's expression), a screen that both conceals women's actions and allows them to appropriate the power of the gaze without being seen, akin to the (male) *flâneur*.

In its subversive state as a screen that allows one to act wilfully, outside of patriarchal precepts, the veil acquires a wilful form. The veil of Wadjda's schoolmate serves to hide her actions from the wary principal (see Fig. 4.2). The schoolmate's body position and insistence upon covering her face and arms in spite of being inside the school (where the veil is not formally required) creates a protected space, 'a space of her own'. As mentioned earlier, in *A Room of One's Own*, Wolff insists on the need for women to have a room of their own for their artistic production, just as men writers do. While this allows women to escape injunctions to perform domestic tasks and have time on their own, the view out of the room's window indispensably nourishes their imagination (Woolf 1945 [1929]). To a certain extent, the veil acquires the form of a room with a window. Similarly, acquiring a bike (or a car) functions along the same lines: it is a vehicle to observe and look at the city from a mediated position. The veil and the bike have more than just meanings; they have forms that modify the power-geometries of space.

4 HOUSES AND WILFUL WOMEN: *WADJDA*   109

Fig. 4.2 The veil takes a wilful form in *Wadjda*

Bending Lines

Wadjda's school figures as a space of docility and discipline—to use Michel Foucault's (1975) terms—with its organisation of space and time, rules, and squared lines. If the organisation of space and time is contingent to power-geometries, wilfulness becomes the bending of fences, the contestation of space, and the production of new lines. Affirmative forms build on the limitations to freedom that the school embodies. As Ahmed writes, education, in the sense of producing docile children, is a matter of 'straightening what is already bent', and putting an end to wilfulness (2014, 71). While the school space figures as a place of order and subservience, the film produces micro-instances of wilfulness through form and the positioning and framing of Wadjda's body.

The opening sequence of *Wadjda* functions as a good example of straightening both children and filmic forms, including space and sound. As a choir of schoolgirls sings along to a recording of a religious song, a fixed camera frames their shiny black shoes and the bottom of their grey robes as they move around. When the teacher stops the tape and orders the girls to stand properly in their place, the camera rises from ground level and stands among the girls, filming their backs and the teacher in front of them, as if the camera was being scolded too. The choir resumes singing, and a static, frontal close-up frames several schoolgirls at shoulder height who look straight ahead, except for one, Wadjda, who looks sideways and waves smilingly at her friends walking by. When the teacher stops the tape again and instructs Wadjda to come to the front, the other girls step aside to let her pass. As Wadjda walks towards the teacher, another close-up concentrates on Wadjda's shoes, a pair of worn-out Converse trainers with purple laces, which are contrasted with those of the other schoolgirls. For not respecting the place she was assigned by the teacher, Wadjda is punished by being assigned another place, under the hot sun on the patio.

In the first part of the sequence, the movement of the pupils' feet and their discordant voices produce disorder within the fixed frame. Remaining at a very low level, the camera focuses on distracted feet, wilful to behave in opposition to imposed norms. As the camera stands among the schoolgirls, the classroom's posters and yellow walls create a somewhat lively atmosphere, suggesting a possibility of escape from the order and discipline imposed by the teacher. This is contrasted with the very dark background seen in the tight frontal shots of the singing girls in grey uniforms. As the teacher calls Wadjda to the front, the camera remains in a corner, filming Wadjda from a low angle while casting the shadow of the teacher upon her—a shadow of docility on her wilfulness.

The various colours, divergent voices, and movements of this scene all produce, as micro-instances, an affirmative space that creates alternatives upon the limitations that the school imposes. On the one hand, the space changes visibly after Wadjda has left the classroom: the entire choir appears in the centre of the frame, well aligned and singing in unison. Without Wadjda in the frame, the cinematic space is 'cleansed' of a disturbing element. Her absence liberates the filmic space from obstruction as the shot becomes wider, excessively ordered, and 'straightened out' (see Fig. 4.3). On the other hand, the overly monotonous grey tones, the low camera angle, and the sudden, vigorous singing ridicule the extreme discipline and docility with which the school space is organised.

The school patio where Wadjda is sent becomes a contested space, at once enclosed within the borders of the school and outside the physical building, offering an opening to the sky behind the high wire fences. Standing on the patio, Wadjda's body disturbs the symmetry of the frame and the geometrical order of the patio. Both the open door aligned with Wadjda's body and the image of the sun above the wires as she looks up

Fig. 4.3 Wadjda's class is straightened out in her absence

Fig. 4.4 *Wadjda*: Micro-instances of wilfulness

create wilful openings: 'lines of flight' ('lignes de fuite', in the words of Deleuze and Guattari 1980). The fence splits the image diagonally and the bright round sun opens up the other half of the frame geometrically, creating a *pointe de fuite* (a vanishing point in painting or photography) that gives form to a micro-instance of affirmation, a line of flight (see Fig. 4.4). Following Deleuze and Guattari, a line of flight is 'deterritorialisation', an escape, a flow, a rupture, a connection to multiplicities that de-organise and de-stratify (1980, 9). There is in Deleuze and Guattari's ideas the appealing sense that the mapping of reality is always modifiable, and that lines of flight are tracings put onto the map (1980, 21). The lines of flight in *Wadjda* are affirmative forms insofar as they aesthetically create possibilities for the order in place to be subverted and transformed.

Like the roof of Wadjda's house (to be discussed later), the patio of the school becomes a space for disobedience and wilfulness. The patio and the roof may be considered as *heterotopias* in Foucault's terms: simultaneously real places conditioned by sociocultural norms and contested spaces, or 'counter-sites':

real places—places that do exist and that are formed in the very founding of society—which are something like counter-sites, a kind of effectively enacted utopia in which the real sites, all the other real sites that can be found within the culture, are simultaneously represented, contested, and inverted. (Foucault 1986, 24)[2]

The cinematography and mise-en-scène construct the patio and at times even the school itself as heterotopic spaces, wherein lines and rules are both implemented and challenged.

Since Wadjda lacks understanding and is not subject to the same degree of restrictions as adult women, her body takes wilful affirmative shapes. When, in a later sequence, she and her classmates are playing on the patio at school and one of the schoolgirls warns the others that as 'respectable girls', they should go inside in case some of the men builders working on a roof overlooking the patio might see them. Wadjda naively replies, 'Why? Are they Superman?' While they all go inside, Wadjda continues to play on the patio. The spatial domination of the male builders conveys their position of power in regards to the schoolgirls and echoes the verbal abuse that Wadjda experiences in the street. Their presence above the patio breaks the homo-social environment and, ironically, calls into question the legitimacy of the girls' presence, despite them being within the school boundaries. In spite of this, Wadjda continues to play hopscotch. Her standing body crosses multiple squared lines as the camera tracks her movement through medium and wide shots. These wide shots, empty of elements except for Wadjda's active body, produce a space that Wadjda controls. The space then expands to another area of the patio and an open door in the background, aesthetically creating lines of flight. While Wadjda's body crosses and bends the lines imposed upon her, the depth of field of these scenes offers alternative spaces potentially beyond social norms—both imaginary and real, as that corner of the patio is also where Wadjda's friends paint their nails and read magazines (that is, perform prohibited activities). Wadjda's and her friends' bodily habitation of the patio de-organises its restrictive heterosocial mapping.

Wilful to Appear Docile

From one generation to the next, wilfulness is passed on or broken up. If the school is a space of the patriarchal state, when the house escapes patriarchal control it becomes an appropriate space for the development of an affirmative politics. Because of generational differences with her daughter, Wadjda's mother understands the sociocultural limitations to her own freedom and the importance of not being perceived as 'against'. As Ahmed underlines, it is often easier to obey than to disobey, so 'a subject can be willing [to obey] in order to avoid being forced' (2014, 139). If docility puts an end to wilfulness, docility also acts as a mask that partially hides wilfulness while it persists in micro-instances. On the one hand, Wadjda's mother's actions and her presence on screen evoke her docility to a socially prescribed idea of 'femininity'. On the other hand, her body in space, like Wadjda's, embodies wilful forms and creates affirmative paths.

When Wadjda's father or any object invoking the father is present (such as his scarf, which the mother irons), the house appears as a divided space that determines gender roles, responsibilities, and labour. After preparing dinner for her husband's guests, Wadjda's mother brings the plate to the living room door, knocks, and hides so that the men cannot see her. The long shot placing her in a dark background enclosed within many door frames suggests a segregated and highly divided space. Later, as the men have left the house, the mother sits alone, surrounded by empty plates, eating the food that the men have left (see Fig. 4.5). Meanwhile, Wadjda

Fig. 4.5 *Wadjda*: Wadjda's mother eats after the men have left

stands, looking at her father's genealogical tree. At this point, her mother comments: 'Interested in your father's glorious family tree? You aren't included, it only includes men's names'. Whereas the father inhabits the living room as a place of entertainment, for the mother, the living room and kitchen are work places—where she irons, tidies up, and helps Wadjda with her homework—which emphasises her subservience to her gendered role as a wife and a mother. Significantly, Wadjda's mother remains unnamed during the whole film. While she dwells in her gendered position, her comments hint at her wilful disagreement with certain sexist sociocultural norms.

In addition to the mother's occasional expression of her own will, her habitation of cinematic spaces creates wilful forms. As the mother sits on the floor eating, the father casts his shadow on the living room in spite of his absence. Indeed, the empty plates in front of her, the genealogical tree on the right of the screen, and the television on the left—which the father alone uses for entertainment—together generate a patriarchal geometry that closes in on the mother. The many surrounding objects and lines frame her in an environment that she can only escape through the open door behind her. This open door, like the open doors at Wadjda's school, produces an opportunity, a micro-instance of affirmation. Similarly, the mother's pensive sideways gaze, off frame through the only spot empty of patriarchal objects, draws a line of flight, another micro-instance of affirmation. The mise-en-scène creates affirmative spaces, which aesthetically allow the mother a space of her own and expose other *rooms* of the house, and indirectly its roof, which the mother inhabits with greater freedom.

Although the mother generally conforms to the 'rules', there is a sense that she possesses an underlying wilfulness. As Deleuze and Guattari write, 'you may make a rupture, draw a line of flight, yet there is still a danger that you will reencounter organizations that restratify everything, formations that restore power to a signifier, attributions that reconstitute a subject' (1980, 9). The mother has thereby learned to mask her wilfulness behind the performance of 'femininity'. In heterosocial spaces, the mother tends to remain silent and in her assigned place; however, on the phone at home, the mother has more 'space' and power to defend herself against her (male) driver and her husband's lack of consideration. Like the veil, the phone acts as a mediatory tool by which she has more 'freedom' to express her thoughts and opinions. Both provide the face with a mask, which partially dissimulates the mother's and daughter's wilfulness, in order to avoid being forced. When the mother is in the same space as her driver in the street or in his car—both 'spaces of patriarchy'—she does not contradict him. On the phone, however, the mother confronts him about his bad manners and threatens to change drivers. Interestingly, it is also on the phone that Wadjda's mother admits to looking at men with desire, as she talks to her friend Leila: 'Come on, he is good looking, isn't he?' Just as the veil allows her a wandering gaze, the telephone allows her to express her wandering thoughts that diverge slightly from sociocultural precepts.

In the only confrontation between the mother and her husband, she angrily tells him, 'I should pay for it? Why can't you pay for it once?'. In this scene she stands facing the camera while her husband sits on the bed with his back to the camera. Her almost full body presence in the frame gives weight to her habitation of space, which the mirror, framed diagonally behind her, reinforces (see Fig. 4.6). The mirror reproduces her domination of space from the opposite angle, showing her back blocking her husband's face from sight. For Foucault, the mirror functions as a heterotopia, allowing him to 'see myself where I am not, in an unreal, virtual space that opens up behind the surface' (Foucault 1986, 24). The mirror draws a connection to the wilfulness in Wadjda's mother that exists behind the surface and awaits to be drawn onto the map. If the mother's body position, with her hands joined and her legs crossed, may suggest insecurity and vulnerability, the cinematography and mise-en-scène of this scene give shape to micro-instances of wilfulness and produce affirmative forms.

When her husband answers back that she should 'bear [him] a son', though he knows she is unable to do so, the characters' spatial habitation is reversed. He is now the one standing, directly behind his wife, who sits sideways on the bed in front of him. The camera's low height, at the same height as the mother, strengthens his vertical occupation of the

Fig. 4.6 *Wadjda*: A formalist confrontation

frame. The direct alignment of his body behind hers also expresses his power over the mother. However, his position, in line with the mirror in the background and the mother's head in the foreground, compresses his body and reduces his spatial power. In addition, as the mother looks sideways and does not appear reflected in the mirror, his spatial domination over her is only partial and leaves her room—out of frame—to escape.

Although Wadjda's mother tends to live her femininity as 'the accumulation of experiences of being silenced; of having to overlook how you are looked over' (Ahmed 2014, 155), her body's micro-relations to cinematic space produce wilfulness. When at the height of the argument she shouts, 'Don't come back! Go to your mother's house and discuss potential brides', she appears in a low-angle shot that grants her authority. After the father has left the house, a medium close-up of the mother from a low angle ends the sequence, confirming her strength, and breaking with the idea that femininity amounts to being silenced.

A Space of One's Own

If Wadjda's house appears divided and gendered, it is also a space of intimacy and affirmation for Wadjda and her mother. Like the school patio, the veil, or the phone for the mother, the roof of the house provides the two characters with a space of their own where they can act freely, hidden from male scrutiny. The roof is a space of leisure, an escape from gendered roles, where only Wadjda and her mother go (as well as Abdullah who, as a young boy, does not invoke a patriarchal presence). Both mother and daughter use the roof to perform acts that would not be acceptable elsewhere in Saudi society. While Wadjda uses the roof to learn how to ride a bike, her mother goes there to be alone and escape from domestic duties, smoke cigarettes, and watch people on the street. This is also a place for the two women to bond, away from patriarchal surveillance and sociocultural norms.

The roof in *Wadjda* may be considered as a 'heterotopia'. Following Foucault's concept, the roof is not a utopia, as it effectively exists as a liminal space in between the outside 'public' space of the street and the inside private space of the house. While the house and the street are both subject to patriarchal control and norms, the roof indeed offers a 'counter-site' to contest the unequal spatialities of Saudi society: it is where mother and daughter can share intimate moments, build an affective and complicit relationship, and can see and act without being seen or heard. One night,

Wadjda and her mother, both unveiled, stand on the roof watching the political meeting organised by Abdullah's uncle across the street, where only men are present. Standing next to her mother, Wadjda makes teasing signs to Abdullah. When an adult man next to Abdullah catches him making signs back at Wadjda, the man looks towards the roof, which causes the two women to crouch down in a swift, playful movement. While Wadjda and her mother's spatial exclusion reflects the fact that women are kept out of politics (see also Aljazeera 2013),[3] the roof, being situated above street level, allows the women look down on the political meeting, which aesthetically contests and modifies the power-geometry of public space. Although this does not allow women to publicly express their subjectivity, their partial invisibility grants the women spatial power to observe without being judged. The spatial supremacy of the women on the roof echoes those of the builders that catcalled Wadjda as well as the male builders working on a roof adjacent to the school, which indirectly forced the female pupils to return to the inside of the school. Like the balcony or the window of Laure's apartment, in *Vendredi Soir* the roof allows the women to build a space for themselves, a space of reflection where one can develop a 'lived body', away from male-dominated urban spaces.

Within and outside a space where patriarchal rules are implemented and enforced, the roof is heterotopic, not completely separate from sociocultural norms; it is a space of deviation that still exists within society. As Foucault explains, 'the heterotopia is capable of juxtaposing in a single real place several spaces, several sites that are in themselves incompatible' (Foucault 1986, 25). At once open onto the sky, looking down onto the street and enclosed by the wall of the house, the roof condenses several 'incompatible spaces' in Foucault's words, allowing its inhabitants to contest the binary sociocultural norms that restrict their existence and mobility when in other places. When her mother surprises Wadjda while she rides her bike on the roof with Abdullah, Wadjda falls off her bike. When she shouts that she is bleeding, her mother panics, 'Where is the blood coming from? Your virginity!' Annoyed, Wadjda replies that it is coming from her knee. The mother then continues: 'Bikes are dangerous for girls! You think you can act like a boy? ... Shame on you: bringing a boy upstairs with no one home! If your father knew, he'd kill you!' By learning how to ride a bike, Wadjda transforms her gendered body into a mobile body and resists oppressive precepts of *femininity*.

Wadjda's micro-instances of affirmation manifest both narratively and aesthetically. As Wadjda is biking, the camera creates a circular panning movement and moves around and *with* her. This contrasts with the panning camera of the first sequence in the street—when Abdulla strips Wadjda of her sandwich and of her veil—which seemed to close up on Wadjda. Now, the slightly elevated angle of the camera and the movement of Wadjda's body create wilful forms. Her body figures as active and capable; instead of being restrained by gender norms, it crosses formal boundaries created by the house's vertical walls, lines that her striped t-shirt crosses again (see Fig. 4.7). When Wadjda's mother comes into the scene, however, the handheld camera becomes static and remains fixed in a corner, filming the altercation between mother and daughter in a long shot divided by multiple frames. While the wide shot of Wadjda biking and the bright colours it captures produce an affirmative space, the divided frame and the shadows cast by the walls of the house give shape to affects of restriction. The forms of the scene suddenly replace Wadjda's wilful actions into a restrictive social context, which the mother's comments also underline. The absence of music also helps create the tension and seriousness of the situation. Medium shots, alternately framing the young protagonist or her mother, emphasise the difference between the mother's and daughter's respectful wilfulness. Whereas the mother's white shirt almost merges with the walls of the house, the red horizontal stripes of Wadjda's t-shirt contrast with the walls' vertical lines. When the mother helps Wadjda stand up and brings her back to the house, a wide medium shot reunites them in the frame and in the common hardships that women have to endure; this is then reinforced by a lengthy silence, only interrupted by their footsteps, as they descend to the house. If the seriousness of this scene and its multiple vertical lines insist on the

Fig. 4.7 *Wadjda*: Crossing boundaries

power-geometries of space and mobility, the door leading on the roof remaining open and Wadjda's striped t-shirt produce micro-instances of affirmation, drawing lines of flight that point towards what is not yet there.

At the end of the film, mother and daughter share a bonding moment on the roof. Instead of buying a sexy red dress to intimidate potential brides for her husband, Wadjda's mother decided to spend her savings on the green bicycle that Wadjda wanted. As she gives it to her on the roof, she also implicitly gives Wadjda permission to ride in the streets, opening up her daughter's (and more broadly women's) spatial experiences, and challenging social conventions. Like her daughter, Wadjda's mother in this scene seems to take the path of the wilful woman, 'reluctant to yield' to men's authority and 'unwilling to participate in sexist culture' (Ahmed 2014, 153–54). She asks Wadjda, 'Why did you have to tell the [principal] that you wanted to buy a bicycle?' She encourages her to lie (or to perform gendered norms) if need be, in order to pursue her will. By choosing the green bike over the red dress, Wadjda's mother also makes a choice in favour of women's mobility as she supports her daughter's choice. This young person embodies the possibility of a different future in which the mother in this instance already partakes. It could be argued that Wadjda's mother is projecting her own feminist battle (aborted with her own adult development) onto her daughter's struggle. *Wadjda* points to the importance of building 'spaces of wilfulness', spaces of their own for women to train wilful bodies and gain the strength to leave prescribed paths.

Housing Wilfulness

The last scene of the film opens up the heterotopic space of the roof onto the street. Wadjda is riding her new bike, passing in front of the house where her father got married the night before. She wins a race against Abdullah, leaves the neighbourhood behind, and heads towards the highway. The film ends with a wide, open-ended shot that creates a seemingly infinite space ahead, as Wadjda bikes towards an affirmative future. Whereas every place in *Wadjda,* whether heterosocial spaces such as streets or homosocial spaces such as the school and the house, embody the apparent fixity of patriarchal sociocultural norms, they also provide the necessary conditions (the negative affects) for these norms to be affirmatively transcended.

It seems impossible to show the wilfulness of women and of forms, and the affirmative paths wilfulness initiates, without simultaneously addressing women's struggle to make a place for themselves in the patriarchal world. This is perhaps because to counter the idea of the happy housewife, that 'happiness is what follows if we do this or that', requires wandering off the prescribed path and becoming what Ahmed calls a 'troublemaker, dissenter, killer of joy' (2010, 14; 17). As Ahmed and Braidotti respectively underline, wilfulness and affirmative ethics arise from being negatively affected. As *Wadjda* shows, however, the power of affirmation and of finding a space of one's own may be contingent upon bonding with other women, and upon having socioeconomic, cultural, and educational resources. If Wadjda can win her wilful battle against oppressive patriarchal and religious ideologies, it is by virtue of her mother's middle-class resources and open-minded attitude. Because she is from a different generation, her mother has a different meaning of empowerment than Wadjda does. While Wadjda's wilful battle concerns women's mobility, her mother's struggle involves her recognising her limitations but asserting her socioeconomic rights and renouncing an abusive marriage.

In this chapter, we have seen how wilful subjects challenge and transform the power-geometry of space by taking different paths away from 'happy' conventions, which, it may be argued, may also become affirmative paths for women beyond the screen. In her search for cinematic meaning and pleasure for women, Lucy Bolton suggests that it is important for women both as spectators and on the screen to bond, to form a community and then return to their individual selves (2011, 198). It is by the association of wilful, multiple, and heterogeneous individuals that Braidotti suggests that creating an affirmative future is possible. As a way to overcome social inequalities, Haifaa Al-Mansour has made an affirmative film that transforms the negative affects produced by the patriarchal status quo into affirmative forces. Transformation takes a number of forms: the veil becomes a disguise of wilfulness in the street, the patio of the school and roof of the house become heterotopic spaces, and wilfulness is emphasised as transformative through micro-relations to space rather than expansive movement. This chapter has shown how affirmative forms may be present on screen through micro-instances, though they may appear difficult to detect at first. Because of the limitations upon women's habitation of the urban space and the punishment of transgressions (as the following chapter explores further), women may hide their wilfulness (unconscious and affectively so) behind the mask of a submissive femininity. The filmic forms of *Wadjda* reveal micro-instances of affirmation—aesthetic lines of flight to be drawn on an otherwise stratified map.

Notes

1. In her article 'Climbing like a girl: An exemplary adventure in feminist phenomenology', Diane Chisholm underlines how gender is a 'background to women's situation in general', thus taking a Beauvoirian view of gender (2008, 12). Echoing Maurice Merleau-Ponty's and Simone de Beauvoir's writings, Chisholm writes that '[Lynn Hill, the first climber to free climb the Nose in El Capitan] understands her body not as an object among objects but as an *embodied intentionality*, a "for-itself", capable of grasping a project and of projecting herself into the world and up the mountain' (17, emphasis mine). Although she does not express it as such, underlying Chisholm's article is the idea that one's embodied spatial habitation *produces* space, thus echoing Merleau-Ponty's idea that 'each sensation gives us a particular manner of being in space and, in a certain sense, of creating space' (Merleau-Ponty 2012 [1962], 230).
2. In the original text: 'des lieux réels, des lieux effectifs, des lieux qui sont dessinés dans l'institution même de la société, et qui sont des sortes de contre–emplacements, sortes d'utopies effectivement réalisées dans lesquelles tous les autres emplacements réels que l'on peut trouver à l'intérieur de la culture sont à la fois représentés, contestés et inversés' (Foucault 2004 [1984], 15).
3. At the time of the film's release, women were not allowed to vote in Saudi Arabia, as 2011 King Abdullah's authorisation of women to vote was to take effect in 2015 (Aljazeera 2013).

References

Ahmed, Sara. 2010. *The Promise of Happiness*. Durham: Duke University Press.
———. 2014. *Willful Subjects*. Durham: Duke University Press.
Aljazeera. 2013. Saudi Women Take Seats in Shura Council. *Aljazeera*, February 19. Retrieved on 20 May 2015 from http://www.aljazeera.com/news/middleeast/2013/02/2013219201637132278.html
Al-Mansour, Haifaa. 2012. *Wadjda*. DVD. Saudi Arabia/Germany: Sony Pictures Home Entertainment.
Al-Rasheed, Madawi. 2013. *A Most Masculine State: Gender, Politics and Religion in Saudi Arabia*. New York: Cambridge University Press.

Bolton, Lucy. 2011. *Film and Female Consciousness: Irigaray, Cinema and Thinking Women.* Hampshire/New York: Palgrave Macmillan.
Braidotti, Rosi. 2011. *Nomadic Theory: The Portable Rosi Braidotti.* Chichester: Columbia University Press.
Brinkema, Eugenie. 2014. *The Forms of the Affects.* Durham/London: Duke University Press.
Chisholm, Dianne. 2008. Climbing Like a Girl: An Exemplary Adventure in Feminist Phenomenology. *Hypatia* 23 (1): 9–40.
Deleuze, Gilles, and Félix Guattari. 1980. *Capitalisme et Schizophrenie: Mille Plateaux.* Paris: Editions de minuit.
Diab, Mohamed. 2010. *678.* DVD. Egypt: Audio Visual Entertainment.
Foucault, Michel. 1975. *Surveiller et punir: naissance de la prison.* Paris: Gallimard.
———. 1986. Of Other Spaces. *Diacritics* 16 (1): 22–27.
———. 2004 [1984]. Des espaces autres. *Empan* 2 (54): 12–19.
Keshavarz, Maryam. 2011. *Circumstance.* Lionsgate: DVD. Iran.
Madsen, Berit. 2013. *Sepideh, un ciel plein d'étoiles.* TV Documentary. Germany/Denmark: ARTE.
Mahmood, Saba. 2005. *Politics of Piety: The Islamic Revival and the Feminist Subject.* Princeton: Princeton University Press.
Meshkini, Marzieh. 2000. *Roozi ke zan shodam* [*The Day I Became a Woman*]. DVD. Iran: Makhmalbaf Productions.
Makhmalbaf, Samira. 2004 [1998]. *Sib* [*The Apple*]. DVD. Iran: Artificial Eye.
Massey, Doreen B. 1994. *Space, Place, and Gender.* Minneapolis: University of Minnesota Press.
Merica, Dan, and Jason Hanna. 2013. In declassified document, CIA acknowledges role in '53 Iran coup. *CNN*, August 20. Retrieved on 9 Oct. 2019 from https://edition.cnn.com/2013/08/19/politics/cia-iran-1953-coup/
Merleau-Ponty, Maurice. 2012 [1962]. *Phenomenology of Perception.* London/New York: Routledge.
Mernissi, Fatima. 1975. *Beyond the Veil: Male-Female Dynamics in a Modern Muslim Society.* Cambridge, MA: Schenkman.
Neshat, Shirin. 2009. *Zanan-e bedun-e mardan* [*Women without Men*]. DVD. Iran: Essential Filmproduktion.
Panahi, Jafar. 2000. *Dayereh* [*The Circle*]. DVD. Iran: Winstar TV and Video.
Pape, Stefan. 2013. Haifaa Al-Mansour Interview - Wadjda. *YouTube.* HeyUGuys, July 16. Retrieved from https://youtu.be/ftLDU-wUSYE
Premiere Scene. 2013. Haifaa Al Mansour on Wadjda - Junket Interview. *YouTube*, July 18. Retrieved on 19 Jul. 2019 from https://www.youtube.com/watch?v=n4MsA4wyZmI
Tlatli, Moufida. 1994. *Samt El Qusur* [*Silences of the Palace*]. DVD. Tunisia/France: Cinétéléfilms.

Wadud, Amina. 2002. Aishah's Legacy: The Struggle for Women's Rights Within Islam. In *The New Voices of Islam: Rethinking Politics and Modernity, a Reader*, ed. Mehran Kamrava, 201–204. Berkeley/Los Angeles: University of California Press.

Woolf, Virginia. 1945 [1929]. *A Room of One's Own*. London: Penguin Books.

Yamani, Mai. 1996. Some Observations on Women in Saudi Arabia. In *Feminism and Islam: Legal and Literary Perspectives*, ed. Mai Yamani, 263–282. New York: New York University Press.

Young, Iris Marion. 1980. Throwing like a Girl: A Phenomenology of Feminine Body Comportment Motility and Spatiality. *Human Studies* 3 (1): 137–156.

Open Access This chapter is licensed under the terms of the Creative Commons Attribution 4.0 International License (http://creativecommons.org/licenses/by/4.0/), which permits use, sharing, adaptation, distribution and reproduction in any medium or format, as long as you give appropriate credit to the original author(s) and the source, provide a link to the Creative Commons licence and indicate if changes were made.

The images or other third party material in this chapter are included in the chapter's Creative Commons licence, unless indicated otherwise in a credit line to the material. If material is not included in the chapter's Creative Commons licence and your intended use is not permitted by statutory regulation or exceeds the permitted use, you will need to obtain permission directly from the copyright holder.

CHAPTER 5

Streets: Freedom, Diaspora, and the Erotic in *Head-On*

> *Cinema, not as a second-order mirror held up to reflect what already exists, but as a form of representation ... is able to constitute us as new kinds of subjects, and thereby enable us to discover places from which to speak.*
> (Stuart Hall 1990, 236–37)

While not all films challenge traditional subject identities, Stuart Hall's idea of cinema as transformative constitutes the premise of a search for affirmative aesthetics that unveil the wilful positions that are born through film. However, these new positions are not always easy to hold, even within representation, as the previous chapter has shown: wilfulness may need to be masked in order not to be brought down. The performance of gender, both unescapable and uninhabitable according to Judith Butler, partly masks wilfulness, which thereby takes shape as micro-instances on screen. Through the analysis of *Gegen die wand/Head-On* (Fatih Akin 2004), this chapter builds on Butler's phrase that gender is 'uninhabitable' (1993), and that habitation of space is always anchored in time and thus context. Although the protagonist of the film may appear stuck in an inescapable spiral of performances of gender, her bodily habitation of the cinematic space suspends gender expectations. Bodies and spaces take forms that produce wilful claims and open up future possibilities for women to fully inhabit the streets. As Stuart Hall's words reflect, the affirmative aesthetic of the film is also the power of cinema: to de-territorialise the Western myth of the subject. *Head-On* constitutes the subject in its multiplicity, complexity, and relationality—as always liminal, always *on the threshold of* rather *than fixed by* categories.

I discovered *Head-On* when I was searching for films depicting mobile and empowered women. I remembered *Auf der anderen seite/The Edge of Heaven* (Akin 2007) because it left its mark on me several years ago. I was struck by the relatively easy movements of the German protagonist in *The Edge of Heaven* compared to the limited or relatively nonexistent mobility of her Turkish friend and that her ease and her ignorance of codes eventually result in her death in the streets of Istanbul. Like other films made by Akin, such as *In the Fade* (2017), *Head-On* seems to make a political statement on issues of gender, space, 'race', and mobility. *Head-On* particularly emphasises how gender, culture, and race as categories of identity affect the subject's habitation of space and the cinematic representations of spaces themselves. In the film, the characters' relations to streets and other so-called public spaces make reference to subjects constituted in gender and dynamics of exclusion. A micro-analysis of the film's formal constitution of spaces and bodies, however, reveals spaces and subject identities as processes, which are fluid and in constant transformation, rather than fixed into gender and racial categories.

Throughout *Head-On,* the desire of Sibel (the film's woman protagonist) to find a home, a place of belonging as a woman and a child of immigrants, haunts the film and Sibel's habitation of space. The film belongs to what Hamid Naficy (2001) calls 'accented cinema': films that integrate the double consciousness of the filmmaker within the film's narrative and aesthetic style, as characterised by the fragmentation, displacement, and tensions of living in between two cultures. Sibel comes from a conservative, patriarchal Muslim Turkish family living in Hamburg, Germany, and like Cahit, the male protagonist, she tries to commit suicide and ends up in a psychiatric hospital. When she meets Cahit and realises that he is Turkish, she pressures him to marry her so that she can leave her parents' house and be free to live as she pleases. Once married, Sibel moves into Cahit's apartment and appropriates the space by redecorating it. Although Sibel and Cahit both live separate (sexually liberated) lives, they become increasingly attached to one another. This attachment has disastrous consequences: out of jealousy, Cahit accidentally kills one of Sibel's former lovers, Niko. Sibel is forced to flee from the city after her brother learns of her unconventional lifestyle and threatens to kill her. Once in Istanbul, she replicates the freedom of movement that she acquired in Hamburg until, after a drunken night, a man rapes her in a bar and a group of men beat her up in the streets. The narrative then returns to Cahit, who has been released from prison and is searching for Sibel in Istanbul. When he finds her, Sibel has a daughter and a partner and lives in a modern luxurious apartment, in stark contrast to her previous life with Cahit. Although they both planned to travel together to Cahit's hometown in Turkey, the film ends with Sibel's last-minute decision to stay with her daughter and partner in Istanbul.

Sibel's habitation of diegetic spaces (such as streets), and how these take shape on screen give form to the difficulties of *inhabiting* gender or race, that is, categories of identity imposed on the subject. If Sibel struggles to fully inhabit space (both public and domestic) because of gender expectations, her cultural hybridity further complicates her sense of belonging to the city. Like the film's director, Fatih Akin, Sibel was born in Hamburg to Turkish parents. She lives in Germany but travels to Istanbul. As a descendent of Turkish migrant workers in Germany, Akin can be considered a diasporic filmmaker, and though it seems cliché to think of Istanbul as a place where the East meets the West, this duality is nonetheless at the core of Akin's films (Dimitris Eleftheriotis 2012, 133–34). Sibel and other characters in the film are profoundly and complexly marked by their ethnic and gender in-betweeness, which is demonstrated by the film's locations and soundtrack. From the very beginning of the film, both Cahit and Sibel are shown as cultural *others* through their performance of traditional gender norms. As subjects of a Turkish–German diaspora (see Hamid Naficy 2001), they neither belong to the Turkish culture nor to the German one. Cahit and Sibel both live 'with and through [cultural] difference', following Stuart Hall's analysis of diaspora (1990, 235). With regard to their Turkish- and German-ness, Cahit and Sibel are hybrid characters 'constantly producing and reproducing themselves anew, through transformation and difference' (Hall 1990, 235). The film itself adopts hybrid forms, mingling German and Turkish languages, Western and Oriental music, and locations in Germany (Hamburg) and Turkey (Istanbul).

As the film deplores the inescapability of gender and cultural codes, it creates what I call 'cracks' (using a Deleuzian vocabulary) in the diegetic punishment of characters who live outside of these codes. The formal representations of bodies and space *crack* open, break, or suspend the status quo apparent in the diegesis, at times only subtly or temporarily. As will be explored, the woman protagonist's search for the erotic and the visual abjection of 'whole bodies' through cuts, blood, and scars are filmic refusals to succumb to conventions, which open up the subject and spatial habitation as deeply liminal. This chapter unveils the film's making of space and bodies as processes in constant transformation. In particular, it focuses on how the woman protagonist wilfully inhabits the city, through walking, dancing, and establishing relations, in defiance of gender and cultural expectations.

Considering women who travel alone in *Gender, Genre, and Identity in Women's Travel Writing*, Kristi Siegel asks, '*What* is at risk [when women travel]—a woman's safety or her morality? Is the amount of risk entirely real or, in part, magnified by its long social and medical history? Most importantly, *what* women are being warned and *what* kind of travel is being addressed?' (emphasis in original 2004, 69). Siegel's questions encapsulate the problematic power-geometries at play in women's habitation of public spaces on both a de facto and rhetorical level. As explored in the previous chapters, gender, sexuality, ethnicity, age, and other socioeconomic factors determine power relations, which in turn determine our habitation of space and the making of space itself (see Certeau 1984; Di Méo 2011; Lefebvre 1974; Massey 1994; McDowell 1999; Rieker and Ali 2008; Rose 1993; Spain 1992). It is in the affirmative representation of space and bodies that subjects appear as essentially liminal, in constant transformation.

A Rewriting of Space-Time

From the start of *Head-on* the focus on space as space-time is manifest within musical tableaux, which structure and interrupt the diegesis. Six scenes of a traditional Turkish orchestra punctuate the narrative with the Turkish-Romani piece 'Saniye'm'. On a representational level, the tableaux-like scenes stress major shifts in the characters' lives, and they divide the film into five parts that could be understood as the five stages of grief, as defined by Elizabeth Kübler-Ross (2005): denial (Sibel's and Cahit's refusal to live), anger (their extreme decisions), bargaining (daily life), depression (Sibel's perception of life in Istanbul as a sort of prison, and Cahit's actual imprisonment), and acceptance (Sibel's new life as a mother in Istanbul and Cahit's return to Mersin, where he was born). The characters' grief is mostly a grief of identity, the inability to inhabit an intercultural and gendered subject. The tableaux's colours and mise-en-scène give form to a circular yet open space-time. When Richard Dyer analyses non-representational signs (that he defines as 'colour, texture, movement, rhythm, melody, camerawork') in musicals, he writes that musical numbers can both reinforce and suggest 'an alternative to the narrative' (2002 [1992], 20; 28). While the tableaux reinforce the specific cultural hybridity of the film, they also imprint a tale-like dimension, placing the film outside of a definite time.

Head-On opens with Turkish-Romani clarinet player Selim Sesler and German-Turksish actress Idil Üner performing 'Saniye'm' with Idil Üner singing and standing in the middle of six seated men playing traditional instruments. A fixed camera films the performance in a medium-long shot that situates the orchestra on the 'Asian side' of the Bosphorus Strait, which divides the city of Istanbul. Meanwhile, the iconic Blue Mosque appears in the background on the 'European side' of the city (the side most-frequented by tourists) and gives this scene and the other muscial-interlude scenes a 'postcard' feel. The tableaux unfold with the stages of day, opening the film with sunrise and closing it with sunset (see Fig. 5.1). Although they appear fixed in a postcard-like space, microchanges within the tableaux and the unfolding day situate the film within both an atemporal and a specific space-time. On the one hand, the song's love tale and the very traditional and classical mise-en-scène—conveyed by the orchestra's long dresses and tuxedos and their immobility 'on stage'—appear to suspend time and give a timeless dimension to the film. On the other hand, the outdoor location, in between the Asian and European continents, mirrors the protagonists' hybrid sociocultural identities and anchors the film in a specific space and time. This outdoor location and the modern texture of the image anchor the scenes in contemporary time, a time of modern, portable cameras polished image and sound.

Fig. 5.1 *Head-On*: Chanting tableaux opening and closing the film

Setting the performance in the course of one day emphasises the unstoppable circularity of time, and thereby the repeatability of tales of impossible love and the inescapability of social codes and expectations. The performance has a clear beginning and end also marked by codes: the film and performance begin with the first chair counting out the tempo and end with the orchestra taking a bow. Performances, live or recorded, are in itself acts that can be repeated, but with variations. Similarly, the film's narrative also appears as a timeless tale—a wilful woman who seeks liberation from a sociocultural jail, finds freedom through the erotic, and is imprisoned back into a timeless gendered role of a mother within the domestic sphere. The female protagonist partly imposes this role on herself, willingly—but this role is also contingent, one of many other possible alternatives or turns the diegesis could have taken. The enclosure of the film within the musical performance, itself enclosed within the passing of the day, gives form to both the inescapability and the variability of history, freedom, and power-geometries.

The tableaux artificially interrupt the fluidity of the narrative with their postcard dimension in a location absent from the narrative, and traditional music contrasting with the film's modern soundtrack. They emphasise the fictional construction process behind the film, one through which stories can be repeated, changed, or manipulated. If the tableaux mirror the performative and ineluctable dimension of heterosexual love stories and gender norms, the micro-changes within the tableaux themselves—the woman singer stands, sits, sings, or keeps silent—also mirror the ever-changing dimension of space and power-geometries. These micro-changes also allow for the possibility to recognise the multiplicities present within the real and to write on the map the real's stratifications and lines of flight. As this chapter will explore, micro-instances of affirmation appear through the (de-)organisation of cinematic spaces and bodies, the erotic, dance, abjection, and finally spaces of pause and transit.

FREEDOM AND THE EROTIC AS POWER

Narratively, *Head-On* focuses on the difficulty of the woman protagonist, Sibel, to inhabit the city as freely as her male counterparts, to walk the streets of Hamburg and Istanbul day and night, and to become a modern *flâneuse*. In her book *Wanderlust*, Rebecca Solnit highlights how walking for pleasure began with modernity, when streets became 'clean, safe and illuminated places' (2001, 177). Yet urban space was, and still is, not safe for and accessible to everybody, as gender, race, age, socioeconomic background, and sexuality play an important role in determining who can access which parts of cities and at what time. In the time of the *flâneur*, women were commanded to be accompanied by men to 'ensure their safety' (read: protect them from other men) or justify their presence in the public sphere, 'defined as the world of productive labour, political decision, government, education, the law and public service, [that] increasingly became exclusive to men' (Pollock 1988, 67–68). Women themselves were also divided according to ethnicity and social class. In her famous essay 'Modernity and the spaces of femininity', Griselda Pollock explains that while bourgeois women could not freely access public places such as masked balls and café concerts without damaging their 'feminine respectability', working women were identified as being outside of 'femininity' (1988, 78). Urbanisation, however, brought about the possibility for promiscuity, economic independence, and revolutionary ideas that undermined patriarchal authority (Wilson 2001, 73). Audre Lorde identifies promiscuity and the discovery of sexuality as a structure of resistance against patriarchy; the erotic is 'the power which rises from our deepest and nonrational knowledge', a 'deep and irreplaceable knowledge of [our] capacity for joy' (1984, 46; 48). Women's connection to the erotic—a resource that Western society has systematically oppressed, abused, and vilified—becomes 'a lens through which we scrutinize all aspects of our existence', which allows us 'not to settle for the convenient, the shoddy, the conventionally expected, nor the merely safe' (Lorde 1984, 48–49). In this first section of the chapter, I will consider how Sibel's connection to the erotic is a source of power against patriarchal domination that takes shape through the film's space.

In *Head-On*, the reclaiming of the erotic in particular figures as a position from which to speak, as a way of taking space, and as a method for making feminist spaces. As Sibel embraces the erotic, she is searching for freedom, the freedom to fully inhabit the streets and other 'public' spaces. Philosopher Elizabeth Grosz defines freedom as 'a process of self-making ... activities one undertakes that transform oneself and (a part of) the world' (Grosz 2010, 152). Sibel's actions, movement, and representation of herself act as liberation from the constraints that her family imposes on her, and, in Grosz's words, as an '[expansion of] knowledge production,... [and] the creation of a future unlike the present' (2010, 154). Grosz's definition of freedom is an affirmative one, not 'freedom from' but 'freedom to', which resonates with Braidotti's idea that freedom arises from the awareness of our limitations. For Grosz, the 'freedom to' is finding a space (albeit small) for innovation amidst present constraints or containment, at the level of both the individual and the species. *Head-On* figures as a rewriting of the present, as innovation, through the characters' actions and the cinematic making of diegetic spaces such as streets, bars, and houses.

Sibel appears in constant innovation, writing herself and the spaces she inhabits outside of gender and racial expectations. After a 'prologue' that focuses on Cahit's suicide attempt, we see a series of unattributable shots edited together: a white ceiling light, two different exit signs, alarm bells, a poster of an insect, and a doctor's plate, all of which locate the scene within a hospital where Cahit has been admitted. After the series of fast-edited objects in close-up, the handheld camera stops on a young woman, Sibel, looking straight into the camera with a deep gaze and subtle smile (see Fig. 5.2). A reverse close-up then reveals the object of her gaze: Cahit, who is looking directly into the camera (and thus at her), and shortly after he looks away, he is visibly embarrassed by Sibel's gaze. Rather than a

Fig. 5.2 *Head-On*: Sibel looking directly into the camera and at Cahit

spectator to Sibel's performance, Cahit becomes her prey, and her exit door from an oppressive system. While Sibel's own suicide attempt did not liberate her from her father's and brother's control over her sexuality and mobility, she hopes that marrying Cahit could be a way to escape the domestic family space.

The centred close-up on Sibel as she looks directly at the camera introduces her as wilfully embodying the screen space. The framing of the characters gives shape to the power geometries existing between them and within the space they inhabit. When Sibel and Cahit later escape from the hospital, they go to a bar for a beer. There, when Sibel ignores one of Cahit's questions, the medium shot of Cahit becomes a close-up as he leans forward and repeats his question authoritatively. The cinematography expresses Cahit's attempt to physically assert his power over Sibel through his occupation of space. In response, Sibel, in a reverse medium shot, leans towards him in a close-up, thereby asserting her own spatial power over the male character. The affective power she has in their conversation and in the previous scene at the hospital merges the power of the erotic and a wilful habitation of space. As he responds to Cahit, 'I want to live, Cahit. To live and to dance and to fuck!', Sibel asserts her will of a 'freedom to', by 'putting her body in the way' of patriarchy (in the words of Sara Ahmed 2014, 163).

As the previous chapter has shown, one sometimes needs to dissimulate wilfulness in order not to be forced (Ahmed 2014, 139). From the start, the film constructs Sibel as a wilful women who refuses to be an object of the gaze and fully inhabits the cinematic space. Naturally, she plays different versions of herself depending upon who she interacts with; her performance varies based on whether she interacts with Cahit, her mother, or her father and brother. On the one hand, she performs a Western image of 'femininity' by wearing shirts that display her cleavage and keeping her long hair untied; on the other hand, when her family comes to visit her at the hospital, she ties her hair back, removes her makeup, and wears loose clothes (see Fig. 5.3). In this scene, the forms of her family's bodies and the multitude of objects in the foreground and background overwhelmingly fill up and fragment the cinematic space. A *topoanalysis* reveals how traditions and gender expectations (embodied by Sibel's family) impose their power on the woman protagonist and crush her wilfulness. With her family, Sibel reproduces a particular 'compulsory repetition' of gender norms (Butler 1993, 21–22), which they require of her. However, Sibel's pink cardigan and her white t-shirt with an orange-coloured figure with raised arms on the front (as if expressing fight or

Fig. 5.3 *Head-On*: Sibel being submissive in front of her father and brother

victory), contrast with her family's darker and sober garments and visually give shape to a micro-instance of resistance. Once the male members of her family have departed, she removes her submissive mask as she pushes her chair back to sit at ease: she crosses her legs, unties her hair, and lights a cigarette. While Sibel's second embodiment appears more in touch with her body and wilfulness to take up space, it cannot but remain what Butler calls 'performative' of another type of 'femininity', an unconscious reiteration of gender norms. Whereas Butler asserts that there is no way out of gender, the mise-en-scène of Sibel's body and the cinematic space indicate otherwise throughout the film, whether through micro-instances or the subversive queer and punk lifestyles of the characters.

By marrying Cahit and thus escaping the strict patriarchal scrutiny of her brother and father, Sibel embraces the erotic as a view of the world, a lifestyle. If the privilege of casual sexual relationships is reserved for men, as Sibel will learn, she establishes a connection to her body, a power to feel and live truly as she pleases. Marriage becomes a gateway to the sexual (which a conversation between Sibel and her female cousins, who ask about her sexual life with Cahit, illustrates); but paradoxically, Sibel finds her sexuality outside of marriage. The erotic works as a subversion, an innovation, and an opening to a possible future beyond conventions. Sibel and Cahit are married in a traditional Turkish wedding, but immediately afterward Cahit throws Sibel out of his filthy apartment when she asks about his deceased ex-wife. Sibel, wearing her wedding dress, goes to a bar to have a drink by herself and then seduces the bartender. Her encounter with the erotic manifests in her habitation of space and her masquerade of gender. Sibel seduces the bartender in an indirect manner, because of an internalised form of 'femininity' that plays with false timidity and the pretense of submissiveness as she waits for him to 'do the last move'. Her indirectness is also necessary because she lacks a space of her own (like Jeanne and Marie in *Messidor*) and thus has to wait for him to invite her to sleep at his place. At no point in the film does Sibel have access to a private space of her own, yet she builds transitional 'homes' through the erotic, 'a freedom to', and a 'lived body' through which she inhabits public spaces such as bars.

The connection to the erotic and Sibel's conversion into a lived body happens at an aesthetic level through the cinematic construction of bodies and spaces. The cinematic space of the bar sequence gives shape to the social and gendered dynamics of Sibel's encounter with the bartender and to Sibel's free, wilful body. On the one hand, the counter of the bar cuts the medium long shot horizontally and places Sibel on the 'demanding' side of the bar—thus indicating the bartender's position of power since he can choose to attend to her demands or not (see Fig. 5.4). On the other hand, Sibel is on the *outside* of the bar; she sits in an open environment free of objects (and is visually free to leave if she wants to), while the counter and numerous bottles and objects spatially enclose the bartender. While the editing of the sequence establishes the conversation and game

Fig. 5.4 *Head-On*: Fluid dynamics of power in the cinematic space

of seduction through a classical shot/reverse-shot montage, a microanalysis of the editing and cinematography reveals more complex power dynamics. The camera's angle, at the same height as the characters, and its deep-space shots connect the two characters socially and spatially. However, the counter that separates the characters, and the bartender's often blurred appearance in contrast with Sibel's invariable sharp appearance, attribute a different degree of power to the characters. The longer takes showing Sibel as opposed to the short takes showing the bartender when he speaks (which sometimes even shift focus mid-sentence) narratively position Sibel as the main character and the one in power. Moreover, when the two characters appear together in the frame, the sharp focus on Sibel as opposed to the blur conferred to the bartender emphasises her as the subject of the gaze and him as the object. This contrast also gives Sibel's figure an embodied shape that is connected to a newly found freedom to fully— unashamedly—inhabit public spaces. A topoanalysis of this scene considers how the cinematic framing of objects and bodies gives affirmative forms to Sibel's habitation of the diegetic space. Sibel's connection to the erotic aesthetically transforms the power-geometries at play within social spaces: not as a product of Sibel's will but rather, as Lorde suggests, a deep sensory knowledge that has the power to subvert patriarchal domination and gender expectations.

When Sibel walks in the street the next morning after spending the night with the bartender, her bodily habitation of the cinematic space is again affirmative. The mise-en-scene and cinematography of the scene embody the wilfulness 'not to settle for the convenient' (in Lorde's words, describing the erotic, 1984, 48–49); it is both an individual wilfulness and that of a generational sociocultural group of women. The well-lit, slow-motion tracking shot of Sibel places her in the middle of the frame and grounds her in an environment that she now happily and fully inhabits. When Sibel crosses the street, the camera films her with a deep focus in a long establishing shot; her body stands in parallel with other vertical objects such as houses, doors, and windows, as she walks across the frame diagonally towards a camera tracking backwards (see Fig. 5.5). Rather than enclosing her, the objects and the lines they create in combination with Sibel's body and the line of her walking direction create what Barthes calls a 'line of flight' (1980), which opens the space onto both the foreground (through the camera tracking backwards) and the background (behind Sibel). Sibel's possession of the erotic gives form to her wilful habitation of the screen and

Fig. 5.5 *Head-On*: Sibel walking in the street

the diegetic environment; the open frame asserts her right to be there as any other body on screen.

Dance and Diaspora

Sibel's full habitation of the screen and of the public space especially manifests through three dancing scenes, which punctuate the film and encapsulate the complexity of wilfulness, space, and subject identity. The difference of narrative outcomes between the scenes emphasises a cultural and gendered difference in sexual freedom. In one way or another, some elements of the scenes condemn Sibel's free sexuality. After the first dance scene in a German danceclub in Hamburg, Cahit destroys his apartment in a fit of jealousy when Sibel leaves to have sex with someone else (although Sibel and Cahit were never involved in a romantic relationship despite being married, and Cahit's own casual sex is never questioned in the film). As we will see, the aesthetic of the scene also negatively portrays Sibel's sexualised dancing style, with a fixed and distant camera that focuses as much on Sibel dancing in the middle of the frame as on Cahit unhappily watching her from afar. After the second dancing scene, Cahit is beaten up for attempting to 'rescue' Sibel from a Turkish man harassing her. And after the third dancing scene, Sibel is raped in a bar in Istanbul. Aesthetically, however, dancing in each of these scenes seems to be an act of freedom, which takes erotic, abject, and intercultural forms.

Sibel's first dance is a celebration of the erotic, a celebration of *the freedom to* 'dance, live, and fuck' (in Sibel's own expression), take control over her body, and inhabit a 'lived body'. As she is coming back from her first day at work with Maren (Cahit's lover), she shows Cahit her new belly-button piercing (just like Maren) and tells him that she is also going to get a tattoo in the small of the back, the same spot where Maren has a tattoo. For Sibel, both the piercing and the tattoo represent erotic power. In contrast with her sober clothing she wears when she meets her family, Sibel embodies a sort of 'feminine' eroticism when she goes out by wearing a shirt that shows her a cleavage; she also fixes her hair and wears makeup on her eyes and lips. Whereas all of the other women in the (Western) nightclub wear jeans and t-shirts, Sibel wears boots with short shorts and a cardigan buttoned only at the middle of her torso, revealing both her cleavage and her new belly-button piercing, which Sibel had previously mentioned she wanted to 'show off'. The scene in the nightclub encapsulates the contradictory nature of gender, its compulsory performative (yet largely unconscious) repetitions of gender norms and its 'radical uninhabitability' (Butler 1993, 25).

> Insofar as heterosexual gender norms produce impossible ideals, heterosexuality can be said to operate through the production of hyperbolic versions of 'man' and 'woman'. For the most part these are compulsory performances, ones which none of us choose, but which each of us is forced to negotiate. (Bulter 1993, 26)

If it could be said that in this scene Sibel performs a hyperbolic form of woman, her dancing is also a form of reaching out for the body and of letting go of control, while—maybe paradoxically so—gaining control. Through dancing, Sibel searches for the freedom (and the power) that the erotic promises. Maren's piercing and tattoo that Sibel appropriates are ways for her to own her body—through a German punk style rather than traditional 'feminine' attributes—ways denied to her by the patriarchs of her family.

Writing about nineteenth-century Paris, Elizabeth Wilson describes the city as an environment 'where women are able to gain freedoms—even if the price of this is their over-sexualisation and their participation in what is often a voyeuristic spectacle': '[cities] are spaces for face to face contact of amazing variety and richness. They are spectacle—and what is wrong with that?' (1991, 56; 158). In the nightclub, Sibel embodies an erotic spectacle from which she does not shy away. She dances in the middle of fixed medium shots looking straight into the camera (see Fig. 5.6). In a partial reverse shot, a handheld tracking camera comes to a close-up of Cahit, who looks steadily at Sibel. The change between fixed and handheld cameras imposes a distance in watching Sibel, while emphasising Cahit's discontent. If Cahit appears as a (jealous) spectator of Sibel's performance, Sibel rewrites herself while dancing and redefines what a 'feminine identity' means. Dance becomes 'a sexual ritual, a form of self-expression … and a way of speaking through the body', in Angela McRobbie's words in her essay on dance narratives (1990, 195). In the previous scene, when she dances in the kitchen while Cahit prepares dinner, Sibel looks at her piercing in the mirror and says that she wants to go out and 'show it off', to which Cahit replies, 'Yes, I want to show *you* off too'. While Cahit's sentence positions Sibel as his possession, Sibel uses

Fig. 5.6 *Head-On:* Sibel performing masquerade while dancing in a nightclub

dance to make her body her own possession, though it also engages the gaze of others. Sibel herself would not be the object of the gaze—her piercing would be the object and act as a sign of her eroticism—and her body lives to the rhythm of music rather than rules of gender.

Dancing at once appears as an act of freedom, an expression of Sibel's individual subjectivity, and an act that makes space. The three dance scenes in the film de-territorialise the categories of gender and 'race' by encapsulating contradictions, subjects, and spaces as processes that constantly remake themselves. These dance scenes encapsulate the cultural hybridity of the film, present in the diegesis as well as in the mise-en-scène, music, and geographical locations. In the film, 'Western' or 'Eastern' elements merge indistinguishably; for example, a hybrid version of 'The temple of love' (a song originally sung by The Sisters of Mercy re-mixed with the voice of Israeli singer Ofra Haza) plays throughout the first dancing scene (both in the kitchen and louder in the nightclub). When Sibel leaves with a young blond man to 'get laid' (in her words), a traditional Turkish chord resonates, superimposed with the music, as if announcing a cultural incompatibility to her free sexuality (an incompatibility that is not only cultural but rather pervasively sexist, as will be explained later). Gender, 'race', and cultural customs also figure as uninhabitable, which becomes especially apparent in the second dance scene in a Turkish nightclub in Hamburg, when a man brutally interrupts Sibel and Cahit as they dance. The close-up of the man placing his body between Sibel and the camera visually interrupts the image and breaks the movement of the frame, which was moving in rhythm with the characters.

The mise-en-scène and cinematography of these two dance scenes both nourish and contradict the diegesis. While the first scene exoticised Sibel and kept her performance at a distance, her erotic power allowed her to exert her sexuality freely, though her sexuality is diegetically punished later in the film. In this sense, the aesthetic of the scene foretells future events of the diegesis and gives shape to the uninhabitability of gender. Similarly, in the second scene, the physical interruption of the characters' dance manifests visually as an interruption of harmony, a denial of the characters' ability to belong to a space. This denial is cultural, because of the characters' hybridity: they do not belong to any particular culture. Rather than being fixed in place (in the film's case, Germany or Turkey), culture is, in the words of Arjun Appadurai, 'an aspect of practice, of social life' that is not static and exists in its 'differences from something else' (2002, 45). The characters' hybrid *German-ness* and *Turkish-ness* is also apparent in the aesthetic of the second dance scene. The sudden changes and dynamics in the cinematography give form to sociocultural difference, the impossibility to get along with the idea of a cultural fixity: First, the transition from moving in rhythm to static close-ups of the unwanted male body when the man interrupts Sibel and Cahit, and then second, the fixed filming in high angle of the Cahit's ensuing beating. The interruption of the man is also an unwanted sexualisation and objectification of Sibel, reinforced by their dialogue. 'What do you want?', she asks. 'You', the man replies, followed by Cahit's 'That's my wife'. Sibel is here denied the ownership of her body and her sexuality; she is rendered as a gendered body and is denied the opportunity to live through the power of the erotic. The characters' inability to fully inhabit space on screen without being interrupted and replaced within a fixed frame, amounts to the inability to inhabit 'race' and gender as subject identities.

The third dance scene gives form to the subject as deeply liminal: always in constant transformation and on a threshold rather than fixed by mediated and cultural categories (such as race, gender, or sexuality). Stuart Hall writes that identity is a 'production, which is never complete, always in process, and always constituted within, not outside, representation' (1990, 222). Through the representation of Sibel and her habitation of space, the film places emphasis on the subject as a process, a body that lives through affects rather than gender, sex, or race. If multiple characters and events of the diegesis attempt to place her on a gender-coded path, the film's aesthetic and cinematic spaces give shape to Sibel's search for the erotic as a way to find freedom, embrace an uncomplete identity, and live outside of conventions. As the next section will explore in more detail, the uninhabitability of subject identities such as race and gender takes form on screen as abjection. After her family blames Sibel for bringing shame onto them through her liberated sexuality and Cahit's murder of Niko, she flees to Istanbul. Her life in Istanbul parallels Cahit's 'messy' life, demonstrated in the very first sequence of the film when he drives his car into a wall. By wandering in the streets at night dressed in black, with dark makeup, short hair, and baggy pants, and through her use of drugs and alcohol, Sibel wilfully disorganises her body and the codes that constitute her as 'feminine'. Sibel's 'cross-dressing' can be described as a way to negotiate gender norms, '[reiterating] a gendered idealisation and its radical uninhabitability' (see Butler 1993, 25). Sibel's presence in 'the interstices of the city' (in the words of Elizabeth Wilson 1991, 8) appears as a punk resistance to a capitalist world, which her cousin Selma embodies (with her 'work, sleep, work' routine that Sibel despises), and to a world in which women are not accommodated in public spaces.

In the third dancing sequence that closes Sibel's punk life, she drinks and dances frantically in a bar in Istanbul to the point of collapse. While Sibel drinks and dances, the song 'I Feel You' by Depeche Mode plays, loudly and extra-diegetically, indicating Sibel's own self-destructiveness and anticipating the ultimate trajectory of her life ('I Feel You' also plays when Cahit drives his car into a wall at the beginning of the film). The lyrics of the song correlate with the diegesis of the film, in its suggested replacement of religion (the Muslim religion of Sibel's family) with sex and drugs ('you take me to and lead me through oblivion'). As Sibel drinks and whirls around, the handheld camera follows her movement in close-up, making a constant effort to reframe her in the middle, and even 'loses' her for a moment. The editing of the scene, through multiple cuts and dissolves of short takes of Sibel in close-up, condense the passing time while giving form to Sibel's wilful liminal subject. If the camera's framing of Sibel obeys the cinematic narrative conventions of keeping the main character *in the frame*—filmically integral to social norms—the disjointed editing gives shape to a resistance to integrate a normative frame of

Fig. 5.7 *Head-On*: Sibel drinks and dances until she falls to the ground, unconscious

identity. The blur of images and loud colours invade the frame and merge with Sibel's body. The aesthetic of this scene formally expresses Sibel's drunkenness (see Fig. 5.7) and participates in a de-territorialisation of the idea of a stable subject identity.

In the third dancing scene, the cinematic space embodies Sibel's resistance to how she has previously been contained, or replaced, in a gendered, sexualised, and racialised identity. The blurring of images and loud colours create a dream-like space, which Sibel angrily inhabits, putting her body in the way of other people's dancing. The protagonist is depicted as a body that has been affected by her habitation of bars (for example, by the man in Hamburg who invaded her space and sexualised her in the second dancing scene), and as a body who affects others (as seen through the reactions of people around her, who push her when she gets in their way and form a circle around her when she collapses). Dark yellow, orange, and red colours seem to merge the tones of the two previous dance scenes, thus visually embodying Sibel's freedom to 'dance, live and fuck' and ability to replace her gendered, sexualised body with a non-gendered, asexual body (in this precise scene). As Senta Siewert writes about this scene, 'just as the consumption of energetic and hallucinogenic drugs brings one into a non-space, a space outside the body, dancing can evoke a delocalization of the body that suspends normal affective relationships and perception of the self' (2008, 204). The filmic space gives shape to an affective—punk—innovation, the forming of a wilful and liminal subject. Her invasive and angry habitation of the bar provokes unwanted interruption of other people's private space, which appears as a destruction of norms and normal affective relationships. For José Esteban Muñoz, queer and punk performances manifest as a materialisation of possibilities and generate 'a utopia… [as] a time and a place that is not there yet' (2009, 99–100). In this view, Sibel's punk and queer habitation of the space-time of this scene opens up a utopia, aesthetically pointing out to 'something missing in the here and now' (in Ernst Bloch and Theodor W. Adorno's words, qtd. in Muñoz 2009, 99). It creates an affirmative opening into the capitalist and sexist structures of society that delineate subject identities and the habitation of space. The cinematography and mise-en-scène of the three dancing scenes give shape to the subject as an ever-incomplete process. While Sibel's rape following this third and last dance scene is a physical destruction of her body and erotic power, Sibel's queerness and the punk aesthetic of the dance scene are inherently affirmative forms in their wilfulness to suspend the myth of the subject as immutably delineated by gender, race, and sexuality.

Punk and Abjection as Affirmative Forms

Like dance, abjection becomes a wilful form, a resistance to the gendering and racialisation of the self. Sibel's punk resistance verges on the abject, both as a fascination and fear for the destruction of the subject—the subject as coded by patriarchal and racial laws. For Julia Kristeva, the abject is the unassimilable: what cannot be assimilated by the 'acceptable', the thinkable (the socially accepted self); abjection is 'a mix of judgment and affect, condemnation and effusion, signs and pulsions' (Kristeva 1980, 9; 17, translation mine). As the characters reject subjectification according to gendered, racialised norms, they embrace what is considered abject. This abjection of the self takes the form of blood in the film, and demarcates the fall of dichotomic and arbitrary boundaries between inside/outside of the body, the self/the other (see Kristeva 1980, 15). By looking at the forms of the abject in the film, we actually look at the forms that displacement takes. Sibel and Cahit's relation to blood, or to the sexual, is a form of internalisation of the abject, of being other, and of not finding space in a place that divides because it is totalising. For Kristeva, the perception of the self as abject is common for people in exile, as it questions the space which one occupies (or can occupy) (1980, 15). Living in a country where one is seen as 'other' and the uninhabitability of gender and racial identities take abject and affirmative forms on screen. Blood manifests as an erotic force, which is, in Lorde's words, 'self-affirming in the face of a racist, patriarchal, and anti-erotic society' (1984, 50).

Both Sibel and Cahit's intercultural situation and their refusal or inability to inhabit idealised gendered identities take the shape of self-abjection: bringing their selves to abjection by acts of self-destruction, or by letting others destroy them. The abject in the film figures at once as a rejection of norms, a symptom of not belonging (neither to the German nor to the Turkish community), a transgression, and a punishment for transgressing. While Cahit drives into a wall, beats people up or is beaten up, destroys his own apartment, has sado-masochistic sex, abuses drugs, smashes glasses with his bare hands, and dances with blood running down his arms, Sibel cuts her veins open three times in the film, takes drugs, gets drunk, and fights until the point of unconsciousness. Psychoanalytically, we can regard the characters as finding affective refuge in abjection, in response to being made 'other'. The abject manifests as a restitution of the body outside of the social codes, determining what is acceptable and unacceptable.

The emphasis the film places on blood, conventionally regarded as abject, as Kristeva underlines, amounts to a suspension of the coded gendered and racialised body, a refusal to exist within these codes, and a recognition of the subject as always being on a threshold, always liminal. Blood also symbolises the boundary between the inside and the outside of the body. Sibel's taped wrists indicate that she cut her veins open, so that, as she admits to her mother, her brother and father would 'leave her alone'. When she cuts her veins open again, the camera films the action in a medium shot while blood dramatically spurts out of Sibel's arm into Cahit's face, which spurs the other customers in the bar to flee. Narratively, this gesture is designed to force Cahit to marry her, and is a result of not being understood (as Sibel says to Cahit, 'You don't understand shit'), of not being able to live her youth as she pleases ('live, dance, and fuck, and not just with one guy', as she says to Cahit). Formally, however, blood becomes an internal fluid that 'reassures the self' (1980, 65); it gives shape to a body of flesh that is, on Cahit and everything around them, is a trace of Sibel, a stain that remains while it exits her body as a rejection of her own self. This rejection is a result of the profound inability to exist within gendered, racial and set cultural codes.

Cahit smashes two glasses with his bare hands, creating a bloodbath—also a result of 'not being understood', as he himself states. His subsequent frenetic dancing to Turkish music while blood runs down his arms, however, appears as an acceptance of his 'otherness' within a German context.

After a group of Turkish men beats Cahit up until he bleeds. When the fight is over, he says to Sibel 'Fucking Turks'. Sibel replies, 'What? But you are one of them'. This opposition between them and us manifests through language, as Cahit cannot speak Turkish, and his statement shows that he considers himself German. Others, however, do not see him that way. The doctor who sees Cahit after his attempted suicide comments on his 'exotic' Turkish name and compares it to 'our' German names, thus positioning Cahit as other. When Cahit and Sibel pay a visit to her family, he says he hates 'all this Turkish crap'. Cahit has internalised racism, and reproduces, through his violent behaviour and self-abjection, the subject identity given by the injunction 'you-other'.

In another occasion, Cahit smashes two glasses with his bare hands... his arms, however, appears as an acceptance of his 'otherness' with a German context; the singer welcomes him on stage in spite of his bloody appearance. Cahit's 'bloody dance' unites the self-other distinction as a movement that embraces the abject. This time Cahit expresses abjection not through violence but instead through dance, as an erotic freedom to express oneself through the body. This is confirmed by the singer, who does not recognise Cahit's interior fluid as abject but welcomes him on stage. One reading of Cahit's and Sibel's relation to the abject would be to consider them 'bodies without organs', in Deleuze and Guattari's term (1980): their actions disorganise the body and the significances and hierarchies imposed on it by experimenting, moving, and dismantle the 'unity' of the subject through self-destructions (Deleuze and Guattari 1980, 197–98). While disorganising the body amounts to dismantling the strata of significances and subjectification that organise subjects within a majoritarian reality of dominations and exclusions, the abject is what remains of the body after it has been codified and ordered according to a particular context (see also Grosz 1994, 192–93). The aesthetic embrace of abjection is affirmative insofar as it participates in constituting the subject as essentially liminal, always in movement, on thresholds.

Several times in the film, Sibel makes herself or is made abject, as a punishment for her transgressions of gender, racial, and cultural codes. Just as in *Vendredi Soir*, the film's narrative and aesthetic constantly oscillate between Sibel's erotic freedom and her confinement within gendered and sociocultural codes. The first climax of the film unfolds from Sibel's empowered habitation of social spaces and the patriarchal and sexist repercussions. After making it clear to Niko that their sexual encounter was a 'one-off', Sibel goes by herself to an entertainment park. The movements of the camera and its long medium shots in slow motion, filled with colourful lights, position Sibel as fully inhabiting the screen space (see Fig. 5.8), similarly to when she walked the streets in her wedding gown after her night with the bartender. The camera follows her body's movement in the roller coaster and portrays Sibel's body as living through sensations rather than gender. Meanwhile, in the bar where the characters usually go, Niko goads Cahit about Sibel's 'whoring around' in a long static, fragmented, and obstructed shot (see Fig. 5.8). While the scenes in the entertainment park give shape to Sibel's ability to move around freely and control her own body and sexuality, the aesthetic of the parallel scene between Niko and Cahit hints at punishment for her transgressions.

Compared to Sibel's fluid and unobstructed habitation of the cinematic space, the cinematography, dialogue, and mise-en-scène of this dark scene

Fig. 5.8 *Head-On*: Parallel editing of Sibel enjoying the city and being confined in gender expectations

between Niko and Cahit attempt to return Sibel to a *socially acceptable* position. As Niko provokes Cahit through violent and racist comments, Cahit smashes a glass of beer on Niko's head, which ultimately causes his death. If Cahit goes to prison for his crime, Sibel is the one who is socially condemned for it and held as a 'dangerous woman' for her liberated sexuality. A dark musical phrase begins when her family realises what has happened. Both they and the media reporting on the event—through an article titled 'Jealousy killing' and a picture of the newlywed couple—blame Sibel for Cahit's violent outburst. Left without a place to call home, Sibel is forced to take refuge with Cahit's friend, Seref, who also blames her for what happened: 'Can't you see what you've done to him? You've ruined his life!' While Cahit's own 'extramarital' sexual life is never questioned, Seref's rebuke reinstates the persistent gendered dichotomy that defines women 'in terms of their sexuality in a way that most men [are] not' (Wilson 2001, 137). While Akin's film at times suggests the cultural nature of the double standards that allow men casual sexual relationships and refuse the same privilege to women (through the difference of outcomes of the three dancing scenes, for example), it also emphasises the pervasiveness and ubiquitousness of sexism: both Niko, a non-Muslim German, and the German media see Sibel's attitude about sex as a problem.

The lyrics of Wendy Rene's soul song 'After laughter comes tears', which plays throughout the sequence, from Sibel alone in the entertainment park to Cahit killing Niko, echo Sibel's predicament. The non-diegetic song seems to sarcastically comment on Sibel's wilful behaviour. As if it was diegetic, the music stops suddenly when Sibel, back at home, opens the compact-disc player and puts on an album by Turkish musician

Agir Roman. The cross-cultural dimension of the soundtrack encapsulates Sibel's self-abjection, as she looks at herself in the mirror, crying, and cuts her wrist open again. The extreme close-ups of the razor blade dripping with blood give shape to what cannot be assimilated: the judgement and affect of her culturally hybrid situation. A lengthy shot in extreme close-up then focuses on the needle with which the doctor sews her wrist up. The needle leaves a trace on her arm—the trace of not belonging. This uncomfortable close-up gives an affective form to the abjected body, both a body that is refused a space and a body that is never complete and always in the making (although this is also true for non-diasporic bodies). This scene gives form to the abject as an affective situation that blends confinement and an impulse out, a will to escape and an inability to do so (see Fig. 5.9). The dark walls on both sides of the door that spatially frame Sibel in the brightly lit bathroom visually parallel the action of the blood and the needle in the next scene, which both go out and stay in. Like her first suicide attempt, Cahit's suicide attempt, and Cahit driving his car into a wall, the abjection of the self results in being admitted to the hospital. The body needs to be 'straightened out' out of the path of the

Fig. 5.9 *Head-On:* Sibel bleeding after cutting her veins open

'melancholic migrant', be put back on the 'right path of happiness', and made 'docile', as Sara Ahmed would write (2010, 2014). One could interpret this scene as the medical institution (a symbol of the German state representing the socially acceptable) attempting to 'fix' Sibel, to bring her back to a socially acceptable state (one that is clean, proper, not opened up). However, looking at the forms of the sequence, following Brinkema's idea that affects have forms, gives us an insight into the affects of the film. The psychological scars of displacement, the inability to go *home* or find a home for oneself, take the form of physical scars.

Throughout the film, both Sibel's and Cahit's bodies are shown as the battleground of the uninhabitability of gender and race. Cahit is physically disciplined for killing Niko (he is sent to prison), and despite Sibel's occasional bouts of freedom, she is still constrained by patriarchal ideas that seek to control women's behaviour and mobility. After the incident, Sibel moves to Istanbul so her family cannot take revenge on her for *bringing* shame onto the family. If the first climax brought Cahit's mobility to a stop, the second climax of the film narratively and aesthetically arrests Sibel's mobility. After Sibel gets drunk (in the third dancing scene) and falls unconscious to the ground in the bar in Istanbul, the bartender rapes her as she lies face down on the floor in a medium-long shot.[1] The frenetically moving camera and the Depeche Mode song that was playing become immobile and silent, respectively, which give shape to Sibel's arrested mobility and foreshadow the last part of the film when Sibel regains a domestic life. The abjection of Sibel's body, through the sperm of the bartender invading her body (and possibly getting her pregnant, although the biological origin of her daughter is not made clear in the film), continues in the following scene in which three men beat her up in the streets and leave her bleeding and unconscious. As she walks down the street after the bartender kicked her out of the bar, three men start shouting sexist comments at her: 'Hey baby! What are you doing out so late? Do you need a man?' These comments position her as an abnormal inhabitant of the so-called 'public' space, a space dominated and controlled by men. Although Sibel undoes binaries through her queering of gender, she is continually repositioned as female, in a body negatively affected by power-geometries. This scene in the streets of Istanbul gives form to the contradictions inherent in gender while it reinforces the body as necessarily gendered, a situation from which the subject can never fully escape following Butler. In addition to constantly changing her 'feminine' appearance in Hamburg and cross-dressing in Istanbul, the deep abjection of Sibel's body gives form to the uninhabitability of gender and to the body's habitation of space through affects and sensations. Rather than being a silent victim of the men's misogyny, Sibel shouts back and starts a physical fight with one of the men, who follows her. As the scene transmits the gendered aspects of mobility, it engenders a political statement, echoing social movements such as 'Take Back the Night'. Sibel's wilfulness is manifest on screen through her full habitation of cinematic spaces. Ahmed also describes the rebellious and disobedient character of those subjects who experience wilfulness: 'wilfulness involves persistence in the face of having been brought down … [and] persistence can be an act of disobedience' (2014, 2). With her face dripping in blood and angrily smiling, Sibel provocatively shouts to the men to beat her up even more, in a gesture of self-abjection (Fig. 5.10). The visual abjection of the self, by bringing out what should be in (her blood), gives form to the destruction of the subject as codified and ordered. As Sibel stands in the street, getting up in spite of having been brought down, she wilfully inhabits the space on screen and the diegetic space (the street). Her embodiment of a punk lifestyle manifests all the more clearly in her

Fig. 5.10 *Head-On*: Sibel in a gesture of abjection

nighttime habitation of Istanbul, by which she embraces a subculture that is in opposition to the neoliberal way of life that she attributes to her cousin Selma. While the diegesis of the film eventually expresses the inability to belong to 'public' space as a woman and an intercultural subject, the aesthetic of the film gives form to abjection as an affective and affirmative resistance to displacement. Similarly to the 'Black Lives Matter' movement, this resistance becomes what remains and leaves traces within and in spite of sociocultural codes, just as blood and scars leave traces on the streets and the body. The abjection as affirmative resistance may once become what transforms the codes.

Windows, Hotels, and a Space for Pausing

In the last part of the film, Sibel inhabits spaces that appear to contain her, as opposed to the streets and nightclub that Sibel 'invaded' through her punk way of life. Her habitation of the domestic space resonates with the predicament faced by women in the road movie genre, as Chap. 2 has shown, who tend to be judged, killed, or taken back to the domestic sphere as a punishment for their transgression into a ('public') sphere where they do not belong. However, as we will see, Sibel's body has not been made completely docile, which becomes apparent through the construction of the cinematic space. While Sibel attempted to build a space for herself in the streets of Hamburg and Istanbul, the final scenes of the film show how home is not anchored in place, but rather in time and social relations. While *Head-On* does not belong to the road movie genre, it retains the protagonist's attempt to find home through mobility, or rather to find an alternative home—home as sense of belonging, a 'home [that] can be "anywhere and everywhere"' (Robertson 1997, 271)—in contrast to the monotonous and family domesticity that home can represent. The domestic space becomes a space of transit, a space for pausing, a space for reflection, and a space for finding one's own self in spite of patriarchal capitalist structures.

The abjection of the body, as explored in the previous section, also figures as a reaction to an unwilling containment within the capitalist system and its disciplinary organisation of time and space. Both Cahit and Sibel embrace a punk lifestyle, one that refuses the concept of career, consumption, and production within the logics of capitalism. In contrast with the neo-feminist figures that Hilary Radner (2010) describes in her book, Sibel is not a woman protagonist who can or wants to 'have it all', but rather who wants to get rid of it all. After she has left Hamburg for Istanbul, Sibel repositions herself in order to (wil)fully inhabit the city, by cross-dressing and adopting a structured, scheduled lifestyle for a period, which allows her to hide her wilfulness. If her cousin Selma associates socioeconomic success with discipline and willpower (as she proudly says to Sibel, 'You just need to believe in yourself'), Sibel's disciplined habitation of the city arises as a consequence of her loss of erotic power; the double standards regarding women's sexuality have negatively affected her.

While the aesthetic of the sequence when Sibel moves to Istanbul appears 'disciplined' in time and space (reflecting the disciplinary structuring of bodies and space that Foucault describes in *Discipline and Punish* [1975]), it also points to Sibel's persistent refusal to integrate capitalist norms. Sibel's temporal acquiescence to the capitalist system is evident in how frames-within-the-frame divide the cinematic space and how repetitive scenes structure the rhythm of the sequence. Fragmented images give shape to Sibel's containment as a docile body, and both the sound of Sibel's alarm clock ringing at 5:00 in the morning and her nighttime walks dictate the division of time. When the camera shows Sibel vacuuming and changing bed sheets in long obstructed and divided shots—marking her movements as repetitive and her attitude as one who is obeying the rules of the job— the bright window in the background creates a visual alternative to Sibel's present habitation of space: it manifests as a micro-instance of her wilfulness. Several times, Sibel looks out the window, with the city made visible by the shot's depth of field, indicating her desire to be part of it. Julianne Pidduck quotes Mikhail Bakhtin in her essay on windows and women's spaces in film when she suggests that windows appear as *thresholds,* as 'chronotopes of *crises* and *breaks* in life' (Mikhail Bakhtin as cited in Pidduck 1998, 382). Windows and mirrors in the takeaway restaurant where Sibel asks where she can find drugs, and the sound of Sibel's alarm clock being suddenly replaced by Turkish Romani music when she turns it off, give form to 'cracks' in the division of space and time. These 'cracks' suggest a wilfulness that persists, which first leads to abjection (as seen in the previous section) and then to building a space of reflection, a room of one's own.

At the end of the film, after Sibel is discovered lying in blood in the street by a taxi driver, the narrative returns to Hamburg, where Cahit is released from prison. Soon after, he leaves for Istanbul with the aim of finding Sibel. When Sibel is informed that Cahit is in town, she secretly calls him, whispers over the phone, and then hangs up hastily. Multiple cross-fades indicate time passing before Sibel and Cahit finally meet again. The portrayal of Sibel here is very different from the first time we saw her;

she has a daughter, wears glasses, does not look directly into the camera, and is dressed in a rather formal, non-sexy manner. As Sibel tells Selma that she is meeting Cahit and will not be coming back for the weekend, her raised chin, calm tone, and confident body posture as she looks straight ahead through the window indicate that she remains wilful (see Fig. 5.11).

If for male road questers, becoming new, empowered subjects means finding a new home on the road, women protagonists on identity quests find themselves in their wilful habitation of space. Rather than defining 'mobility' as the road travelled and possessed, a 'democratic right' of access to the public sphere ('a sphere of personal freedom, leisure, and freedom of movement' Habermas 1989 [1962], 129), *Head-On* shows us the limitations of freedom for both women and men (an essential part of Braidotti's affirmative politics). The affirmative critical thinking and activism of *Head-On* relies on the recognition that 'humanity does not stem out of freedom, but rather that freedom is extracted out of the awareness of our multiple limitations … affirmation [being] about freedom from the burden of negativity, through the understanding of these limitations' (Braidotti 2011, 269). At the end of film, Sibel appears less 'resistant', less

Fig. 5.11 *Head-On:* Sibel enjoying the sun on her face as she confidently looks over the city

'against' in her wilfulness and habitation of space. She inhabits space more confidently and in a more peaceful and negotiated way than in her earlier iterations. Because the street could not provide Sibel with a home, windows now protect her from the world 'out there', a world that has continually threatened and violated her body, reminding her of her designated gender and position in society.

While the windows that separate Sibel from the city may indicate a retirement into the domestic sphere that is typical of women protagonists in road movies, they also give shape to a wilful desire to escape the exhaustion of having 'to insist on what is simply given to others' (Ahmed 2014, 149). As Ahmed explains about wilful subjects, 'a desire for a normal life does not necessary mean identification with norms' (149). Like the windows in *Vendredi soir* and the roof in *Wadjda*, the windows and balconies of Sibel's apartment and of the hotel room she shares with Cahit give form to a certain type of spatial power. While standing 'above' the city she sees without being seen, therefore escaping the male gaze that has threatened her in the past (and threatens Wadjda's and Laure's full habitation of social spaces). Likewise, Sibel's glasses act as mediators between herself and the urban space. Mary Ann Doane writes that women wearing glasses in films acquire an 'intellectual' appearance and become empowered as (female) spectators, gaining a right to look (1990, 50). Sibel's glasses function as a (cinematic) way to avoid sexist comments or as a barrier to those who might question the legitimacy of her presence in the street. Her ability to stop, be a spectator, look at the city from above or through the mediation of her glasses, figure as both acceptance of her limitations and her freedom to inhabit space, as a subject who pauses and reflects before acting and taking decisions, similarly to Jeanne and Marie in *Messidor*.

The windows of Sibel's apartment and the hotel room she shares with Cahit have replaced the windows of the hotel room that she was cleaning earlier in the film. Instead of embodying Sibel's desire to find a home the streets, windows have become mirrors of a space of belonging that she has found within herself. Sibel's contented smile and the light of the sun on her face that the window lets through give form to a peaceful inner space, a *home* (see Fig. 5.11). The bright lighting of this scene, her white flowery clothes, her subtle smile, and her proud body posture contrast with the dark and cloudy Istanbul of the previous sequence. Her glasses echo the double movement of 'taking in' the outside world and reflecting it, simultaneously welcoming its brightness and letting it bounce back out. Rather than a body inhabiting streets at night, hiding oneself behind dark makeup and dark clothes, Sibel has found a 'home' within herself, as the mise-en-scène of this last sequence in Sibel's apartment and in the hotel room with Cahit suggests.

Just as social geographer Doreen Massey and film theorist Giuliana Bruno assert, home is always a space in transit, one that is constantly constructed and transformed through time and social relations. The hotel room in Istanbul where Sibel meets Cahit becomes a kind of home through the affective encounter of bodies. The mise-en-scène and cinematography of the scene show how home is located within affective exchanges and timely relations, rather than in a physical place. The sequence opens with a shot-reverse shot series of close-ups, positioning the characters' faces and naked shoulders in the middle of the frame. The close-ups, the warm light on the two bodies, and the micro-movements of both the camera and the characters give form to an intimate cinematic space, where time seems to stop and give place to desire. When Sibel and Cahit start touching, soft gasps and rustles rupture the silence, and the handheld camera filming them in close-up follows the slow movement of their faces kissing and hiding in each other's necks. The cinematography of this scene creates affects of belonging, a sort of home, and a room for their own selves where they are not abjected by being deemed 'other'.

The hotel allows a pause out of time, a pause for reflection, and an inquiry into the erotic. The hotel room acts as a sort of 'neutral' space, which encompasses numerous past and future stories (as seen in Chap. 3 on *Vendredi soir*); the absence of sounds from the city below also emphasise embodied micro-relations that temporarily suspend gendered power-geometries. In the following scene in which the characters have sex, two beds and a painting in between the beds symmetrically structure the fixed frame. It is a structure that Cahit and Sibel interrupt as they inhabit the space. As Cahit and Sibel's lovemaking breaks the symmetry of the image (see Fig. 5.12), the warm light on their naked bodies contrasts with the dark, cold colours of the room, which create an affirmative 'crack' in the setting of the diegetic space (the room) and in the socially structured reality. Sibel's introverted expression during the whole sequence—she either does not smile or only does so subtly—contrasts with her portrayal at the beginning of the film in Hamburg. The hotel room appears as a space in between inner and outer space, and as a space in transit between the domestic and the city, which the windows and balcony somehow join together. It gives Sibel a space to suspend, at least temporarily, power-geometries and her gendered situation as a mother and as a woman who lives through 'the

Fig. 5.12 *Head-On:* Sibel and Cahit making love and disturbing the spatial symmetry

accumulation of experiences of being silenced. At night, she is shown inside the hotel room with Cahit, looking at the city from the wide-open window, experiencing the air of the night on her naked skin, albeit protected and removed from the 'dangers' of the city (as the previous chapters also suggest regarding balconies). The rupture of the hotel room's symmetry, along with the warm tones of the characters' skin, suspend the neutrality of the room, *make space,* and create a sort of home. It becomes a space of wilfulness to not follow the prescribed path, a location to reconnect with the erotic, and an arena of belonging, which gives both characters a space to exist outside of their intercultural situation.

The sound of the scene also seems to create a pause, a place for reflection, and at once situates the protagonists in the present space-time and removes them from it. Asynchronous dialogue suddenly merges with their panting and rustling and progressively replaces the sounds of their lovemaking. Several pieces of asynchronous dialogue disrupt linear time and situate the characters in between present, past, and future space-times. When the city of Istanbul emerges in the previously dark and nearly silent room through a medium shot of the open window, the sounds of the

5 STREETS: FREEDOM, DIASPORA, AND THE EROTIC IN *HEAD-ON* 157

Fig. 5.13 *Head-On:* Sibel and Cahit looking at the city from above

evening adhan (an Islamic call for prayer) and the sight of the setting sun bring a concrete sense of time into the space. When the camera then films Sibel and Cahit as they sit on the balcony, looking at the city from above with their backs to the camera (see Fig. 5.13), Cahit's asynchronous question to Sibel and her synchronous but post-synchronised response continues to disjunct the linear idea of space-time. The window and the balcony of the room produce thresholds in the space-time and mark a difference between the time outside the room and the characters' time, a space-time lived through affects. While the characters attempt to plan a possible future together, they live through a nostalgic image of the past. Their absence of physical contact with the exterior world, of which the balcony and the window offer a distanced viewpoint, signifies creating a space-time for themselves away from the present space-time and away from being characterised as 'other' or in-between—neither belonging to Germany nor to Turkey. This sequence is affirmative in the sense that it suspends a linear and fixed idea of time and space and presents space as always remaining in transit, in constant transformation through time and social relations.

Domestic Space and Gender Roles

While the diegesis concentrates on the critique of the status quo and seems to conclude that women can neither freely inhabit public spaces nor aspire to freedom and independence, the aesthetic choices and musical tableaux of *Head-On* point to the continual transformation of space and power-geometries. When faced with the choice of staying at home with her partner and daughter at the end of the film, or following Cahit on the road to his hometown, Sibel decides to remain in Istanbul. This dilemma is actually an absence of choice, since in one instance she would remain in a stable domestic situation for her daughter's sake, and in the other instance, leaving with Cahit may mean entrapping herself in another heteronormative relationship. Going alone to Cahit's place of birth, Mersin, amounts to renouncing the life she has built in Istanbul and leaving behind her only remaining relative, her cousin Selma. There she might also have encountered similar kinds of spatial regulations to the ones she experiences with her current partner based on conventional heterosexual norms and expectations. As the film ends before this situation unfolds, and refuses to show Sibel's current partner, it does not visually cluster Sibel within the domestic sphere. Two bright establishing shots of Sibel in the street (one when she pushes her daughter's stoller, the other one when she walks, alone, to meet Cahit at the hotel) suggest that she is able to freely inhabit her environment, albeit within the limitations of her gendered situation.

Sibel's and Cahit's last appearances on screen give form to their sociocultural entrapment and to the limitations upon their freedom. The last scene with Sibel opens with a tight medium shot filmed by a handheld camera that follows her body movement as she packs her suitcase (presumably, with the intention to leave with Cahit). This brief shot then cuts to a fixed close-up of Sibel sitting on her bed in silence and with her head down. As music from a musical box and her partner's and daughter's joyful voices are heard, Sibel raises her head, only to lower it again slowly in the next shot, this time filmed in a fixed tight medium shot from behind (see Fig. 5.14). Sibel's plain grey t-shirt and its white rims echo the grey tone and thick white edges of the wardrobe in front of Sibel, the geometrical lines of which visually divide the image and enclose her body within multiple frames. The bareness of the mise-en-scène and Sibel's few movements within the fixed frame give shape to her resignation and limitation to her freedom, as a mother. Her body almost merges with the space. As Giuliana Bruno would put it regarding women's habitation of domestic spaces, the house is her dress expressing her own motions and emotions

Fig. 5.14 *Head-On*: Sibel's limitation to freedom expressed through her habitation of cinematic spaces

(2002, 91–92). The cracks that Sibel's wilful body created on screen through eroticism, dance, and abjection seem to have closed down on her, only leaving the sound of the musical box as a hope for generational wilfulness.

The musical box creates a sound bridge that links Sibel's last scene to Cahit's and narratively expresses Sibel's decision to remain in Istanbul with her daughter and her partner. When Cahit last appears on screen, a close-up frames him alone inside a bus about to depart for his hometown of Mersin. As the bus reverses, the camera zooms out and pans slightly to keep the bus in the frame while filming Cahit from an increasing distance, contained by frames and behind windows. The cinematography sets a distance from the character, who is slowly leaving the frame of the shot. When Cahit's bus has left the frame, the camera keeps filming the passing traffic on the highway as another sound bridge featuring traditional Turkish music links the scene to the last tableaux of the film. While the woman singer kept silent during the three preceding tableaux—echoing, it seems, the institutionalised sexist punishment of Sibel for her possession of the erotic and her cross-dressing—her singing of the oral tale resumes in the final tableaux.

The tableaux, along with the distancing cinematography of Cahit's last scene, take away the personal and places emphasis on the commonality of Sibel and Cahit's love story, and on the collective—human—limitation to freedom. As singing resumes in the final tableaux, it seems to introduce a wilful hope that a woman's voice can be heard in a world dominated by men. *Head-On* aesthetically introduces 'cracks' or lines of flight within the norms and expectations that its diegesis exposes. Despite uninhabitable subject identities that may appear inescapable, the hybrid, erotic and abject forms of the film's bodies affirmatively emphasise the possibility to conceive of subjects as deeply liminal. If mobility may not be the solution to transform oneself and one's environment, *Messidor*, *Vendredi soir*, *Wadjda*, and *Head-On* all show that the making and habitation of fluid spaces offer glimpses of hope and filmic ways to suspend the status quo.

Note

1. Sibel is not only punished for her queer appearance and moving around unchaperoned in public spaces, but also for drinking, which is not seen as acceptable for women, as film director Ulrike Ottinger also shows in *Bildnis einer trinkerin/Ticket of no return*.

References

Ahmed, Sara. 2010. *The Promise of Happiness*. Durham/London: Duke University Press.
———. 2014. *Willful Subjects*. Durham: Duke University Press.
Akin, Fatih. 2004. *Gegen Die Wand [Head-On]*. DVD. Germany/Turkey: Strand Releasing.
———. 2007. *Auf Der Anderen Seite [The Edge of Heaven]*. DVD. Germany/Turkey: Strand Releasing.
Appadurai, Arjun. 2002. The Right to Participate in the Work of the Imagination. In *Transurbanism*, ed. Joke Brouwer and Arjen Mulder. Rotterdam: NAi Publishers.
Barthes, Roland. 1980. *La chambre claire: note sur la photographie*. Paris: Gallimard.
Braidotti, Rosi. 2011. The New Activism: A Plea for Affirmative Ethics. In *Art and Activism in the Age of Globalization*, ed. L. De Cauter, R. De Roo, and K. Vanhaesebrouk, 264–270. Rotterdam: NAi Publishers.
Bruno, Giuliana. 2002. *Atlas of Emotion: Journeys in Art, Architecture, and Film*. London/New York: Verso.
Butler, Judith. 1993. Critically Queer. *GLQ: A Journal of Lesbian and Gay Studies* 1 (1): 17–32.

de Certeau, Michel. 1984. *The Practice of Everyday Life*. Berkeley: University of California Press.
Deleuze, Gilles, and Félix Guattari. 1980. *Capitalisme et Schizophrenie: Mille Plateaux*. Paris: Editions de minuit.
Di Méo, Guy. 2011. *Les murs invisibles: femmes, genre et géographie sociale*. Paris: Armand Colin.
Doane, Mary Ann. 1990 [1982]. Film and the Masquerade: Theorizing the Female Spectator. In *Issues in Feminist Film Criticism*, 41–57. Bloomington/Indianapolis: Indiana University Press.
Dyer, Richard. 2002 [1992]. *Only Entertainment*. London/New York: Routledge.
Eleftheriotis, Dimitris. 2012. *Cinematic Journeys: Film and Movement*. Edinburgh: Edinburgh University Press.
Foucault, Michel. 1975. *Surveiller et punir: naissance de la prison*. Paris: Gallimard.
Grosz, Elizabeth. 1994. *Volatile Bodies: Toward a Corporeal Feminism*. Bloomington/Indianapolis: Indiana University Press.
———. 2010. Feminism, Materialism, and Freedom. In *New Materialisms: Ontology, Agency, and Politics*, ed. Diana Coole and Samantha Frost, 139–157. Durham: Duke University Press.
Habermas, Jürgen. 1989 [1962]. *The Structural Transformation of the Public Sphere: An Inquiry into a Category of Bourgeois Society*. Malden: Polity Press.
Hall, Stuart. 1990. Cultural Identity and Diaspora. In *Identity: Community, Culture, Difference*, ed. Jonathan Rutherford. London: Lawrence & Wishart.
Kristeva, Julia. 1980. *Pouvoir de l'horreur: Essai sur l'abjection*. Paris: Point.
Kübler-Ross, Elisabeth, and David Kessler. 2005. *On Grief and Grieving: Finding the Meaning of Grief through the Five Stages of Loss*. New York: Scribner.
Lefebvre, Henri. 1974. *La production de l'espace*. Paris: Anthropos.
Lorde, Audre. 1984. *Sister Outsider: Essays and Speeches*. Berkeley: Crossing Press.
Massey, Doreen B. 1994. *Space, Place, and Gender*. Minneapolis: University of Minnesota Press.
McDowell, Linda. 1999. *Gender, Identity and Place: Understanding Feminist Geographies*. Minneapolis: University of Minnesota Press.
McRobbie, Angela. 1990. *Feminism and Youth Culture: From 'Jackie' to 'Just Seventeen'*. Hampshire: Macmillan International Higher Education.
Muñoz, José Esteban. 2009. *Cruising Utopia: The Then and There of Queer Futurity*. New York: New York University Press.
Naficy, Hamid. 2001. *An Accented Cinema: Exilic and Diasporic Filmmaking*. Princeton: Princeton University Press.
Ottinger, Ulrike. 2008 [1979]. *Bildnis Einer Trinkerin. Aller Jamais Retour*. DVD. West Germany: Women Make Movies.
Pidduck, Julianne. 1998. Of Windows and Country Walks: Frames of Space and Movement in 1990s Austen Adaptations. *Screen* 39 (4): 381–400.
Pollock, Griselda. 1988. *Vision and Difference: Femininity, Feminism, and Histories of Art*. London/New York: Routledge.

Radner, Hilary. 2010. *Neo-Feminist Cinema: Girly Films, Chick Flicks, and Consumer Culture*. New York: Routledge.
Rieker, Martine, and Kamran Asdar Ali, eds. 2008. *Gendering Urban Space in the Middle East, South Asia, and Africa*. New York: Palgrave Macmillan.
Robertson, Pamela. 1997. Home and Away: Friends with Dorothy on the Road in Oz. In *The Road Movie Book*, ed. S. Cohan and I.R. Hark, 271–286. London: Routledge.
Rose, G. 1993. *Feminism and Geography: The Limits of Geographical Knowledge*. Cambridge: Polity Press.
Siegel, Kristi. 2004. Intersections: Women's Travel and Theory. In *Gender, Genre, and Identity in Women's Travel Writing*, ed. Kristi Siegel, 1–14. New York: Peter Lang.
Siewert, Senta. 2008. Soundtracks of Double Occupancy: Sampling Sounds and Cultures in Fatih Akin's *Head On*. In *Mind the Screen: Media Concepts According to Thomas Elsaesser*, ed. Patricia Pisters Jaap Kooijman and Wanda Strauven, 198–208. Amsterdam: Amsterdam University Press.
Solnit, Rebecca. 2001. *Wanderlust: A History of Walking*. London: Penguin Books.
Spain, Daphne. 1992. *Gendered Spaces*. Chapel Hill: University of North Carolina Press.
Wilson, Elizabeth. 1991. *The Sphinx in the City: Urban Life, the Control of Disorder, and Women*. Berkeley: University of California Press.
———. 2001. *The Contradictions of Culture: Cities, Culture, Women*. London: SAGE Publications.

Open Access This chapter is licensed under the terms of the Creative Commons Attribution 4.0 International License (http://creativecommons.org/licenses/by/4.0/), which permits use, sharing, adaptation, distribution and reproduction in any medium or format, as long as you give appropriate credit to the original author(s) and the source, provide a link to the Creative Commons licence and indicate if changes were made.

The images or other third party material in this chapter are included in the chapter's Creative Commons license, unless indicated otherwise in a credit line to the material. If material is not included in the chapter's Creative Commons licence and your intended use is not permitted by statutory regulation or exceeds the permitted use, you will need to obtain permission directly from the copyright holder.

CHAPTER 6

Conclusion: Forms of Affirmative Aesthetics

Optimism and positivity are often associated with naivety or a lack of critique. On the contrary, negativity may be seen as either leading to fatalism or essential for the production of critical art. Affirmative aesthetics integrate the critique of the present while also producing a complex relational reality that points to other possibilities beyond the status quo, and to alternative futures. This book has argued that affirmative production does not necessarily happen at the narrative level but rather at an aesthetic level. Affirmative forms may indeed remain invisible as affects in the *en-deça* of visual arts. As Bersani and Dutoit have argued, it is the work of spectators and critics to see and reveal the invisible. If diegesis and narrative are indivisible from representation and filmic form, extented attention to filmic aesthetic may unveil affirmative forms; forms that are critical, transformative, and that may remain hidden if one only looks at dieges and characters' representaion alone.

To sustain my point further, I would like to briefly compare two films that consider women's relationship to space, power-geometries, and emancipation: *Wild* (Jean-Marc Vallée 2014) and *Roma* (Alfonso Cuarón 2018). The focus on a woman character's problematic habitation of space and their U.S.-based production are the only common aspects of these films. On the one hand, *Wild* seems to show a positive representation of a woman's emancipation, through the protagonist's resolve to overcome

© The Author(s) 2020
M. Ceuterick, *Affirmative Aesthetics and Wilful Women*,
https://doi.org/10.1007/978-3-030-37039-8_6

the difficulties for women to walk into the wild and occupy 'public' spaces. On the other hand, it closes on the neoliberal idea of an individual woman working for and by herself in order to attain her goals, thereby leaving unrecognised the privileged background that has allowed this. The final scene of *Wild* confirms this interpretation. As the main protagonist Cheryl (interpreted by well-known American actress Reese Witherspoon) visually and metaphorically leaves the woods, through which she has travelled for the last four months and almost the entirety of the film, she reaches and stands on the Bridge of the Gods, which unites the states of Oregon and Washington. Both her final monologue in voice-over and the film's aesthetic emphasise the individual and transcendental (religious) dimensions of her emancipation. The camera's close-up on her feet walking towards the camera do not point to a wilful move forward beyond the duration and spaces of the film, but rather a journey inward that is completed within the character and on the bridge. The character's future marriage and the children that will result from that marriage, which she mentions in voice-over, figure as a neofeminist rehearsal of a gendered and heteronormative history, whereby women's achievements are measured in terms of taking on a gendered and domestic role. Before the conventional black screen that closes the film, the camera closes up on Cheryl from a high angle as she looks up towards the sky and then closes her eyes (suggesting a Christian idea that her mother/God was looking after her from Heaven during her adventures, and that her/His force has been within her all along). This ending reinforces the neoliberal idea that achievement is ultimately individual and to be found within oneself (with the help of God, not socioeconomic privilege). If the diegesis promotes a positive and emancipatory view of women (which the film was critically celebrated for), the filmic forms of this ending scene reveal a certain fatalism in the modification of power-geometries, which is contingent on individual will, heteronormative gender roles, and the 'sacred' advantage of socioeconomic belonging.

Roma has been regarded as displaying the fatalism of class inequality and the impossibility of emancipation from ideological chains (Slavoj Žižek 2019), because the film's indigenous woman protagonist Cleo works as a caretaker of a rich Mexican family. I argue, however, that the aesthetic of the film creates affirmative moments. Long takes of Cleo standing in silence and looking off frame abound in the film; the length of the takes demonstrate that Cleo gets lost in her thoughts. A framing of Cleo looking through a window of the family's house, enclosed between lines, edges, and a multiplicity of objects, with the foreground sound of hail falling outside, contrasts with a low angle image of Cleo standing on the balcony of the family's holiday house and a reverse shot showing the object of her vision. The reverse shot shows, fairy lights shining in the night, and produces an audible atmosphere, of ambient sounds of waves, crickets, and distant singing. The length of the take allows the spectators to get lost in their thoughts just as Cleo does. Whereas the first scene of Cleo next to the window emphasised her imprisonment in a precarious situation, the aesthetic of the second scene gives shape to a sensuous self. Following the balcony scene, another lengthy take shows Cleo as she recalls the sound and smell of the village where she grew up. As she points her face towards the sun in the upper-right corner of the frame and enjoys its warmth with her eyes closed, the camera begins a tracking shot towards the right, which extends the direction of her body. Although very little about Cleo is articulated through the diegesis, a micro-analysis of space and the filmic forms reveal aspects of her subjectivity. Rather than a continuous display of positivity, it is the formal suggestion that things could be otherwise that produces moments of affirmative aesthetics. Similarly, when Cleo saves one of the children from drowning, the overwhelming sound of the rough sea and the still image of the entire family surrounding her on the beach afterwards produce the bodily and emotional involvement of Cleo as a member of the family, more so than the relentless and unconditional subservience of the poor, as Žižek asserts. As Cleo admits while sobbing that she never wanted the stillborn child she gave birth to, she blames herself for her death as if her wish engendered divine punishment: 'Yo no la quería, no quería que naciera, pobrecita' ('I did not want her, I did not want her to be born, the poor one', translation mine). Saving Sofi from drowning is just like saving her own baby girl. The composition of the frame and geometrical shape of the family's bodies surrounding Cleo in this scene may recall Théodore Géricault's painting 'Le Radeau de la Méduse/The Raft of the Medusa' (1818–1819); the mise-en-scène annihilates the social hierarchy present within the family and on the Medusa raft, at least for a moment (see Fig. 6.1). In contrast with the closing scene of *Wild*, the cinematography of the final scene of *Roma* points to future possibilities. As Cleo hangs up the family's clothes, the camera tilts upwards to film her as she slowly climbs the stairs that lead to the roof but it stays at the level of the house, one of the few times in the film that the camera does not eventually follow the character (see Fig. 6.2). As Cleo exits the frame, she

Fig. 6.1 *Roma*: The family surrounding Cleo as a member of the family

Fig. 6.2 *Roma*: Ending image after Cleo has left the frame

penetrates a space that may not be in view yet, but one that she creates for herself, through her embodied habitation. The social realism of the film does not grant an easy access to Cleo's subjectivity (something that other critics have deplored, such as Brody 2018), which is reinforced by her use of the indigenous Mixtec language that the family and the majority of the audience do not grasp. The aesthetic of the film, however, participates in the creation of Cleo's embodied subjectivity in a discreet fashion. The metal bars of the stairs (and the direct sound of Cleo's steps) and the plane in the sky represent at once the bars of Cleo's prison, the unattainable escape from her situation, and the possibilities to reach up, socially and emotionally (if not economically). The deeply low angle of the camera as she leaves the frame and the accentuated sound of the plane and of the singing birds reinforce these symbols as the dedication and the title of the film are superimposed on the still image at the film's end. While the narrative emphasises the negative affects of colonial power-geometries, other filmic forms bring the virtual into the real and present the affirmative multiplicities present within Cleo's life.

While feminist film theory and films such as *Wild* may formulate a critique, they also indirectly contribute to maintaining women in their conventional place, or rather, *out of place* (to echo Doreen Massey). Whereas *Wild* displays the positive affects of travel, it also depicts the class, racial, and gender status quo as somewhat immutable. As *Roma* critiques the collective negative affects of class disparities (through Cleo's situation and the student protest that indirectly leads to Cleo's stillborn baby), its aesthetic choices also bring affirmative forces to the fore, thereby creating subjects and spaces in continual transformation. Instead of presenting subjects caught in the spiral of gender and race performance, *Roma* emphasises the timely, contextual, and relational aspects of bodies and spatial habitation. Like the other films examined in this book, *Roma* works 'with the time and in spite of the time' rather than pursuing 'a quest for meaning', in Braidotti's words (2011, 292). The analysis of *Messidor* and the brief consideration of *Wild* show us that focusing on the diegesis and narrative success of the characters and their mobility sometimes obscures other aspects of the film, which may be revealed through the reading of affects as forms.

I have suggested that mainstream cinema (chiefly the road movie genre) and the scholarship dealing with space, gender, and cinema participate in creating socio-spatial binaries. Such binaries oppose in a seemingly immutable manner masculine with feminine, public with private, and travel with stasis. The analysis of *Messidor,* a film made in the wake of second wave feminism in Europe, appeared as an adequate point of departure from which to study the conditions that have rendered women's travel difficult and refused them the mobility that generally 'propel the usually male characters along the road of discovery' within the road movie genre (Corrigan 1992, 144). Chapter 2 concluded that the denial of growth for the female protagonists was anchored in the sociocultural gendering of both their bodies and the spaces they intended to inhabit. Women's freedom to fully inhabit space could not be measured in terms of travel, as it could for men. The 'mobility' of women should instead be thought of in terms of how their bodies' micro-relations to space produce affirmative forms. The chapter has introduced the idea that wilfulness takes different forms on screen. In *Messidor,* it is the insatiable search for mobility, the pause for reflections, and the habitation of space on screen rather than movement through it that produce moments of affirmation.

Affirmative aesthetics finds different models through which cinema suspends the gendering of space, the normative relations of gender and power, and the idea that gender, ethnicity, or sexuality determine subject identities and spatial habitation. *Vendredi soir, Wadjda,* and *Head-On* have served as case studies of a transnational narrative cinema – anchored in realism rather than genre – that questions and critiques women's difficult relations to mobility and 'public' spaces and (aesthetically) situate spatial habitation within fluid relations instead of within fixed normative identities. All the films analysed reveal the importance for women to have a space of their own, that is, a certain degree of social, economical, and spatial freedom. In their own ways, the films give form to a collectivity of wilful women. The haptic aesthetic of *Vendredi soir* converts bodies into lived bodies, and the imaginative and the virtual into the suspension of gender roles and expectations. *Wadjda* shows the generational and contextual dimensions of wilfulness, and the power of performance and masquerade to avoid being identified as wilful and being forced to comply. In *Head-On,* performing gender as a cultural form of 'femininity' or cross-dressing turns into the abjection of one's body and a connection to the erotic—as well as deep forms of knowledge and the refusal of conventions. In the four films explored in this book, it is a collective absence of home, of spaces that accommodate the women protagonists, that gives rise to thresholds, liminal subjects, and the recognition of the inadequacies of binary categories.

Though an examination of different films would have produced different models of affirmative aesthetics, this book has sought to make available an analytical model that may help other scholars develop an affirmative kind of critique, which detaches space and subject identities from the negativity of binaries. A greater variety of cinemas, such as local cinemas not aimed at an international audience, and a greater variety of contextual relations to space, such as those of transgender, lesbian, or ageing bodies, would certainly introduce other reactions to the trauma of not being accommodated. In Bridgette Auger and Itab Azzam's documentary film *We Are Not Princesses* (2018), exiled bodies, bodies in displacement, refugees living in camps—people always in between, with nowhere to call home—find a temporary home and alleviation to their trauma within movement and artistic production (such as singing or theatre). This is also the case for the transgender woman protagonist in the fiction film *Una mujer fantástica* (Sebastián Lelio 2017), who has to face constant humilliations and refusals of being granted a place to call home. Similarly, the ending scene of Lelio's earlier film *Gloria* (2013) uses dance to break with the expectations linked to women of old age. As with *Head-On*, dance allows the body to unravel through the senses and suspend codes linked to gender, age, 'race', or sexuality.

On screen, wandering off the prescribed path counters the idea of girls and women being 'natural caretakers' or 'happy housewives', just as shown in Marzieh Meshkini's film *Roozi ke zan shodam/ The Day I Became a Woman* (2000). The resistance to spatial constraints of three generations of wilful women (Hava, Ahoo, and Hoora) takes place through movement: the young Hava goes to play with her male friends on the beach one last time before being housebound because she has turned nine years old and 'become a woman', Ahoo persists in cycling in a competition even when her husband threatens to divorce her because she will not quit, and the old Hoora travels from the countryside to the city with the money of her deceased husband to buy all the domestic appliances she missed out on during her married years. These three women inhabit space in a way that differs from the norm. As wilful women, they will 'what is not present', they march 'with angry feet', and 'put their bodies in the way' of patriarchal imaginaries (Ahmed 2014, 8; 163). As with women who participate in the 'Slut Walks' or 'Reclaim the Night' marches, women's will not to go with the flow involves taking space and making space for themselves in places that do not naturally accommodate them. Instead of offering a lament, the films briefly described here manifest as affirmatively political; while the protagonists recognise the limitations to their freedom, the aesthetic forms that their actions take suggest the multiple possibilities of the present and alternative futures.

This leads us to consider another latent aspect of this book, namely the political aspect of art, the possibility that affirmative forms affect how space, subject identities, and bodies are lived and perceived in the material world. In his book *Post-cinematic affect,* Steven Shaviro borrows Raymond Williams' concept 'structures of feeling' to look at the expressiveness of film: how films give voice to 'ambient, free-floating sensibility that permeates our society today, although it cannot be attributed to any subject in particular' (2010, 2). While Shaviro's thinking resonates with Braidotti's affirmative ethics in that it favours transforming forces over genealogies or causes of negative affects, Shaviro rejects the idea that 'media works, or [his] discussion of them, or the reception of them by others, could somehow constitute a form of "resistance"' (2010, 138). If Shaviro states that 'aesthetics does not translate easily or obviously into politics', he argues that the role of art is to explore the future, while his role as a critic lies in the affective mapping of films' rearticulation of social processes (2010, 138–139). *Affirmative aesthetics and Wilful Women* also serves as an affective mapping and a rearticulation process of the ordinary trauma that pulls women in particular in uninhabitable gendered directions. A micro-analysis of how forms and bodies shape affirmative spaces on screen reveals aesthetic navigations of negative affects and their rewriting as productive forces. If aesthetics cannot be directly translated into politics, affirmative films *are* political insofar as they provide alternatives, albeit sometimes subtly, to disempowered collectivities.[1]

As this book has explored the 'forms of the affects' (as per Brinkema's expression) that give rise to women's habitation of fluid space-time, it has ignored the human body of the spectator that may somewhat *live through* these affections. If the role of the spectator and the critic is to see the invisible forms of visual arts beyond their characters and diegetic structures, it may also be the role of the spectator to adopt an embodied position: the spectator's 'body [thus becoming] a source not just of individual but of cultural memory' (Marks 2000, xiii). In that case, film viewing would be an embodied experience that affects our spatial imaginary and may ultimately transform collective (cultural) memories of space and the habitation of space itself.

As explored in the introductory chapter through the works of Deleuze, Massumi, Ahmed, Hemmings, Berlant, Dyer, and Brinkema, affects function at different interwoven and simultaneous levels. As affects emerge from filmic forms (from the film's aesthetic), it may bring the spectators' bodies in the image, spectators who also affect each other through their co-presence in the movie theatre (creating an 'atmosphere', in Ben Anderson's words, 2009). As Ahmed writes about affective events and situations, the film's body would *touch* the surface of the viewers' bodies, drawing them into emotional-affective-intellectual experiences, connecting with them by 'moving' them or 'holding [them] in place', and 'giving [them] a dwelling place' (2004, 11). Similarly, Vivian Sobchack asserts that the cinematic creates a 'habitable *world* ... a lived space and active possibility ... a space that is deep and textural, that can be materially inhabited' (2004, 151). Sobchack situates the affective experience of cinema in two specific aspects: its preserving of the present 'always presently constituting itself' (146) and the reversibility of the seer and the seen, the *onscreen* and *offscreen* (referring too to Merleau-Ponty's reversibility of the touching experience). Sobchack writes:

> All the bodies in the film experience—those onscreen and offscreen (and possibly the screen itself)—are potentially subversive bodies ... each arguably becoming the 'grounding body' of sense and meaning since each exists in a dynamic figure-ground relation of reversibility with the others. Furthermore, these bodies also subvert their own fixity from within ... so that meaning, and where it is made, does not have a discrete origin in either spectators' bodies or cinematic representation but emerges in their conjunction. (2004, 67)

By engaging the body in present and reversible situations, films create textural spaces that can be inhabited, 'lived and re-membered' (Sobchack 2004, 152), and *responded to* with new possibilities of being-in-the-world and inhabiting the material world. This cultural, individual, and collective mediated habitation of the film's (social) spaces both physically affects our bodies (insofar as affect is contagious Gibbs 2001; Ahmed 2004; Brennan 2004; Probyn 2005) and, in the accumulative dimension of experiences, affects our ways of being in the world, our socio-spatial existence.

From this phenomenological notion of affective (or embodied) spectatorship, two lines of thought emerge. The first one is embedded in Nigel Thrift's work on the collective transmission of affects: 'soaking' space 'with a combination of affects... [that] become bodies of influence', *a political form* (2008, 222). In this sense, cinema can be seen as an accumulation of 'like-minded' film bodies potentially provoking political movement by affecting (individual and) collective spectators in a particular way. The second line of thought involves the spectators' micro-relations to, and modification of, space. As seen in Massey and Braidotti's writings, such micro-instances participate in structures of power and may indeed become the foundations for a larger (affirmative) movement. Braidotti calls for affirmative politics as a movement of 'autonomous but mutually connected communities or group-multitudes … or complex singularities … engaged in the project of constituting alternative structures', as a result of having been (individually and collectively) negatively affected by unjust politics (2011, 272). It may be a valid concern to ask whether the films explored in this book have an impact on spectators' habitation of space, even only at a micro-level, and whether their affective charges would eventually modify existing structures of power.

When Bachelard studies how poetic imaginaries create certain spaces as 'intimate', such as the house, he underlines the 'movement' of the poetic image, which carries the imagination along, brings the reader to experience its language, and potentially creates a new 'nerve fiber' (1994 [1964], xxviii).[2] The poetic image provides us with an affective experience, and a contact with things; between the 'new image' and the adhesion it invites, there is a transfer of imaginaries between the producer (poet or filmmaker) and receiver (reader or viewer) of the images, an 'inter-subjectivity'; readers thus fully *live* the poetic image, which *takes root* in them (Bachelard 1961, 15; 13; 8). Applying Bachelard's theory and topoanalytical method to film allow us to recognise how filmic aesthetics produce affective and lived spaces, which may create new connections and accumulatively transform our own habitation of the world (at once affective and embedded within dynamic discourses and power-geometries). As such, every film affects the viewer with more or less intensity through its position as an 'aesthetic object'. Both the poetic and the filmic languages invite an embodied spectatorship; they invite us to enter into contact with the affective and material spaces they create.

As Chapter 1 detailed further, I first and foremost consider films and works of art as maps of social and spatial relations, maps that are dynamic, that may show us different paths and lines of flight, and open our imagination and desires. As Shaviro explains about the post-cinematic media that he himself analyses, they are 'best regarded as affective maps, which do not just passively trace or represent, but actively construct and perform, the social relations, flows, and feelings that they are ostensibly "about"' (2010, 6). Establishing a transfer of affects between the bodies of the film and the spectators requires further study, as does any attempt to answer the complex question: What does art do to us? I concur with Deleuze and Guattari that 'maps [thereby works of art] are not static representations, but tools for negotiating, and intervening in, social space. A map does not just replicate the shape of a territory; rather, it actively inflects and works over that territory' (Shaviro 2010, 5–6). Post-cinematic media or digital media in a broader sense offers a freer access to a variety of platforms, forms, and languages than cinema has offered and therefore opens the art of cartography to a broader multiplicity of voices.

Virtual reality, augmented reality, locative art, art video, gallery films, and experimental cinema are in some ways denominations of cinema, a confirmation of its constant mutability. Similarly, blogs, electronic literature, and social media are extensions of the written press, the book, and the telephone. While these 'digital media' may only be prolongations or rewritings of codes that already existed, their advanced technology offers a non-linearity, portability, and interactivity, as well as the embodiment of and exchanges between spectators and 'users' that were somewhat restricted by the cinematic apparatus. As a follow-up to this book, it would be worth exploring whether and how the new aesthetic forms developed by 'post-cinematic' media, specifically its juxtapositions, assemblage, and fragmentation, give rise to a different mapping of gender, power, and spatial relations.

Notes

1. As Lauren Berlant writes in Cruel Optimism, 'Aesthetics is not only the place where we rehabituate our sensorium by taking in new material and becoming more refined in relation to it. But it provides metrics for understanding how we pace and space our encounters with things, how we manage the too closeness of the world and also to have a desire to have an impact on it that has some relation to its impact on us' (2011, 12).

    I read in Berlant's text the double idea that one's body and sensations transform with aesthetic experiences, and that aesthetics is also a way to measure and cope with the limitations to our freedom, the 'too closeness of the world'. In turn, critical writing and artistic production through film and digital media allow us to take part in the mapping of the world, and thereby, perhaps, have an impact on it.

2. 'The verse always has a movement, the image flows into the line of the verse, carrying the imagination along with it, as though the imagination created a nerve fiber ... the poetic image furnishes one of the simplest experiences of language that has been lived' (Bachelard 1994 [1964], xxviii).

References

Ahmed, Sara. 2004. *The Cultural Politics of Emotion*. Edinburgh: Edinburgh University Press.
———. 2014. *Willful Subjects*. Durham: Duke University Press.
Anderson, Ben. 2009. Affective Atmospheres. *Emotion, Space and Society* 2: 77–81.
Auger, Bridgette, and Itab Azzam. 2018. *We Are Not Pincesses*. Motion Picture. UK/USA: Noerlum Studios, Open Art Productions.
Bachelard, Gaston. 1961. *La Poétique de l'espace*. 1st edition in 1957. Paris: Presses Universitaires de France.
———. 1994 [1964]. *The Poetics of Space*. Boston: Beacon Press.
Berlant, Lauren Gail. 2011. *Cruel Optimism*. Durham: Duke University Press.
Bersani, Leo, and Ulysse Dutoit. 2004. *Forms of Being: Cinema, Aesthetics, Subjectivity*. London: BFI Publishing.
Braidotti, Rosi. 2011. *Nomadic Theory: The Portable Rosi Braidotti*. Chichester: Columbia University Press.
Brennan, Teresa. 2004. *Transmission of Affect*. London: Continuum.
Brody, Richard. 2018. There's a Voice Missing in Alfonso Cuarón's "Roma". *The New Yorker* (Online), December 18. Retrieved on 20 Aug 2019 from https://www.newyorker.com/culture/the-front-row/theres-a-voice-missing-in-alfonso-cuarons-roma
Corrigan, Timothy. 1992. *A Cinema Without Walls: Movies and Culture after Vietnam*. London: Routledge.
Cuarón, Alfonso. 2018. *Roma*. Motion Picture. Mexico/USA: Netflix.
Gibbs, Anna. 2001. Contagious Feelings: Pauline Hanson and the epidemiology of Affect, *Australian Humanities Review* 24. Retrieved on 9 Oct 2019 from http://australianhumanitiesreview.org/2001/12/01/contagious-feelings-pauline-hanson-and-the-epidemiology-of-affect/
Géricault, Théodore (1818–1819) Le Radeau de la Méduse [Oil on Canvas]. Musée du Louvre, Paris.
Lelio, Sebastián. 2013. *Gloria*. DVD. Chile/Spain: Fabula.
———. 2017. *Una mujer fantastica* [*A Fantastic Woman*]. Motion Picture. Chile/Germany/Spain/USA: Participant Media.
Marks, Laura U. 2000. *The Skin of the Film: Intercultural Cinema, Embodiment, and the Senses*. Durham/London: Duke University Press.
Meshkini, Marzieh. (2000). *Roozi ke zan shodam [The Day I Became a Woman]*. DVD. Iran: Makhmalbaf Productions.

Probyn, Elspeth. 2005. *Blush: Faces of Shame*. Minneapolis: University of Minnesota Press.
Shaviro, Steven. 2010. *Post-Cinematic Affect*. Winchester/Washington, DC: 0 [zero] Books.
Sobchack, Vivian. 2004. *Carnal Thoughts: Embodiment and Moving Image Culture*. Berkeley/Los Angeles/London: University of California Press.
Thrift, N.J. 2008. *Non-representational Theory: Space, Politics, Affect*. New York: Routledge.
Vallée, Jean-Marc. 2014. *Wild*. DVD. USA: Fox Searchlight Pictures.
Žižek, Slavoj. 2019. *Roma Is Being Celebrated for All the Wrong Reasons*. Essay Online. Retrieved on 21 Aug 2019 from https://blogs.spectator.co.uk/2019/01/roma-is-being-celebrated-for-all-the-wrong-reasons-writes-slavoj-zizek/

Open Access This chapter is licensed under the terms of the Creative Commons Attribution 4.0 International License (http://creativecommons.org/licenses/by/4.0/), which permits use, sharing, adaptation, distribution and reproduction in any medium or format, as long as you give appropriate credit to the original author(s) and the source, provide a link to the Creative Commons licence and indicate if changes were made.

The images or other third party material in this chapter are included in the chapter's Creative Commons licence, unless indicated otherwise in a credit line to the material. If material is not included in the chapter's Creative Commons licence and your intended use is not permitted by statutory regulation or exceeds the permitted use, you will need to obtain permission directly from the copyright holder.

Index[1]

A

Abjection, 24, 27, 128, 130, 141, 144–146, 148, 149, 159, 168
  as refuge, 145
  See also Resistance
Aesthetics, 9, 13, 16, 17, 21–27, 40, 41, 44, 46, 49–51, 53, 59–62, 69, 70, 72, 76, 77, 79–83, 85, 87, 88, 90, 91, 99, 100, 104, 106, 107, 111, 112, 114, 117, 118, 121, 126, 135–138, 140, 141, 143, 146, 149, 150, 152, 158, 160, 163–165, 167, 170–173, 173n2
  filmic, 23, 27, 163, 172
  and politics, 170 (*see also* Affirmative)
Affect, 4, 5, 8–10, 12–16, 19, 23, 24, 29n10, 30n12, 30n14, 37, 57, 61, 62, 67, 80, 91, 99, 101, 104, 105, 126, 144, 148, 170
  affirmative ethics (*see* Braidotti, Rosi)
  as filmic forms, 2, 12, 16, 28, 167, 171
  as form, 12, 13, 167

negative, viii, ix, 1, 4, 5, 10, 14, 18, 19, 22, 26, 27, 51, 52, 67, 72, 75, 82, 91, 93n12, 119, 120, 167, 170
  as passage, 12, 67
  as productive forces, 4, 170
  theory, 8–13, 29n9
  See also Space, and affect
Affirmative, 2, 11, 12, 14, 26, 37–54, 74–78, 89, 100, 110, 112–114, 118–120, 128, 131, 155, 157
  aesthetics, v, 4, 5, 10, 16–19, 21, 23–25, 27, 47, 53, 60, 62, 82, 91, 107, 125, 126, 163–174;
  and microanalysis, 17
  ethics (*see* Braidotti, Rosi)
  forces, 21, 22, 27, 37, 40, 120, 167
  forms, ix, 10, 23, 27, 40, 42, 43, 106, 109, 111, 115, 120, 136, 143–150, 163, 168, 170
  politics, 2, 4, 19–23, 94n19, 113, 153, 172 (*see also* Braidotti, Rosi)
Agency, 19, 39, 51, 103

---

[1] Note: Page numbers followed by 'n' refer to notes.

© The Author(s) 2020
M. Ceuterick, *Affirmative Aesthetics and Wilful Women*,
https://doi.org/10.1007/978-3-030-37039-8

Ahmed, Sara, vi, viii, 2, 8, 10–13, 19–22, 26, 30n14, 87, 100, 104, 109, 113, 116, 119, 120, 133, 149, 150, 154, 169–171
  The Promise of Happiness, 21
  Queer Phenomenology, 11, 21, 28
  Willful Subjects, 11, 21, 28
Akin, Fatih, 5, 27, 38, 101, 125, 126
Althusser, Louis, 11
American Honey, 38
Anderson, Ben, 70, 82, 171
Apartment, *see* Home
Appadurai, Arjun, vii, 24, 57, 140
The Apple, 100
Arendt, Hannah, vi
Atmosphere, 8, 43, 46, 64, 69, 70, 76, 79–82, 84, 110, 165, 171
  See also Affect
Auf der anderen seite/The Edge of Heaven, 126

B

Bachelard, Gaston, 16, 59, 69, 77, 92n8, 172, 173n1
Balcony, *see* Space
Banet-Weiser, Sarah, 51
Bar, 127, 135, 138, 142, 143, 145, 146, 149
  cafés, v, 46, 51
Barker, Jennifer, 8, 12, 15, 60–62, 92n3
Belonging, 27, 73, 107, 126, 127, 144, 148, 151, 154, 156, 157, 164
Berlant, Lauren, 8, 10, 12, 19, 170, 173n2
Bernheim, Emmanuèle, 68, 87, 94n20, 95n25, 95n26
Bersani, Leo, 16, 17, 163
Beugnet, Martine, 61, 64, 79, 85, 92n9

Bicycle, vi, 26, 100, 101, 104–108, 119
  See also Vehicle
Bike, vii, 71, 104, 105, 107, 108, 116, 117, 119
Binaries, 1, 2, 4, 6, 11, 13, 18, 21, 23, 26, 27, 53, 58–60, 67, 70, 78, 82, 86, 95n23, 117, 147, 149, 168, 169
Black Lives Matter, 150
  See also Resistance
Blood, 117, 128, 144–146, 148, 150, 152
Body, vi, 5, 8–18, 20, 22–25, 27, 29n7, 29n10, 29–30n12, 40, 44–46, 49–51, 53, 57–95, 92n3, 93n14, 94n19, 94n21, 99–102, 106–110, 112, 113, 116, 118, 121n1, 125–128, 130, 133–137, 139–141, 143–146, 148, 151–155, 158, 160, 165, 167–173
  and affect, 9, 13
  and desire, 27, 59
  docile, 151
  female, 2
  gendered, 12, 19, 26, 42, 149
  lived, 60, 80, 89, 117, 135, 138
  position of, 115
  as shape, 11, 47
  wilful, v, 6, 19, 22, 42, 119, 135, 159
Bolton, Lucy, 18, 120
Bonding, 42, 52, 94n19, 119, 120
Border, 48, 49, 77, 82, 89, 93n11, 110
Boundary, 3, 4, 7, 25, 26, 46, 59, 67, 78, 86, 92n6, 112, 118, 144, 145
  blurring of, 75
  See also Threshold
Bovenschen, Silvia, 18

INDEX

Braidotti, Rosi, 2–5, 18–22, 27, 29n6, 45, 91, 94n19, 106, 120, 132, 153, 167, 170, 172
  politics (see Braidotti, Rosi)
Brennan, Teresa, 8, 9, 171
Brinkema, Eugenie, 8, 12, 13, 106, 149, 170
Bruno, Giuliana, 23, 29n6, 37, 39, 40, 42, 60, 62, 65, 78, 155, 158
Butler, Judith, 8, 11, 27, 83, 94n21, 125, 133, 134, 138, 141, 149
Butterfly Kiss, 45, 38, 52

C

Capitalism, 47, 48, 99, 151
Car, v, 2, 5, 7, 16, 23, 25, 42, 44, 46, 48–53, 57–95, 92n10, 93n11, 93n13, 93n14, 93–94n17, 94n22, 101, 105, 108, 115, 141, 142, 148
  in traffic jam, 60, 71
  See also Godard, Jean-Luc
Child, 101, 104, 107, 119, 126, 165
  docile, 109
  innocence of, 104
  wilful, 108
Chisholm, Diane, 100, 121n1
The Circle, 20, 100
Circumstance, 100
City, v, vi, 3, 6, 14, 23, 26, 28n3, 28–29n5, 29n8, 45–48, 57–60, 64–66, 68, 71–73, 75, 77, 78, 82, 89, 91, 92n6, 92n10, 93n11, 93n14, 101, 102, 108, 117, 120, 126–131, 135–139, 141, 147, 150, 152–158, 160n1, 164, 168, 169
Codes, see Culture
Colebrook, Claire, 11
Commodification of women, 51

The Company of Wolves, 20
Confinement, 146, 148
Control, viii, 7, 17, 18, 29n5, 40, 51, 94n17, 102, 107, 108, 112, 116, 138, 146, 149
Crash, 58
Cresswell, Tim, 6, 7, 28n2, 40
Cruising Utopia, 28
Culture, vii, ix, 7, 14, 21, 27, 57, 61, 89, 101, 112, 119, 121n2, 126, 127, 140
  as codes, 151
  as subculture, 151

D

Dance, 27, 48, 75, 130, 133, 137–146, 159, 169
Dangerous women, 41, 42
The Day I Became a Woman, 20, 23, 100, 169
de Certeau, Michel, 6, 13
De Lauretis, Teresa, 18, 39
Deleuze, Gilles, 9, 11, 12, 16n16, 22, 26, 29n11, 30n12, 30n15, 67, 68, 84, 87, 110–111, 114, 146, 170, 173
Denis, Claire, 5, 16, 25, 26, 57–59, 61, 65, 71, 72, 76, 78, 80, 81, 85, 91, 92n9, 93n11
Desire, ix, 4, 15, 18, 19, 21, 22, 27, 28n5, 42, 46, 58, 59, 61, 67, 71, 78, 80–82, 84, 85, 91, 93n14, 102, 103, 115, 126, 152, 154, 155, 172, 173n2
Di Méo, Guy, 29n8, 93n12, 128
Diaspora, 125–160
Dichotomy, see Binaries
Digital media, 173, 174n2
Discipline, 5, 93n14, 109, 110, 149, 152
  See also Foucault, Michel

Disobedience, *see* Resistance
Displacement, 69, 124, 126, 144, 149, 150, 169
   See also Diaspora; Race
Docility, 26, 109, 110, 113
   See also Foucault, Michel
Domestic, viii, 42, 91, 102, 108, 116, 127, 130, 133, 149, 152, 154, 155, 164, 169
   labour, 102, 120
   space (*see* Space)
   sphere, vii, 1, 3, 29n7, 39, 42, 61, 63, 66, 68, 71, 72, 75, 78, 89, 130, 150, 151, 154, 158–160
Donaldson, Lucy Life, 70, 79
Door, 73, 79, 87, 110, 112–114, 119, 133, 148
Drive, 59
Duration, 11, 12, 49, 50, 67, 164
Dutoit, Ulysse, 16, 17, 163
Dyer, Richard, 12, 128, 170

E
The Edge of Heaven, 126
Eleftheriotis, Dimitris, 127
Empowerment, 22, 25, 51, 53, 66, 120
Endurance, *see* Persistence; Resistance
Erotic, 10, 24, 27, 67, 68, 70, 77, 79, 80, 83, 85, 87, 91, 125–160, 168
Everyday Sexism Project, 14
   See also Social media

F
Far from Heaven, 20
Femininity, 47, 83, 86, 92n8, 94n20, 116, 117, 131, 133, 134, 168
   as aesthetics, 18
   dangerous, 58
   as docility, 110, 113
   and happiness, 120
   as identity, 139
   and submissiveness, 121, 135
   and subservience, 114
Feminism, 24, 168
   feminist theory, 5, 18
   and Islam, 102
   post-feminism, 18
   through comics, 15
Film theory, 11, 18, 24, 28, 167
   and accented cinema, 126
   and affect, 8, 12
   and ethics, 15
   feminist, 17
   and phenomenology, 15
      (*see also* Phenomenology)
Fire, 20
Flâneur, 2–4, 28n5, 108, 130–131
Flâneuse, *see* *Flâneur*
Foucault, Michel, 19, 26, 109, 111, 112, 115–117, 121n2, 152
Freedom, 1, 18, 19, 38, 42, 46, 51, 57, 58, 71, 113, 114, 125–160, 168
   limitations to, 15, 22, 23, 26, 45, 70, 101, 109, 110, 113, 120, 132, 153, 154, 158–160, 169, 173n2
Frozen River, 46, 52
Fullwood, Natalie, 10, 18, 39

G
Gaze, 3, 18, 28n5, 66, 75, 78, 81, 84, 85, 92n10, 108, 114, 115, 132, 133, 136, 140
   male, 3, 17, 45, 154
Gegen die wand/Head-On, 27, 125
Gender, v–viii, 1–30, 39, 40, 42, 45, 51, 58, 60–62, 68, 70, 78, 80, 83, 84, 86–89, 91, 94n21,

94n22, 99–103, 106, 113, 118, 121n1, 125–128, 130–136, 138, 140, 141, 144, 146, 147, 149, 150, 154, 158–160, 164, 167–169, 173
and inequality, vi, 105
and labour (*see* Domestic)
and mobility, v, 1, 2, 5–17, 19, 24, 58, 61, 150 (*see also* Flâneuse)
norms, 25, 26, 59, 62, 79, 80, 83, 89, 91, 99, 118, 119, 127, 130, 133, 134, 138, 141, 144
performance of, 24, 27, 83, 84, 114, 125, 127
as performative, 114, 130, 134, 138–141
role, vi–viii, 29n7, 40, 64, 103, 113, 130, 158–160, 164, 168
as situation, 26, 60, 67, 70, 105, 155, 158
theory of, 1, 2, 24
uninhabitability of, 83, 138, 140, 141, 144, 149, 150
Generational lines, 20
Geography, 24, 29n6, 29n7
cultural, 5, 7
Germany, 126, 127, 140, 144, 147, 157
Germany, Pale Mother, 20, 38
Gesture, vi, 51, 63, 67, 79, 89, 93n17, 108, 145, 150, 151
Ghost, 3, 28n5, 73
Gloria, 169
Godard, Jean-Luc, 58, 71, 93n11
Grosz, Elizabeth, 11, 131, 132, 146
Guattari, Félix, 110–111, 114, 146, 173

H

Habermas, Jürgen, 58, 92n2, 153
Hall, Stuart, 127, 141

Happiness, *see* Ahmed, Sara; Femininity
Haptic, 24, 26, 29n6, 60–62, 67–70, 79–88, 91, 92n3, 95n23, 168
Haunting, *see* Ghost
Head-On, 5, 21–25, 27, 46, 62, 64, 66, 72, 82, 89, 91, 92n10, 94n20, 125–160, 168, 169
Hemmings, Clare, 8, 10, 12, 170
Heterotopia, 111, 115–117, 119, 120
Hole, Kristin Lené, 15, 16, 28
Home, 25, 38, 39, 45, 46, 59, 60, 62–73, 79, 82, 87–89, 91, 92n10, 93n13, 117, 126, 127, 135, 154–156
in the road movie, 1, 19–21, 24, 25, 27, 28n1, 37–54, 57, 58, 71, 150, 151, 154, 167, 168
as *transito*, 39, 66
Hotel room, 59, 60, 62, 66, 68, 69, 71, 79, 80, 82, 84–89, 94n20, 154
House, v, 1, 2, 5, 7, 14, 16, 23, 25, 26, 40, 41, 46, 59, 60, 62, 63, 66, 68, 69, 75, 77, 92n8, 99–121, 126, 132, 136, 158, 164, 165, 172
Hybridity, 140
cultural, 127, 129, 140, 148, 151, 156

I

Imaginaries, 9, 16, 22, 24, 26, 29n6, 59, 62–64, 76–78, 93n11, 112, 169, 172
patriarchal, 22, 169
spatial, 4, 5, 17, 21, 24, 65, 71, 73, 82, 83, 170
Imagination, v, vii, 4, 14, 16, 18, 19, 22, 24, 30n12, 57, 63, 66, 67, 70, 78, 82, 87, 92n8, 108, 172, 173n1

Immobility, *see* Mobility
Ince, Kate, 40
Ingraham, Chris, 51
In July, 38
In the Fade, 126
Intimacy, 16, 25–27, 38, 42, 44, 59, 60, 62–64, 67–71, 73, 77–81, 87–89, 91, 116
 See also Desire; Space
Irigaray, Luce, 18
Islam, 102, 103
 See also Feminism, Islam
Istanbul, 126–130, 138, 141, 149–152, 154–156, 158, 159

J
Johnston, Claire, 18
Jonas qui aura 25 ans en l'an 2000, 48
Journey, *see* Travel

K
Kabeer, Naila, 51
Kings of the Road, 41–42
Kristeva, Julia, 144, 145
Kübler-Ross, Elizabeth, 128

L
La Captive, 92n6
La Promesse, 19
Le derrière, 86
Lefebvre, Henri, 5–8, 29n8, 128
Les rendez-vous d'Anna, 20, 23
Les visiteurs, 92n5
Liminal space, 25, 26, 62, 67, 74, 78, 82, 89, 100, 116
 balcony as, 67, 89, 154, 155, 157
  (*see also* Threshold)
 patio as, 110
 roof as, 67, 111, 114–119
  (*see also* Threshold)
 See also Space

Limitations, 15, 22, 23, 26, 45, 70, 101, 109, 110, 113, 120, 154, 158–160, 169, 173n2, 132153
Line of flight, 111, 112, 114, 119, 130, 136
Lluvia, 58, 93n13
Locke, 59
Lorde, Audre, 10, 27, 131, 136, 144

M
Magical realism, 62–67, 71, 74–76, 78, 82, 88
Mahmood, Saba, 102
Marks, Laura U., 60, 61, 67–70, 95n23, 170
Marseilles, 23, 38
Mask, *see* Wilfulness
Massey, Doreen, viii, 5–8, 14, 15, 29n7, 60, 69, 104, 128, 155, 167, 172
Massumi, Brian, 8–10, 12, 22, 24, 170
McDowell, Linda, 7, 29n7, 128
Medusa, Raft of the, 165
Merleau-Ponty, Maurice, 13, 81, 82, 94n18, 94n19, 121n1, 171
Mernissi, Fatima, 101, 102, 107, 108
Messidor, 5, 20–25, 27, 37–53, 57, 58, 72, 73, 80, 91, 135, 154, 160, 167, 168
#Metoo, Micro-instances of affirmation, 14, 23, 101, 118, 119, 121, 130
Mirror, 18, 115, 116, 129, 130, 139, 148, 152, 154
Mobility, v, vi, viii, 1, 2, 5–19, 22–25, 28n2, 37–40, 42, 44, 53, 57–61, 68, 71–75, 78, 82, 90, 91, 101, 104, 105, 108, 117–120, 126, 133, 149–151, 153, 160, 167, 168
 as democratic right, 58, 153

and immobility, 18, 25, 40, 49, 58, 64, 68, 71, 73, 74, 79, 82, 93n17, 105, 129, 149
uninhabitability of, 149
See also Gender
Monster, 38, 52
Mortelle randonnée, 38
Morvern Callar, 38, 40
Motel, *see* Hotel room
Movement, viii, 3, 9, 12, 14, 16, 18, 20–22, 25, 27, 28n1, 28n2, 37, 38, 40, 45–50, 53, 70, 76, 78, 79, 82, 85, 90, 94n18, 94n20, 100, 101, 104–107, 110, 112, 117, 120, 126, 129, 131, 140, 142, 146, 150, 152, 154, 155, 158, 168, 169, 172, 173n1, 180
freedom of, 1, 18, 46, 51, 57, 58, 101, 153 (*see also* Mobility)
micro-movements, 62, 155
Muñoz, José Esteban, 28, 143
Music, 12, 15, 41, 48, 64, 65, 67, 76, 80, 90, 105, 118, 127–130, 140, 142, 145, 147, 148, 152, 158, 159
as interlude, 129
My Blueberry Nights, 38

N
Naficy, Hamid, 126, 127
Nature, 6, 29n7, 47, 91, 103, 138, 147
Negation, 4, 19
Neoliberalism, 151
Night on earth, 58
Nominalisation, 11
Non-representational theory, 12, 13, 128
No sex last night, 58

O
The Odyssey, 50
Offside, 20

Optimism, ix, 8, 46–48
and positivity, 163
See also Berlant, Lauren

P
Paris, 58, 59, 64, 66, 77, 138
Pause, 24, 25, 51, 53, 63, 130, 154–156, 168
Persistence, 20, 45, 49–51, 53, 100, 107, 150, 152
See also Resistance; Wilfulness
Phenomenology, 11, 16, 24, 26, 40, 121n1
and mobility, 24 (*see also* Mobility)
See also Spectatorship
Pidduck, Julianne, 18, 152
Place, practiced, *see* Space
Political, 10, 19, 21, 51, 58, 61, 62, 78, 94n19, 99, 102, 103, 117, 126, 131, 150, 169, 170, 172
Politics, 2, 4–7, 10, 12, 19–23, 53, 58, 94n19, 113, 117, 153, 170, 172
Pollock, Griselda, 131
Possible future, 19, 135, 157
Post-cinema, 172, 173
Power, v, vi, viii, 5–9, 11–16, 18–22, 24, 28n5, 29n7, 29–30n12, 37, 40, 41, 57, 58, 60, 61, 68, 77, 78, 81–87, 91, 94n20, 102, 104, 107, 108, 112, 114, 116, 117, 120, 126, 128, 130–144, 152, 154, 168, 172, 173
micro-politics of, 6
and structural inequalities, 6
Power-geometries, viii, 5–8, 14–16, 21–23, 26, 28, 40, 46, 50, 58, 62, 79–81, 88, 93n17, 100, 104–109, 117, 119, 120, 128, 130, 136, 149, 155, 158, 163, 164, 167, 172
Public space, *see* City

Public sphere, vii, 2, 21, 29n7, 39, 49, 51, 57, 58, 75, 92n2, 102, 131, 150, 153
Punishment, see Transgression
Punk, 134, 138, 141–151

Q
Queerness, 126, 143
A Question of Silence, 52

R
Race, 2, 5, 7, 16, 27, 58, 104, 119, 127, 131, 141, 149, 167, 169
 and double consciousness, 126
 internalisation of racism, 145
 as racialisation, 10
 uninhabitability of, 140, 144
Al-Rasheed, Madawi, 101–103
Recollection-object, 67–70, 73, 85, 87, 89
Resistance, vii, 3, 4, 6, 19, 20, 22, 24, 28, 47–49, 52, 53, 70, 100, 106, 111, 131, 134, 141–144, 150, 169, 170
Road, 1, 2, 25, 37–43, 45, 46, 49, 50, 53, 58, 59, 70, 153, 158
Road movie, 1, 19–21, 24, 25, 27, 28n1, 37–54, 57, 58, 71, 150, 151, 154, 167, 168
Robertson, Pamela, 39, 151
Roma, 163–167
A Room of One's Own, 108
Rose, Gillian, 7, 29n7, 128
Rosetta, 19

S
Sans toit ni loi, 20, 23, 38
Saudi Arabia, 101, 103, 104, 121n3
Sensations, 13, 14, 24, 59–62, 65, 67, 69, 70, 79, 80, 82, 89, 92n9, 121n1, 146, 150, 173
 See also Haptic
Sense-memories, 67, 68, 70, 71, 85
Sexism, v, viii, 45, 51, 52, 147, 149
 and misogyny, 14
 and sexualisation, 141
Sexuality, v, 2, 10, 16, 27, 68, 102, 103, 107, 126, 128, 131, 133, 134, 137, 140, 141, 144, 146, 152, 168, 169
 of men, 147
 of women, 3
 See also Transgression
Shaviro, Steven, 12, 61, 170, 172, 173
Sheller, Mimi, 21, 58, 75, 79, 93n14
Siewert, Senta, 143
Silences of the Palace, 100
678, 20, 23, 100
Slut Walks, 14, 169
 See also #metoo
Sobchack, Vivian, 12, 15, 60, 61, 92n3, 171
Social media, 15, 173
Solnit, Rebecca, vi, 130
 Wanderlust, 3
Space, v–viii, 1–30, 38–51, 53, 57–95, 99–102, 104, 106, 108–119, 121n1, 125–137, 140, 141, 143, 144, 146, 148–160, 163, 165, 167–173, 173n2
 and affect, 5, 8, 13, 19, 79
 any-space-whatever, 84
 and the body, 100 (*see also* Affect)
 of containment, 63, 66
 domestic (*see* Domestic)
 as filmic forms, 165
  (*see also* Film theory)
 gendering of, 23, 25

habitation of, viii, 1, 2, 4, 8, 11, 16, 19, 20, 23, 24, 26, 27, 29n8, 62, 70, 80, 82, 83, 87–91, 93n17, 115, 121n1, 128, 167, 168
  of intimacy, 16, 25, 26, 60, 62, 85
  liminal (*see* Liminal space)
  as lived, 5, 6, 70, 171, 172
  micro-relations to, 5
  of one's own, 66–69
  as practiced place, 6
  public, 3, 14, 23, 28n3, 45, 52, 58, 66, 80, 91, 101, 102, 107, 116, 117, 126, 128, 131, 135–137, 141, 149, 150, 158, 160n1, 164, 168
    (*see also* Bar)
  semi-private, 64
  as space-time, 2, 157
  of transito, 65
Spain, Daphne, 7, 29n7, 128
Spectatorship, 16, 17, 171, 172
Spinoza, Baruch, 8–9, 12, 22, 29–30n12, 30n13
Streets, v, 2, 3, 5, 7, 14, 16, 20, 23, 25–27, 59, 60, 62, 63, 72, 74, 84, 85, 89, 90, 92n7, 93n17, 100–102, 104–108, 112, 115–120, 125–160
See also City
Subject, v, 4, 6, 11, 13, 16, 17, 19, 20, 23, 27, 28, 30n12, 30n14, 39, 51, 71, 81, 83, 94n21, 104, 112–114, 116, 125–127, 136, 137, 144–146, 149, 150, 154, 160, 168–170
  gendered, 59
  as liminal, 128, 141–143, 145, 146, 160
Subjectivity, 2, 12, 24, 75, 76, 83, 89, 93n14, 117, 140, 165, 167, 172

T
Tableaux, 128–130, 158–160
Ten, 23, 58
Texture, 12, 13, 15, 23, 24, 60, 62, 65, 67, 69, 70, 76, 80, 81, 84, 85, 88, 89, 91, 129, 171
Thelma and Louise, 20, 38, 45, 53
Thornham, Sue, 18
Threshold, 2, 9, 62, 64, 73, 74, 78, 91, 126, 141, 145, 146, 152, 157, 168
  See also Liminal space
Thrift, Nigel, 7, 12, 13, 29n10, 171
Topoanalysis, 16, 133, 136
Touch, sense of, 13, 19, 60, 67, 70, 81, 83–85, 87–89, 94n19, 134, 155, 171
Towards a Feminist Cinematic Aesthetic, 28
Traffic jam, *see* Car
Transformation, 2, 6–8, 11, 12, 21–24, 37, 40, 42, 48, 53, 58, 59, 64, 66, 69–71, 74, 78–80, 82, 83, 88, 89, 91, 104, 120, 126–128, 141, 157, 167
  political, 4
  of space, 4, 27, 62, 158
  See also Imagination
Transgression
  punishment of, 120, 127, 144, 146, 150, 159, 165
  See also Resistance
Transylvania, 38
Trauma, 5, 169, 170
Travel, v, 1, 2, 5, 7, 21, 24–26, 28n2, 37–42, 45, 46, 48, 51, 53, 58, 66, 75, 77, 79, 91, 127, 164, 167, 168
  failure to, 48
  and risk for women, 128
  See also Mobility; Space
Turkey, 127, 140, 144, 157

U

Una mujer fantástica, 169
Urban space, *see* City
Urry, John, 21, 58, 75, 79, 93n14
Uteng, Tanu Priya, 7, 28n2, 40
Utopia, 12, 112, 116, 143

V

Vehicle, 25, 42, 44, 45, 70–74, 80, 92n10, 107, 108
   and docility, 109
   poetic, 59
   See also Bicycle; Car
Veil, 26, 66, 102, 104–109, 114–116, 120
Vendredi soir, 5, 21, 22, 24, 25, 27, 46, 57–95, 99, 117, 146, 154, 155, 160, 168
Villenet, Jane, 77, 93n15
Virtual, 4, 11, 13, 22, 53, 75, 77, 91, 115, 167, 168, 173
Virtual (*vs.* actual), 26, 68
Virtual reality, 91, 173

W

Wadjda, vi–viii, 5, 21, 22, 24–27, 46, 62, 66, 71, 82, 83, 89, 91, 94n20, 99–121, 154, 160, 168
Wadud, Amina, 103
Walking, vi, 16, 27, 47, 48, 50, 72, 104, 105, 107, 110, 128, 130, 136, 137, 164
   See also Wandering
Wall, 89, 100, 110, 117, 118, 141, 142, 144, 148
Wanda, 20, 38

Wandering, viii, 2, 19–21, 23, 24, 28n1, 37–54, 73–78, 115, 120, 141, 169
   camera, 63, 64, 73–75, 77, 82, 89
We Are Not Princesses, 169
Weekend, 5, 20–25, 27, 37–53, 57, 58, 71, 93n11
Wendy and Lucy, 38, 58
Wild, 163–167
Wilfulness, vi, 2, 11, 19–25, 28n1, 30n14, 42, 52, 83, 101, 106, 107, 109, 110, 112–116, 118–121, 125, 134, 136, 137, 143, 150, 152, 154, 156, 168
   as affect, 45, 104
   dissimulation of, 99, 111, 133
   mask of, 26, 99, 114
      (*see also* Resistance)
   as persistence, 99, 100
   shape of, 51
Wilson, Elizabeth, 3–4, 28n5, 47, 73, 75, 78, 131, 138, 141, 147
Window, 15, 43, 62, 63, 65, 66, 69, 71–76, 78, 79, 83, 89, 92n6, 108, 136, 151–156, 159, 164, 165
   See also Liminal space
Wolff, Janet, 2, 3, 108
Women Without Men, 20, 100
Woolf, Virginia, 3, 65, 108
   A Room of One's Own, 108

Y

Yamani, Mai, 103
Yella, 38
Young, Iris Marion, 78, 100

Z

Žižek, Slavoj, 164, 165

The manufacturer's authorised representative in the EU is Springer Nature Customer Service Centre GmbH, Europaplatz 3, 69115 Heidelberg, Germany. If you have any concerns regarding our products, please contact ProductSafety@springernature.com

Printed and bound by CPI Group (UK) Ltd, Croydon, CR0 4YY

23/03/2026

02076661-0001